Literature-Based Learning Activities Kit

Ready-to-Use Whole Language Lessons & Worksheets for Grades 2–6

Janice Jensen

illustrated by Susan Jerde

THE CENTER FOR APPLIED
RESEARCH IN EDUCATION
West Nyack, New York 10995

10 9 8 7 6 5 4 3 2

Library of Congress Cataloging-in-Publication Data

Jensen, Janice.
    Literature-based learning activities kit : ready-to-use whole
language lessons & worksheets for grades 2–6 / Janice Jensen :
illustrated by Susan Jerde.
        p.   cm.
    Includes bibliographical references.
    ISBN 0-87628-545-0
    1. Reading (Elementary)—Language experience approach.
    2. Literature—Study and teaching (Elementary)   3. Education,
Elementary—Activity programs.   4. Children—Books and reading.
    I. Title.
    LB1573.33.J46   1991
    372.4—dc20   90-29012
                                                                      CIP

The author and publisher gratefully acknowledge permission to use
the following:

Excerpts from *Kenneth Lilly's Animals* by Kenneth Lilly, Text by Joyce Pope; Maps & Text ©
1988 by Walker Books, Ill.; © 1988 by K. Lilly; *The Warrior and the Wiseman* by David
Wisiewski; © 1989 by the author; by permission of Lothrop, Lee & Shepard Books, a division
of William Morrow & Co., Inc. *Scaly Babies: Reptiles That Grow Up* by Ginny Johnston and
Judy Cutchins; © 1988 by the authors; by permission of Morrow Junior Books, a division of
William Morrow & Co. Excerpts from *Steven Caney's Invention Book*, © 1985 by Steven
Caney; and from *The Bug Book*, © 1987 by Somerville House Books Ltd., Text by Hugh
Danks; reprinted by permission of Workman Publishing Company. All rights reserved.
Excerpts from *The Whipping Boy* by Sid Fleischman; © 1986 by the author; and *Drugs: What
They Are, What They Do* by Judith Seixas, © 1987 by the author; by permission of
Greenwillow Books, a division of William Morrow & Co. Excerpts from *Eyewitness Books:
Rocks & Minerals* by R.F. Symes and *Eyewitness Books: Skeleton* by Steve Parker are used
with permission from Alfred A. Knopf, Inc., a division of Random House, Inc.; © 1988.
Outline of pear, flower, and seed from *Flowers, Fruits, Seeds* by Jerome Wexler; © 1988 by
Prentice Hall Press.

ISBN 0-87628-545-0

**The Center for Applied
Research in Education**
Business Information & Publishing Division
West Nyack, NY 10995

Simon & Schuster, A Paramount Communications Company

Printed in the United States of America

to CAROLINE FELLER-BAUER
for igniting the spark

to BYRON SKAUG
for fueling the flame

special thanks to my
DEDICATED AND TALENTED COLLEAGUES
and to my ENTHUSIASTIC STUDENTS
—the real literature experts

ABOUT THE AUTHOR

Janice Jensen, an elementary teacher and consultant based in Eugene, Oregon, has taught at both the primary and intermediate levels. She conducts literature-based inservices throughout the United States and overseas, but continues to love the classroom because, "the rewards are so great for helping children learn basic skills through good books and for witnessing their sheer enjoyment."

Ms. Jensen has studied the classics, including mythology, researches and writes articles for professional magazines, teaches literature-related classes at the university level, and appears on television—all for the purpose of capturing the excitement of literature and passing it on to others.

She is the co-author of *I Love Library Books,* literature-based lessons for primary students.

ABOUT THIS KIT

Literature-Based Learning Activities Kit brings a new dimension to the teaching of basic subject area concepts while providing exciting, ready content for reading instruction and literature appreciation. These outstanding fiction and nonfiction books, interesting skills-oriented lessons and activities, and lively illustrations all showcase the elements of creative, innovative teaching.

All of your students in grades 2–6 will benefit from the excellent books and the over 100 lessons and activities that provide reinforcement, review, and application for basic skills. The activities are designed to be challenging and enjoyable at all ability levels. Lower and average performers will benefit from the step-by-step directions and carefully sequenced worksheets, while all levels of students can use the books and activities as springboards for further exploration. You, the teacher, will benefit by receiving help in:

- teaching important basic skills in a novel and appealing manner
- introducing good literature to students within a subject-matter context
- integrating the curriculum through the different skills incorporated in each activity
- having a handy source of high-quality reproducibles

There are eleven sections, each representing a different subject or curriculum area, although each lesson contains multiple skills spanning several subject areas. Note that the primary skill is listed in both the Table of Contents and on the teacher directions pages. There are both picture books and full-length books, and the lessons provide complete teacher information for directing them. These lessons and activities require full teacher and student participation. They have been field tested in regular classrooms and have been successfully used with a full range of ability levels.

THE BOOKS

What Kind of Books

These top-quality books are from a variety of genres and topics representing a wide range of grade levels and interests. There is an abundance of picture books and full-length books for both the younger and older student. The books were carefully chosen for their appeal to students at the particular grade levels designated, but many can be extended. Selection was also based on potential for staying in print. A large portion are award-winning titles, many of which are library staples. Most are recent to brand-new titles.

"Yes" to Picture Books for Older Students

In recent years, many excellent picture books have been written that greatly appeal to the intermediate and older student. In fact, a large group of top-quality titles have been written and illustrated specifically for the older student's interests and needs. Picture books have a distinct advantage: because of the shorter length, a larger amount and a greater variety of quality literature can be presented to students.

Availability of the Books

Before deciding on the lessons and activities to complete, assess the availability of the books in the library and potential for purchasing, including edition(s) and number of copies available. All but a few of the titles are available in at least one hardcover edition, and many are also available in paper. A few—mostly full-length novels—are only available in paper. Check the annotated bibliography at the back of this book for ordering information. Also, check book clubs, such as Scholastic and Trumpet, for availability of specially priced copies.

Single vs. Multiple Copies of Books

All of the lessons and activities can be successfully executed using only one copy of the book. In many cases, multiple copies are preferable for: (1) full-length books, (2) older students, (3) review of concepts for content areas, and (4) added interest, flexibility, and efficiency.

COMPONENTS OF THE LESSONS

Teacher Read vs. Independent Student Reading of the Books

Books can be read: (1) totally by the teacher to students, (2) partially by the teacher and partially by the students (orally, independently, or both), or (3) in some cases, independently by older, higher performers.

Most commonly, the picture books are read to students, with or without multiple copies. Usually, the full-length book reading is completed by a combination of teacher and student reading.

Where multiple copies are available, determine the purpose for the reading and activity, and the students' reading level, and then decide what book-reading procedure to use.

Book Reading Level

Books designed to be used with primary-age students were not necessarily selected for independent reading by the students. However, depending on the level of the performers, some could be at least partially read independently. Books selected for the intermediate level can be independently read by the students.

Grade-level designations in the Table of Contents are for the book and lesson based on typical student reading level, interests, and needs.

Reading Books to Students

Research has demonstrated the effectiveness of reading aloud to students, regardless of their age or ability. Many books, particularly picture books, can be read rather quickly to the students. Included are a few full-length novels and nonfiction titles that are more time-consuming, requiring from one hour to twenty hours of oral reading time.

Choices of reading completion include:

1. Total book reading by the teacher to students.

2. Partial oral reading (divided by chapters, pages, paragraphs) by the teacher to students and partial reading by students, orally, independently, or both. (Students can prepare a paragraph or page ahead of time to read to the group.)

3. Complete reading of the book by students independently. This option is not recommended for most books and most settings. Even older, high-performing students enjoy and benefit from the quality teacher performance, as opposed to total solo work.

Remember, the choice between partial and total independent reading depends on the availability of multiple copies.

Lesson and Activity Purposes

Each lesson includes: (1) list of any materials needed, (2) background information for students, (3) how to execute the reading of the book(s), and (4) directions for worksheet completion or, in some cases, the activity without a worksheet.

All of the lessons and activities are meant to *follow* initial teaching of a skill or concept. Their purpose is *reinforcement, review,* and *application. None are intended to replace the beginning teaching through the basic textbook.*

Much of the preparation for implementation of the lesson has been done. However, at the discretion of the teacher, introduction of vocabulary and comprehension questions may be added to the lesson.

All lessons and activities have been designed for adaptability to a large age and ability range, and to varied teaching styles, thus facilitating wide usage.

Teacher Preparation

Follow the sequence here to prepare for the lesson and activity:

1. Assess availability of book(s).

2. Read the book(s) to be presented.

3. Become thoroughly knowledgeable of the teacher information given.

4. Decide on a book reading option and on how to utilize the directions for the particular group and purpose.

5. Add a section for vocabulary development as needed.

6. Write additional comprehension information and questions as applicable.

7. Assess the time allowed and needed for completion. Lessons may vary from approximately one-half hour to several class periods. Most fall between 45 minutes and 90 minutes.

Completing the Worksheets

The large variety of activity formats is intended to capture student interest in learning basic skills. Included are board games, puzzles, riddles, and hands-on working with materials.

Most lessons and activities contain optional ways to extend the book or skills. These activities are of three types:

1. *Follow-up*, which provides more practice with the theme, topic, or skill

2. *Extended*, which applies the skill, topic, or theme to other situations

3. *Additional*, which takes the skill, theme, or topic to other subject areas

The worksheets have specifically been designed to accommodate varied teaching styles, purposes of instruction, and student needs, including age, ability, and type and size of group. Therefore, select completion options from the following: entire completion by the total group; partial completion by the whole group and part by small groups, pairs, or independently; small group completion; or entire completion done independently.

Answer Keys

Answers to the worksheets are included on the teacher pages. No answers are given when student interpretation is needed.

A FINAL WORD

Literature-Based Learning Activities Kit pairs high-impact fiction and nonfiction books with creative lessons and activities encompassing all of the major subject areas—the purpose being to instill in students both basic subject area knowledge and a love of literature. The rate of teacher/student success and enjoyment is high because important interests and needs are met with innovative and exciting methods and materials. The material in *Literature-Based Learning Activities Kit* will capture the imagination of all children!

Janice Jensen

TABLE OF CONTENTS AND SKILLS INDEX

Section 1 READING WITH CHILDREN'S BOOKS   1

Section 2 LITERATURE ANALYSIS & APPRECIATION WITH CHILDREN'S BOOKS 35

Section 3 WRITING WITH CHILDREN'S BOOKS 65

Section 4 LISTENING, SPEAKING, AND NONVERBAL COMMUNICATION WITH CHILDREN'S BOOKS   89

Section 7 SCIENCE WITH CHILDREN'S BOOKS   159

Section 8 HEALTH WITH CHILDREN'S BOOKS   191

Section 9 CREATIVE ARTS WITH CHILDREN'S BOOKS   215

Reading with Children's Books

Viorst, Judith. *Alexander and the Terrible, Horrible, No Good, Very Bad Day.* **New York: Atheneum, 1972.** Some days are bad—even in Australia.

Optional But Recommended Additional Books: *Sing a Song of Popcorn,* selected by Beatrice Schenk deRegniers, Scholastic, 1988; *If All the Seas Were One Sea,* etchings by Janina Domanska, Macmillan, 1971; *The Random House Book of Poetry for Children,* selected by Jack Prelutsky, Random House, 1983. See #4 below.

Directions

1. Read and enjoy the book with students, and talk about its contents.
2. Discuss the following:
   A. Why this is such a popular book (character, events, theme).
   B. How to prevent problems and accidents from occurring, and how to accept those that are not preventable.
   C. *Optional*: Role-play positive reactions to bad situations, for example, your best friend rejects you, you didn't like your lunch, you missed problems on the math quiz even though you tried your best.
3. Students complete the activity sheet as follows:
   A. Read and discuss the information at the top of the sheet with the students, as reinforcement for understanding the cause and effect concept.
   B. Point out that the word *so* is often used at the beginning of an effect.
4. Optional but highly recommended extension of the cause and effect concept:
   A. Enjoy poems beginning with the word *if* from the sources given above. Refer to the Index of First Lines, for "If babies could speak . . .", for example. Lead students to discover the cause and effect sequences.
   B. Read the poem from *The Random House Book of Poetry for Children,* "If We Walked On Our Hands" on page 105.
   C. Students create whole group, pair, or individual additional incongruent situations.
   D. *Optional*: Illustrate or act out the new poetry.

Extended Activities

1. "Good Day" and "Bad Day" Badges

   Students cut out a badge from construction paper and write on it: "(name)'s Good (or Bad) Day." After the badge is decorated, students describe an especially good or bad day on the back of the badge. The badge is worn for the day.
2. A Good Day At School Chart

   Students describe positive events to be displayed for positive reinforcement, OR students give positive descriptions of a math or reading lesson, OR students give positive descriptions of a good book or game.

Answer Key to Activity Sheet: 6, 4, 1, 3, 2, 5

Directions: Alexander did things that made other things happen. He had a cavity when he went to the dentist, so he had to go back and have it fixed. The cavity was the *cause* of the problem, going back to the dentist was the *effect,* or result.

If you close your eyes, you cannot see. Closing your eyes is the cause; not being able to see is the effect.

Below are more things Alexander did that caused other things to happen. Match the correct cause with the correct effect by writing the number from the cause in the first part on the line in front of the effect in the second part.

CAUSE:

1. I had gum in my mouth when I went to bed,

2. In the car, the other kids got seats by the window,

3. I wasn't Paul's best friend now,

4. Anthony made me slip in the mud and cry,

5. I punched Anthony for calling me a crybaby,

6. The shoe store was out of blue and red shoes,

EFFECT:

_____ so I had to get plain white shoes.

_____ so Anthony called me a crybaby.

_____ so I woke up with gum in my hair.

_____ so he has two better friends than me.

_____ so I was squished between everyone.

_____ so my mom got angry at me for fighting and getting muddy.

Now, write something YOU did that caused something else to happen.

CAUSE:

_____

_____

_____

EFFECT:

_____

_____

_____

MacLachlan, Patricia. *Sarah, Plain and Tall*. New York: Harper & Row, 1985. The tender bonding between Sarah, plain and tall from Maine, and a motherless prairie family. Newbery, 1986.

Directions

1. Introduce the book by showing the cover and telling students that this book received the award for the best full-length children's book of 1986. Ask students to find, as the story is read, characters and events that made the story interesting.

2. Read the book orally to students. (*Note:* For older students, if multiple copies are available alternate oral and silent reading.) As the reading progresses, include the following story elements and questions in the discussion (in keeping with age and ability of students):

   A. *Setting*. Relate the time and place to other studies and books about that time period; compare with modern times

   B. *Characters*. Establish descriptions of how each acts and behaves, their likes and dislikes, and their attitudes towards life and each other. Trace the unfolding of Caleb's and Sarah's personalities. Note probable ages of children—Caleb, 5 or 6, Anna, 11 or 12. Point out the subtle humor in things the characters say and do

   C. *Themes*. Point out how the characters and plot show a growing love, security, and companionship

   D. *Point of View*. Identify the fact that Anna tells the story and presents the ideas and events as she sees and understands them

   E. Point out the concepts contained on the activity sheet, as they occur throughout the story.

   F. Specific questions for specific chapters:

   • end of chapter 1: Papa wanted a wife, but what other reason did he have for wanting Sarah to come?

   • end of Chapter 3: Why was Caleb more anxious and afraid about Sarah than Papa and Anna?

   • end of Chapter 5: What are two things Sarah said that would give Caleb reason to believe that she might stay?

   • end of Chapter 7: How was Maggie being a good friend to Sarah?

   • chapter 8, page 48: Why did Sarah bring her shells to the barn?

   • chapter 9, page 52: Why do you think Sarah wanted to go away alone?

   G. Questions for the end of the book: (oral or written)

   • Describe how Sarah's three favorite colors—blue, gray and green—were important to what happened in the story.

   • What things did Sarah do and say that made Anna and Caleb like her?

   • In what ways did Papa have to adjust to Sarah's ways of doing things?

   • What things would you like about having a mother or friend like Sarah?

   • What characters and events made the story interesting? How?

   • For older students: How is Sarah different than the typical pioneer woman? Compare her to modern women.

3. Completion of the activity sheet:
   A. Review concepts as needed.
   B. Students work individually or in pairs to complete the sentences.
   C. Stress that, except for sentence 2, there could be several different good answers.
   D. Tell students that in the first two sentences, Anna *and* Caleb are talking. In the following ones, only Anna is talking.

Related Book   *Iva Dunnit and the Big Wind,* by Carol Purdy (Dial Books, 1985)

Additional Activities

1. Language: "Deliciously Descriptive Nouns"

   Brainstorm nouns from the story, for example, Caleb, Seal, wagon, windmill, and use adjectives to describe them, patterned after "Sarah, Plain and Tall," or "Caleb, Loud and Pesky."

2. Writing: "Mother Wanted"

   Students write a want-ad, advertising for a mother, assuming the character of Anna or Caleb. Consider: Anna's and Caleb's likes and dislikes and qualities they would like in an adult.

3. Writing: "Sarah Sees It This Way"

   Students take an incident, for example, Sarah's going to town, and rewrite it from *Sarah's point of view.*

4. Art: "What Isn't Missing From the Picture"

   Students create a picture of a prairie landscape and home during a storm (see *Iva Dunnit and the Big Wind*) using "Sarah's sea colors" of blue, gray and green, in addition to yellows, etc.

5. Social Studies: "Sarah's Diary"

   Students assume the character of Sarah and write a diary page, telling of the happy but unexpected similarities of the sea coast and the prairie.

©1991 by The Center for Applied Research in Education

Directions: After Sarah said she would stay, Anna was so happy that she wrote her this letter. Finish each sentence as ANNA would have.

Name :

_____

Dear Sarah, Plain and Tall,

We love you, and we're so glad you're here. We know you answered the ad because _____

_____

We also know that you miss the sea, but are staying because you would miss _____

Papa cares a lot about us, so he didn't tell Caleb and me about the "ad" until you said "yes." That's because _____

Papa will try hard to be a good husband. One thing he's done to show that is _____

Caleb is "pesky" and asks lots of questions. We let him do it because we _____

He should get even more time with a loving mother than me because _____

_____

Your singing is very special! We used to want to sing to remember Mama, but now we all want to sing so _____

Thanks for loving us!

Anna

The Tortoise and the Hare. **Adapted and illustrated by Janet Stevens. New York: Holiday House, 1984.** Tortoise eats right, works out, and jogs over the finish line, while watching Hare in his pink jogging shorts try to catch up.

Directions

1. Read the book to students and enjoy the humor and action. *Optional*: compare with other versions.

2. Discuss the *character* differences between Tortoise and Hare:

    A. List *descriptions* of both (Tortoise: short, solidly built; Hare: long-legged).

    B. List *traits* of both—how each acts and behaves (Tortoise: friendly, quiet; Hare: flashy, rude).

    C. Compare and contrast.

3. Completing the activity sheet:

    A. Define and give examples of antonyms and synonyms. See activity sheet.

    B. Students work independently or in pairs to complete the task. Synonyms part optional for younger or lower-performing students.

    C. Suggested time limits for each part—grade 3: six minutes; grades 4 and 5: four minutes

Extended Activity   Students alphabetize a list, for additional winners.

Additional Activities

1. Math: "Tortoise and Hare Facts Race"

    Students compete with themselves for an improved rate for given math facts. Winners: "Terrific Tortoises," Losers: "Horrible Hares."

2. Health and Fitness: "Finish a Line for Fitness"

    Students each talk for thirty seconds about keeping healthy and fit, then call on another student to continue.

See also Activity 5–9, "Hare, Tortoise and Friends to the Finish!"

THE BIG ANTONYM AND SYNONYM RACE

Name _____

Directions:

1. An *antonym* is a word that means the opposite of another word. Example: hot, cold.

   Write one or more antonyms for each word on the left.

   No prefixes—example: un(healthy)

   No "not" words—example: not big

2. *Synonyms* are words that mean the same or almost the same as another word.

   Write one or more synonyms for each word.

Winner(s): most antonyms, most synonyms, and grand total correct.

ANTONYMS

big _____

stop _____

last _____

win _____

slow _____

work _____

late _____

asleep _____

day _____

cool _____

run _____

move _____

friend _____

healthy _____

victory _____

TIME: _____

ANTONYMS CORRECT: _____

GRAND TOTAL CORRECT: _____

SYNONYMS

start _____

run _____

walk _____

stop _____

eat _____

go _____

end _____

work _____

big _____

hare _____

finish _____

fast _____

slow _____

TIME: _____

SYNONYMS CORRECT: _____

Estes, Eleanor. *The Hundred Dresses*. San Diego: Harcourt, Brace, Jovanovich, 1944, 1973. A poor Polish girl is teased because she wears the same blue dress every day but says she has one hundred others all lined up in her closet. Good material for discussion of stereotyping, prejudice, teasing, and friendship.

Directions

1. Introduce the book by asking students: "How many of you have

   A. been teased and couldn't figure out how to get it stopped?"

   B. tried unsuccessfully to stop someone else from teasing a friend?"

   Tell students that if their answer was "yes" to either or both questions, they will understand the feelings expressed in *The Hundred Dresses*.

2. Read and discuss the book with students by sharing it aloud with them. For older students, if multiple copies are available, combine oral and silent reading.

   A. Discuss key concepts by including the following questions:

      * page 18: Why did Peggy tease Wanda?

      * page 36: What are some possible reasons Wanda couldn't read very well?

      * page 46: Why did Wanda's father write the letter? Why did the kids holler "Polack" and make fun of Wanda's name?

      * page 48: Why is it as bad to stand by as to actually tease someone?

      * page 49: Why did Peggy decide to try to find Wanda, too?

      * page 51: Why did the girls think Wanda was dumb?

      * page 63: Why didn't the girls say they were sorry in the letter?

      * page 64: Why is it easier to role-play defending someone against teasing than to do it in real life?

      * page 70: What new things do you learn about Wanda from the letter?

      * page 74: Why is it important to be nice to people each day?

      * page 78: How did Peggy and Maddie each feel differently about what had been done to Wanda?

   B. Define and discuss the themes of stereotyping, prejudice, and friendship by:

      1. using book examples

      2. making a list of the prejudices shown when the students decided why Wanda wasn't "smart." Include: nationality, accent, couldn't read, where sat in room, name, shyness, where lived.

   C. Discuss and list ways Wanda was "smart." Then list ways individual students in the class are smart.

3. Provide the focus and structure for the role-playing activity as follows:

   A. Focus: Students role play appropriate responses for common teasing situations.

   B. Students choose one of the following types of situations:

      (1) Start with a scene from the book where Wanda is being teased. Rewrite the script so that Peggy or Maddie, or both girls, find nice things to say to Wanda, and defend her against others. Example: "Wanda, you always look so neat and clean! How do you do it?"

      (2) Use the same (or different) characters as the book, but write a different scene— either at or away from school. Example: Peggy, Maddie, and Wanda are at the

the beach. Peggy teases Wanda about her faded blue bathing suit. Maddie talks to Peggy and gets her to apologize.

(3) Think about a time at school when someone is being teased (about their clothes, lunch, hair, etc.). Write what would be a good way to get the people to stop the teasing. Example: Kyle is being teased about his turtleneck shirt. Kyle, Matt, and Justin ignore the teasing the first time. Then Matt says: "We could find something to tease you guys about, but we won't. Come on Kyle, let's go play."

4. Students now write and practice the skit(s):

A. Younger students write group skits as follows:

(1) Brainstorm appropriate responses for a situation(s)

(2) Set up guidelines for performance:

(a) memorize important ideas

(b) ad-lib the rest

(c) practice

B. Older students are formed into groups of three (possibly four) students to write and practice a skit. Steps for completion:

(1) Make an outline. Include the problem, characters, and solution.

(2) Add the details.

(3) Write in skit form. Add props.

(4) Set up guidelines for presenting the skit.

(5) Practice for the performance. Memorize important ideas, ad-lib the rest.

C. IMPORTANT NOTE TO TEACHER: Make sure the skits are structured so that "pat solutions" or responses are given at least a second round of solutions. When kids are asked to stop teasing the first time, they often continue the teasing a second or third time. Include appropriate follow-up responses.

Manes, Stephen. *Be a Perfect Person in Just Three Days!* **New York: Bantam-Skylark, 1983.** Is being perfect the answer to Milo's and everyone's problems? Read and find out!

Cobb, Vicki and Kathy Darling. *Bet You Can't!* **New York: Avon, 1983.** A collection of over sixty mostly impossible-to-do, but highly-motivating-to-try tricks.

Directions

1. Complete reading of the book to students, as follows:
   A. Read through to the end of the first step to perfection.
   B. Now, ask students to predict what the next steps are (students who have already read the book can share their own creative "three steps to perfection").
      (1) Share in groups of two, four, whole class.
      (2) Help students differentiate ideas that are humorous from those that are silly.
   C. Finish reading book.
2. Perform two science activities from *Bet You Can't!*—one that cannot be done and one that can, with practice, become "perfectly done."
   A. Do page 36, tearing a piece of paper into 3 pieces. (Impossible if directions are followed correctly!)
   B. Do page 103, making two pencil points meet. (Can be done—after the first time!)
3. Complete the activity sheet. Note the following:
   A. For problem 1, give students guidance in choosing and planning.
      Group option for choosing, writing, or demonstrating activity to class: students work in pairs or small groups.
      Note: Activity could be done outside of class and steps presented.
   B. The list for item 4 can be ingredients, steps, or both.

Follow-Up Activities

1. "The Perfect Sundae"
   Students choose a class favorite, easy-to-prepare food, such as a sundae. Students each make and eat the "perfect" one.
2. "A Perfect Interview"
   Student interviews someone who hasn't read the book, who wants to be perfect. Record the response. After the book has been read, student interviews again, and records response.

1–5 IT'S PERFECT

©1991 by The Center for Applied Research in Education

1. Think about something you do rather "perfectly," something you could show the steps for, or explain how to complete, to the class.
   Examples: turn a cartwheel, catch a ball, perform a science experiment, put together a model, draw a picture, play an instrument.
   WRITE HOW TO DO IT IN THREE STEPS:

   A. _____

   _____

   _____

   B. _____

   _____

   _____

   C. _____

   _____

   _____

2. Now, do it for your class!

3. The "perfect" friend is one who:

   A. _____

   B. _____

   C. _____

4. My favorite food is _____
   For it to be perfect, it has to:

   A. _____

   B. _____

   C. _____

   D. _____

12

Gibbons, Gail. *Sunken Treasure.* **New York: Thomas Y. Crowell, 1988.** Treasures from *Atocha,* a Spanish galleon sunk in 1622, are found in 1985. Very readable, interesting nonfiction!

Note: This is a reinforcement or review lesson for outlining skills. Teach the basics before starting this activity. Also see Activity 1–10, "Turtle Topics."

Materials

Light blue 12-by-18-inch construction paper, one piece per student; scissors; glue.

Directions

1. Read and enjoy the book with students, including the author information.
    A. *Optional*: Stop at the end of page 9 and ask students: *What would be some problems with finding and excavating a treasure from a sunken ship?* Students write the problems, or share with a partner or the large group.
    B. Point out the following:
        • Why it costs so much money to conduct such searches.
        • Why the treasure is sketched and photographed twice—both before and after recovery.
        • The importance of the historical and scientific information learned.
        • Why the found treasure does not now belong to Spain.
2. To provide a focus for the activity, complete a short outline with the group.
    A. Review the purposes of an outline:
        • Is an efficient way to take notes on important ideas.
        • Makes it easier to remember facts in their correct order.
    B. Choose a familiar general topic. Examples: planning a class party or other event, electing class officers.
    C. Label the outline parts. Suggested labels: topics, subtopics, details.
3. Reinforce and review book chapters as needed for completion of the activity.
4. Complete the outline activity: pieces from activity sheet.
    Note: See Extended Activity at end for optional treasure hunt after cutting pieces from activity sheet.
    A. Students follow cutting and folding directions on the activity sheet. (Teacher completes a sample of the components and steps as the sequence progresses. Teacher also displays the Roman numerals and the eight chapter headings for students to copy—I. The Sinking, II. The Search, and so on.)
    B. Next, teacher gives these directions:
        (1) Head paper with "General Topic: Sunken Treasure."
        (2) Write Roman numerals. (Check for alignment.)
        (3) Write the eight chapter headings. These chapter headings are the *topics*. Topics tell in a word or two what the chapter is about.
        (4) Place the *subtopics* (some with details included) under the appropriate topics. *Subtopics* are the most important ideas in the chapter. (Check for correctness.)
    C. Students glue the subtopics with one or two drops of glue.
    D. Students label subtopics and details.

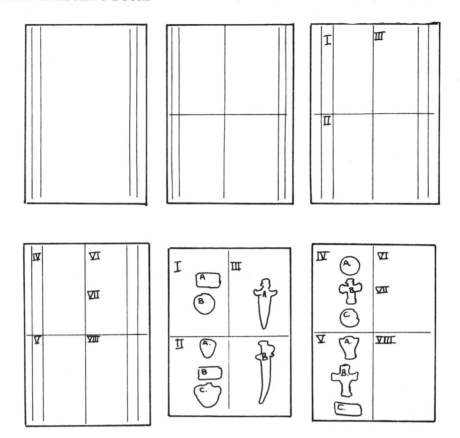

E. Students complete the subtopics for chapters 6, 7, and 8 with group input. Example:
  VI. Restoration and Preservation
      A. First the treasure must be sorted.
      B. Next it must be preserved/restored.
  VII. Cataloging
       Cataloging is done through picture taking, computer scanning, and artists' drawing, for future study
  VIII. Distribution
       The treasure is distributed fairly between museums, investors and the crew

Extended Activity   *"Atocha* Treasure Hunt"

1. Students cut out the thirteen treasure pieces on the activity sheet.
2. Pieces are hidden around the room.
3. Students retrieve hidden pieces four at a time and receive a reward—gold candy coins, for example.

   Hint for hiding pieces: After they are cut out, students stack them in groups by shape. Several pieces of one shape can then be hidden together.

Related Article   *National Geographic Magazine,* June 1988, page 804, "Yorktown Shipwreck." A vessel from the Revolutionary War is being excavated.

Related Book   *Exploring the Titanic* by Robert D. Ballard, Scholastic, 1988.

1–6 FOUND TREASURES AND TOPICS

Name _____

Directions: 1. *Carefully* cut out each treasure. Put aside. 2. Lay large paper lengthwise. Fold left edge twice (only 3/4″ each fold). Fold right edge the same way. 3. Next, fold whole paper in half once lengthwise and once widthwise. Open.

—Salvage goes on for years.

—The *Atocha* and sister ships sink.
• 260 people drown
• 5 people survive

—In 1970, a new location is found.
• Silver bars, brass cannons found.
• No main ship or treasure.

—Salvage boats with divers bring the treasure to the surface.

—The treasure is found!

—At first, the treasure is not disturbed.

—Divers take pictures and make drawings.

—Most of the cargo is there.

—The *Santa Margarita* is found, but the *Atocha* is not.
• It's almost forgotten.
• Treasure is scattered.
• Ship rots.

—The information will be used to learn about the past.

—The treasure ship *Atocha* is caught in a hurricane.
• Wind rips sails.
• Wave reefs boat.
• Hull breaks open.

—Mel Fisher begins a new search.
• Investors provide money.
• Search boats explore.
• Only litter is found.

—The treasure must be accounted for, sketched, and photographed.

©1991 by The Center for Applied Research in Education

Gardiner, John Reynolds. *Stone Fox.* **New York: Harper & Row, 1980.** Ten-year-old Willy is determined to save his grandfather's farm—and his grandfather—by entering a dog sled race against the legendary Indian, Stone Fox.

Materials

1. Duplicated activity sheets with the bottom part ("Chapter 10") folded under (to prevent students from knowing ending)

2. List of race times, four or more sets, for the team game: "The Winner Is . . ." (See 4 below.)

Directions

1. Introduce the book by showing the front cover and asking students to predict who the *main characters* will be, and what the *plot*—the *problem* and the *solution*—might be. *Note:* If students have seen the TV version of the story, substitute other motivational ideas.

2. Next, preview the Table of Contents and ask students to relate experiences about races won or lost.

3. Read and discuss the book with students, either by reading aloud to them, or preferably, if multiple copies are available, by combining oral and silent reading.

   A. Chapter sections on the activity sheet are reasonable divisions for completing both the book and the activity sheet.

   B. Students complete the activity sheet by following directions contained there plus these additional hints:

      1. Inform students that you will tell them when to unfold the bottom part of the paper.

      2. Go over all the sections of the activity sheet with students before starting the questions.

      3. Question 3: Students give different kinds of setting details—snow, crisp air, frozen rivers

      4. Questions 4 and 5: Identify the pictures for students before completing the puzzle:

         • grapes, ampersand, feather, can, haystack, taxi, bow, hand, pot, stick
         • well, center (of circle), ace, doors that go out and in, monkey (Note for "feather (-) e," the first *e* is the one to leave out)

      5. Answers to rebus puzzle:

         Problem: Grandfather can't pay taxes so he got sick.

         Solution: Willy enters a race to win money.

   C. Point out additional key story concepts by asking the following questions:

      CHAPTER 1: Give a possible reason for why Grandfather didn't want to live. If you were Willy, what would you do if something like this happened to someone you loved very much?

      CHAPTER 2: What are two things that Searchlight does that makes him a believable character?

      CHAPTER 3: Point out details about the setting. Why didn't Willy want to go to college?

CHAPTER 4: Why is this chapter called "The Reason"?

CHAPTER 5: "What does a state use tax money for? What word would you use to describe Willy's wanting to save the farm? What possible reasons could Grandfather have for shedding the tear? (last paragraph)

CHAPTER 6: Describe Stone Fox with words and phrases from pages 50 and 51. Discuss the justice or lack of it in taking tribal lands from the Indians.

CHAPTER 7: Why did Stone Fox hit Little Willy?

CHAPTER 9: (beginning of chapter) Who do you think will win the race? Why?

CHAPTER 10: Why was winning more important than "running a good race" in this story? How are Little Willy, Searchlight, and Stone Fox *all* heroes? What would have happened if: (1) Grandfather had become well just before the race? (2) Searchlight had not died? (3) Stone Fox had not helped?

4. *Play team game "THE WINNER IS . . ."*

A. Divide students into two or three teams, selecting a spokesperson for each.

B. Tell students that you will read off ten timings for races finished by Stone Fox or Little Willy.

Example: 33 minutes
32 minutes
34 minutes . . .

C. Each student on the team adds up the scores. A consensus team score is then reached and the spokesperson raises his/her hand to report the score.
The first team reporting correctly gets a point. *Hint*: no talking allowed in group.

D. Complete additional rounds in the same manner. *Optional*: Add seconds to times (29 minutes 7 seconds, for example)

E. Alternative method of winning points: One person from each team is at the board to add the numbers.

1–7 FINISHING A RACE

CHAPTER 1

1. Match up the characters
   and their descriptions.

Little Willy	dressed up as a scarecrow
Doc Smith	wore bib overalls
Grandfather	had a white spot on her forehead
Searchlight	had snow white hair and a long, black dress

Directions: Answer the questions at the end of the given chapters. Write *small*.

CHAPTER 2

2. A *character trait* tells how a character *acts*. For example,
   when Willy hugs Searchlight and tells her he loves her, he's being
   caring.
   Write *two* character traits, that show how Willy acts. (one or two words
   each)

_____   _____

CHAPTER 3

3. The setting of a story tells its *place* and the *time*. The story, *Stone Fox*, takes
   place in (where?) _____ (when? season) _____
   Give three details (three to five words each) from the first two paragraphs about the
   setting.

A. _____ , B. _____
_____ , C. _____

CHAPTER 5 Find first the *problem* of the story and then its *solution* with the rebus puzzle.

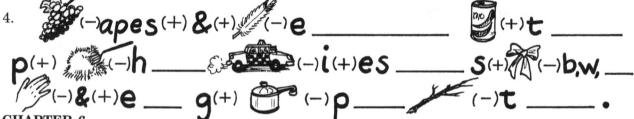

4. 🍇(−)apes(+) & (+)🪶(−)e _____ 🥫(+)t _____
p(+) 🌰(−)h _____ 🚕(−)i(+)es _____ s(+)🎀(−)b,w, _____
🤚(−)&(+)e ___ g(+)🍲(−)p _____ 🌿(−)t _____ .

CHAPTER 6

5. *Solution:*

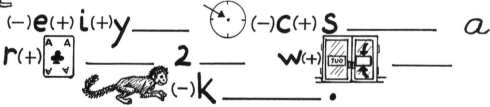

🪣(−)e(+)i(+)y ____ 🕐(−)c(+)s _____ a
r(+)♣ _____ 2 w(+)▣ _____
🐒(−)k _____ .

6. Did Stone Fox have as good a reason for wanting to win the race as
   Willy? _____ Why? _____
   _____
   _____

CHAPTER 10

7. List three good reasons why it was or was not right for Stone Fox to let
   Willy cross the finish line with Searchlight. (Think about this: Could or
   should something else have been done to help Willy?) Write your
   reasons on the back of this page. Start with: "It was right . . ."

Smith, Robert Kimmel. *The War With Grandpa.* New York: Dell, 1984. First-person account of a ten-year-old boy who struggles to maintain two separate emotions—his love for his grandfather and his independence.

Directions

1. Introduce the book by:

   A. telling students that Peter thought it unfair that he had to give up the room he loved so much to his grandfather.

   B. role-playing the decision made by the parents to have Peter give up his room. Assign the roles of the parents, the brother, and the sister. Coach students in the appropriate dialogue for the roles.

2. Read and discuss the book as follows:

   A. If multiple copies are available, alternate oral reading by the teacher with silent reading by the students. *Optional:* Select passages or chapters for oral reading by students.

   B. Students summarize and write the battle points (activity sheet) either as the story progresses or after completing the book.

   C. Point out, discuss, or otherwise present the following concepts:

   * page 1: Point out that Peter is telling the story in the first person.

   * page 10: Peter says that when you live in a room your whole life, it's yours. Do you agree? Why?

   * page 16: Students role-play possible solutions to the problem. Then ask: Which solution do you think is the best? Why?

   * page 19: Why is Dad making Peter move upstairs?

   * page 21: Write a letter to your best friend telling the friend three or more things you would never make your children do.

   * page 25: What could be some reasons for liking the upstairs room?

   * page 42: Discuss the historical context of guerrilla warfare with students.

   * page 63: What was the important reason why Grandpa wasn't interested in giving Peter back his room? Do you think he was right?

   * page 71: What name did Grandpa give the problem? Why do you think Grandpa's definition of war was different than Peter's?

   * page 74: Why *did* Grandpa hit Peter? Do you think Peter could have tried harder to settle the problem with his parents? With Grandpa? What could he have done? Is it ever OK to fight a war? When? What did Grandpa mean when he said, "War is no game . . ."?

   * page 128: Why do you think Peter's parents didn't talk to him about giving his room to Grandpa?

   * page 138: What do you think was the best thing that happened because of "the war"? Why?

After finishing the book:

1. What makes this an interesting book even for kids who have never had a "war" with a grandparent?
2. If Grandpa had told the story, how would he have told it differently?

Extended Activities

1. "Hug-O-Gram": Read "Hug O' War," from *Where the Sidewalk Ends*. Students cut out enlargements of the bear and write a Hug-O-Gram to someone special.
2. "A Perfect Room": Students design a perfect room on graph paper, or in a shoe box.

1–8 PARTS OF THE BATTLE

Name _____

Write what happened at each "battle point" in one to three sentences. Write the ideas in your own words, using complete sentences. Pages tell when battle is told or begins.

 p. 47 _____
_____
_____
_____

 p. 56 _____
_____
_____
_____

p. 61 _____
_____
_____
_____

 p. 64 _____
_____
_____
_____

 p. 81 _____
_____
_____
_____

p. 89 _____
_____
_____
_____

 p. 93 _____
_____
_____

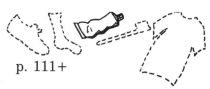 p. 111+ _____
_____
_____
_____

 p. 122+ _____
_____
_____
_____

 p. 131+ _____
_____
_____
_____

Hess, Lilo. *That Snake in the Grass.* New York: Scribner's, 1987. Engaging facts are elaborated while superstitions are dispelled in this accounting of snakes in the wild and as pets.

Materials

1. *Guinness Book of World Records,* several copies, if possible. Refer to pages giving the oldest, heaviest, and longest snakes. (See 6 below and "Find the Answer" parts on the activity sheet.)
2. Yardstick, or other device to measure students' heights.
3. *Optional, but recommended*: additional large, colored pictures of snakes, such as in Sylvia Johnson's book, *Snakes,* Lerner, 1986.

Directions

1. Introduce the book by presenting the cover and asking the following questions:
   - Will some snakes bite you even if you run away and leave them alone?
   - Can a snake run faster than you can?
   - Can a snake put its tail into its mouth and roll along like a hoop?
   - Can a snake sneak into a barn and drink milk directly from a cow's udder?
2. Review the definitions of *true*-or-*false statements* as needed. (See the activity sheet.)
3. Give students the activity sheet for preassessing their knowledge. Directions are followed from the sheet. *Note:* Students fill in the blanks for the "find the answer" sections later.
4. Read and discuss the book with students, from pages 8 through 27—the pages where information on the activity sheet is contained. Students check and correct wrong answers as the pages are read. Follow-up questions: #2: Why does it seem that snakes move so fast? #9: Why do snakes eat only when warm?
5. Ask students to write three reasons for why they think snakes are popular pets. Then read the book information on pages 37 and 38.
6. After reading the book and coloring the snake sections, students complete the "Find the Answer" part of the activity sheet using the *Guinness Book* pages, either as a total group, small group, or individually, depending on the number of *Guinness Book* copies available and the skills of the group. Recommended for younger or lower performers: Make enlarged copies of the pages with the information and underline the needed information.
   - Oldest snake: boa, living for 40 years 3 months 14 days in the Philadelphia Zoo.
   - Heaviest snake: anaconda of South America, weighing 500 pounds.
   - Longest of all snakes: reticulated python of Southeast Asia, Indonesia, and the Philippines, which regularly exceeds 20 feet 6 inches (32 feet for one snake of this kind)

   Note: The records information is from the 1989 edition. Answers from other editions may vary.

   Students measure themselves and compare the snake's length with their height. Additional records: shortest snake, most venomous snake . . .

Related Title *A Snake's Body,* by Joanna Cole, Morrow, 1981.

Extended Activity Students write their own true-or-false statements about snakes.

Additional Activity Students study an animal and develop a similar activity for the animal they studied.

Answer Key to Activity Sheet

 1. T
 2. F
 3. T
 4. T
 5. F
 6. T
 7. F
 8. T
 9. T
10. T
11. T

Directions: A statement is TRUE if all of the information is correct. A statement is FALSE if *some* or *all* of the information is not correct. 1. Before reading, write *T* beside TRUE statements, and *F* beside FALSE statements. 2. After reading, lightly color TRUE statements green and FALSE statements gray. 3. Complete Find the Answer parts and color them yellow.

1. Snakes bite people only when the snakes can't get away.

2. Snakes can move so fast that they can outrun people. (How fast can you run?)

3. A snake moves by means of its strong muscles and the scales on its belly.

4. Snakes have a "third eye," called the Jacobson's organ, through which they can recognize a mate, find food, and detect enemies.

5. Snakes that are not hungry will sometimes strike at other animals.

6. Snakes "hear" through vibrations they feel through the skull bone.

FIND THE ANSWER:

Ⓐ The oldest snake that ever lived was a _____ . It lived for _____ years. Ⓑ The heaviest snake is the _____ . The highest recorded weight is _____ lbs.

FIND THE ANSWER:

Ⓒ The longest kind of snake is the

_____

_____

It's _____ feet long.

Ⓓ I am _____ feet tall.

7. A snake can put its tail into its mouth and roll along like a hoop.

8. Snakes are very useful to farmers because they eat many harmful rodents.

9. Snakes eat only when they are warm.

10. All snakes have teeth, even though they swallow food whole.

11. All snakes can swim.

Johnston, Ginny and Judy Cutchins. *Scaly Babies: Reptiles That Grow Up.* New York: Morrow, 1988. Photographs and text describing interesting physical and behavioral characteristics of young reptiles.

Note: This is a reinforcement or review lesson for outlining skills.

Materials

1. Copies of statements in 2A for each student
2. Transparencies of pages to be outlined from chapter 4.
3. *Optional:* Large pictures of baby reptiles to display while reading chapters 1 and 2. (Sample source: *Zoobooks—Snakes, Turtles,* published by Wildlife Education, Ltd., 3590 Kettner Blvd., San Diego, California 92101); Live baby snakes, lizards, or turtles to study.
4. Duplicate activity sheet on tag for ease in game playing.

Directions

1. Introduce the book by:
   A. Asking each student to write five words describing reptiles. (Give examples of reptiles: turtles, lizards, snakes, crocodilians.)
   B. Ask: Why do many people think reptiles are ugly, slimy, and dangerous?
2. Present the information for chapters 1 and 2 as follows:
   A. To help focus student attention during the book reading, distribute copies of the following animal groups and statements:

Newborn Humans H	Kittens K	Reptiles R	Snakes S	Lizards L	Tree Boa T	Gila Monster G

_____ Most are harmless to humans

_____ Drink milk from mother

_____ Are on their own from the moment of birth

_____ Swallow their food whole

_____ Born with instincts to hide

_____ Have an amazing tail that "pops" off

_____ Look like a tiny copy of their parents

_____ Mother takes care of baby when first born

_____ Born with instincts to escape enemies

_____ Can climb a tree minutes after birth

_____ Are affected by extreme hot and cold temperatures

_____ Are usually hatched from an egg

_____ Are born with instinct to find food

_____ Have no eyelids to close eyes

_____ Uses tail to store extra fat

_____ Scales are dry and moist to protect from the heat

_____ Young develop inside the mother's body for 240 days

_____ Scales called "scutes" help them move

_____ Uses venom and powerful jaws for defense

B. Give students these directions to follow for completing the statements before reading chapters 1 and 2 to them:
   1. Read each statement and write the letter for the group(s) that the statement is true for.
   2. Statements can be true for more than one animal group.
   3. Write the letter(s) in front of the statement.

C. Next, read or tell the important information in chapters 1 and 2, especially the concepts contained in the statements above. As the information is shared, instruct students to add to, change, or correct statements by putting symbols to the right. Discuss and compare student analysis. *Note:* Information about the Asian Cobra is optional, as it is not included in the above statements.

   Optional: Draw illustrations of concepts on the overhead or board. (See examples.)

D. Chapter 3: reading is optional.

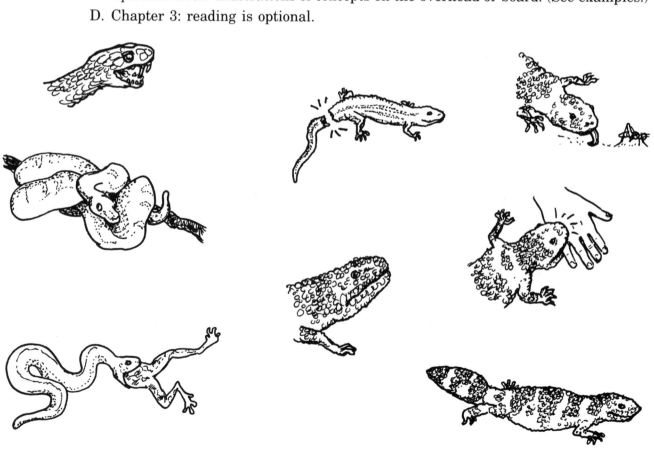

3. At another time period, read or tell the important information from the Introduction to chapter 4.

4. Review outlining skills, including the terms *topic, subtopic,* and *details.*

5. Present the activity sheet and complete with students the outlining for the *first* and *third* topics, "Loggerhead Sea Turtle" and "Gopher Turtle."

   A. Present information one topic at a time, using transparencies if possible. Read the information to students.

   B. Present the information a second time, paragraph by paragraph, with students reading silently.

   C. Students write the topic, subtopics (paragraph topic), and key details.

   D. Tell students to write *small!*

   Optional, but recommended: Sample outline on transparency.

6. Chapter 5 is optional.

7. Play "Pin the tail on the turtle."

   (1) Either enlarge the turtle image, or use a transparency of the drawn turtle and project it onto a wall.

   (2) Students tape their tails to the wall or chalkboard.

Answer Key to Activity Sheet

On left side of turtle

I. Loggerhead Sea Turtle
   A. Laying eggs
      1. in sand
      2. one hundred
   B. Dangers of hatching
      1. many nests destroyed
      2. hatch in 60 days
   C. Journey to the ocean
      1. instinct
      2. some die
   D. Survival in the ocean
      1. strong swimmers
      2. eat on own
      3. hide in seaweed

On right side of turtle

II. Gopher Tortoise
   A. Hatching
      1. seven hatchlings
      2. dig through sandy soil
      3. soft claws, sturdy legs
   B. Nest & burrow
      1. nest at burrow entrance
      2. burrow—20 feet
      3. mother ignores babies
   C. After hatching
      1. wander off
      2. dig burrow
   D. Food
      1. plant eater
      2. bite: "scissor" teeth
      3. food gives water
   E. Protection
      1. burrow protects from sun, not enemies
      2. tortoise pulls in head, tail, legs
      3. camouflaged
      4. can survive 40 years

Name _____

Directions: Write the first topic, *Loggerhead Sea Turtle* and its subtopics and details on the LEFT side of the turtle. Outline the second topic, *Gopher Tortoise*, on the RIGHT.

©1991 by The Center for Applied Research in Education

Write your name and your favorite turtle fact on the tail and cut it out. Play "Pin the tail on the turtle."

Fleischman, Sid. *The Whipping Boy.* **New York: Greenwillow, 1986.** Newbery-winning novel about a spoiled prince and his whipping boy. They run away and are caught by two ruffians who are fooled as to their identities.

Note for Fourth-Grade Use   Use later in the year with good to excellent students.

Materials

Large area to play game "Get Away Jemmy." (See 3B below.)

Teacher Preparation

1. Read the book before presenting it to students.
2. List key ideas relating to setting, character, plot, and style that reflect both the story concepts and the time period.
3. Be prepared to point out specific details related to the above areas, *even if students appear not to have questions.*
4. Note use of similes.
5. See 3C below for broad comprehension concepts to discuss.

Directions

1. Introduce the book by noting the Newbery award given to the book in 1987. Ask students to consider, during the reading, why this book was selected by a group of children's literature experts.
2. Read and discuss the book with students, either by reading aloud to them, or preferably, if multiple copies are available, by combining oral and silent reading. *Note:* When reading aloud, be prepared to supply the name of the person being quoted when it may be confusing.
3. Conduct the reading and completion of the activity sheet as follows:
   A. For a reasonable division of both book and activity sheet completion, follow chapter sections on the activity sheet.
   B. Additional directions for activity sheet questions 1, 2, and 3:

   Question 1: Give non–book-related examples of jokes, pranks, or "annoying other people."

   Question 2: Game, "Get Away Jemmy": Select a large play area (gym, outside). The persons who are "it" keep going back and forth until everyone is caught. Everyone has to get to the other end of the game area before a new round can begin.

   Question 3: Hints—(a) the *words* are in the correct order; (b) the message is not in the exact words of the book; (c) message is a sentence; (d) optional help: supply word divisions or selected letters. Message: "Send a cart full of treasures."

   C. Comprehension discussion concepts, starting with chapter 8:
   * after chapter 8: Why do you think the author "mixed up" Jemmy and Prince Brat?
   * after chapter 9: What was Jemmy's plan for tricking the villains?
   * page 40: Why does Prince Brat betray Jemmy?
   * page 49: How has the prince changed?
   * page 58: Why didn't the prince bawl? Why did he want Jemmy's friendship?

- page 66: Discuss the differences between "school knowledge," or "book learning," and "street knowledge." What are the advantages of each?
- page 69, bottom: Discuss the meaning of what's important in life—status and clothes, or concern for others and leadership.
- page 77: What does it take to trust someone?
- page 89, last paragraph: Define the word *convict,* then ask: Why is this idea funny?

D. Large issues for discussion:

(1) What are the two social classes depicted in the story? What social classes exist today?

(2) What dangers would Jemmy and Prince Brat face if they ran away today?

E. Additional oral or written discussion questions:

(1) What makes the characters humorous?

(2) Describe two or three humorous events.

(3) Which of the two boys would you choose for a friend, and why? OR: Which would you choose to take on a trip with you? Why?

(4) Why would you like to, or not like to, live in a castle?

(5) Why did the Newbery committee vote this as the "top book" for 1987? (Point out that personal taste and the *kind* of story are part of a person's evaluation of a book.) OR: You are on the Newbery committee: Would you vote for this book? Why or why not?

Additional Activity   "A Letter for a Friend—'Gaw'!" Students assume one of the two characters, Jemmy or Prince Brat, and write a letter to the other character:

- thanking for the help he gave you when you were kidnapped by the rogues;
- describing how to catch a rat *or* how to cause mischief in the palace;
- describing what the other does to help you in your daily life; or
- your choice.

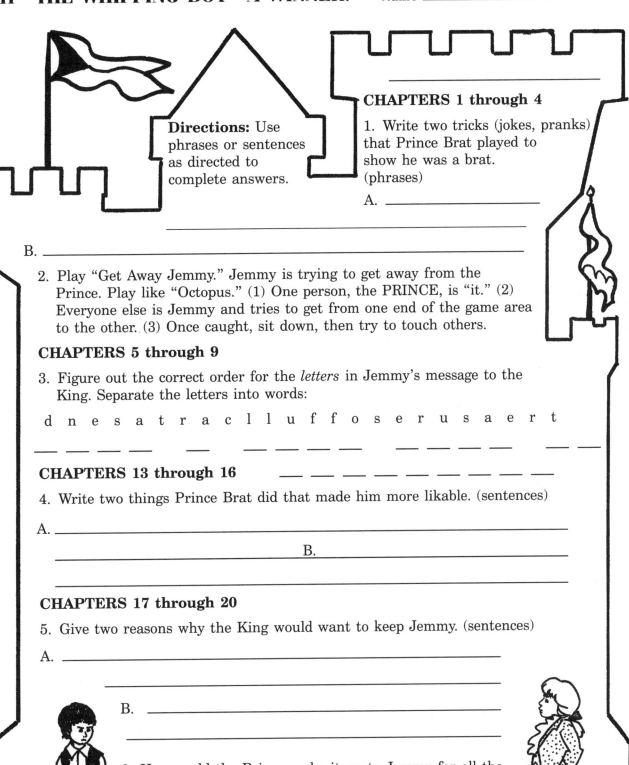

Directions: Use phrases or sentences as directed to complete answers.

CHAPTERS 1 through 4

1. Write two tricks (jokes, pranks) that Prince Brat played to show he was a brat. (phrases)

A. _____

_____

B. _____

2. Play "Get Away Jemmy." Jemmy is trying to get away from the Prince. Play like "Octopus." (1) One person, the PRINCE, is "it." (2) Everyone else is Jemmy and tries to get from one end of the game area to the other. (3) Once caught, sit down, then try to touch others.

CHAPTERS 5 through 9

3. Figure out the correct order for the *letters* in Jemmy's message to the King. Separate the letters into words:

d n e s a t r a c l l u f f o s e r u s a e r t

__ __ __ __   __   __ __ __ __ __ __ __ __ __

CHAPTERS 13 through 16   __ __ __ __ __ __ __ __

4. Write two things Prince Brat did that made him more likable. (sentences)

A. _____

_____ B. _____

_____

CHAPTERS 17 through 20

5. Give two reasons why the King would want to keep Jemmy. (sentences)

A. _____

_____

B. _____

_____

6. How could the Prince make it up to Jemmy for all the spankings he got when the Prince wouldn't do his lessons? (Write one to three sentences on back).

7. Tell how FRIENDSHIP (or LOYALTY, choose one) is important in this book. Begin with "Friendship (or Loyalty) is important because _____ ." (three or more sentences on back)

D'Aulaire, Ingri and Edgar Parin D'Aulaire. *D'Aulaires' Book of Greek Myths.* **New York: Doubleday, 1962.** The gods, goddesses, and heroes of ancient Greece come to life with all of their heroic, powerful, mischievous, tricky, and winsome characteristics.

Additional Reference Evslin, Bernard. *Gods, Demigods & Demons: An Encyclopedia of Greek Mythology.* Scholastic, 1975.

Note: This is a *follow-up activity* to Activity 2–10, To Tell the Truth: Zeus and His Family, or other study of Greek mythology.

Directions

1. Discuss with students the idea that many words and terms in use today come from the Greeks and their mythology. For example: The name *Electra*, the daughter of Agamemnon, shares the same root as our word *electricity*. *Cronus* turns up in *chronograph* and *chronology*.

2. A. Read about and/or review the information about the following characters in the D'Aulaires' book: Python, Arachne, Clotho, Echo, Atlas, Achilles, Hermes, the Titans.

   B. Tell students that there are more characters and terms originating with Greek mythology that have modern day applications. Reinforce the information presented that is contained on the activity sheet.

   C. Alternative teacher presentation of material: Organize students into cooperative groups and assign each group a character to study and present to the large group. *Note:* If several copies of the D'Aulaires' book are not available, make copies of the appropriate page(s) for each group.

3. Present the original Greek meanings for the three remaining terms on the activity sheet: *Marathon, Biblis,* and *Hypnos.*

4. Review information contained on the activity sheet as needed.

5. Facilitate completion of the activity sheet:

   A. Students read directions contained on the sheet.

   B. Students complete the sheet individually, in pairs, or small groups.

   C. Depending on the skills of the group, and the purpose for using the sheet, names or correct sentence completions can be written in random order on the chalkboard for students to refer to.

6. When the activity sheet is completed, introduce other terms and expressions rooted in mythology, such as: Calliope, Pandora's box, by Jove, mentor.

Follow-Up Activity Students collect objects, pictures, and ideas from their everyday lives with origins in Greek mythology, from newspapers, magazines, TV, purchased products. Make a bulletin board display!

Answer Key to Activity Sheet

- PYTHON—crush their prey
- ARACHNE—arachnid
- MARATHON—foot race of 26 miles or any long-distance race

- CLOTHO—cloth, clothes
- ECHO—sounds
- ATLAS—maps or bound book of charts, plates, or tables
- BIBLIS—Bible, bibliography
- ACHILLES—hurt
- HERMES—hermit
- TITANS—Titanic
- HYPNOS—hypnosis, hypnotism

GREEK HEROES LIVE NOW!

Name _____

"IT'S GREEK TO ME"

Directions: Fill in the correct letters for each Greek name beside the pictures. Write the letter from each *box* on the blanks at the top, matching correct numbers. Spell a mystery sentence! Complete the sentences with the correct word or words.

GREEK _ _ _ _ _ _ _ _ V _ _ _ W !
　　　　1 2 3 4 5 6 7 8　9　10 11

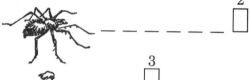

1
_ _ _ _ [ ] _ _ _

The dragon killed by Apollo at Delphi. Today, this is the name of some snakes that

_____

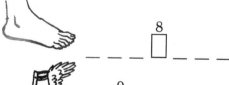

2
_ _ _ _ _ _ [ ]

Athena won the weaving contest and changed this girl who challenged her into a spider. Today the class name for spider is arachn _ _.

3
_ [ ] _ _ _ _ _ _

A plain in SE Greece where the Greeks defeated the Persians. A runner ran 26 miles from here to Athens to give the news. Today, a marathon is

_____

4
_ _ [ ] _ _ _

One of the three Fates. She spun out the thread of each life on her spindle. Our modern word _____ is related to her name.

HELLO
HELLO

5
[ ] _ _ _

Hera took away this mountain nymph's ability to form words. She could only repeat words of others. Today, the word describes the repeating of _____.

6
_ _ _ _ [ ]

The Titan who was punished by being forced to hold the sky on his shoulder. Today, an atlas is a book of

_____

7
_ _ _ [ ] _ _

Ancient Phoenician city that shares its name with a word for "books." Other modern related words are

_____

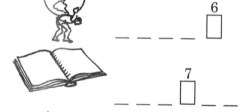

8
_ _ _ _ _ [ ] _ _ _

Greatest of all Greek warriors who could only be hurt on his heel. Today, a part or a trait of a person that can be especially _____ is called the Achilles heel.

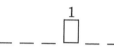

9
[ ] _ _ _

Messenger and god of magic who sealed air into a bottle to keep it from outside influence. Today, a person who stays away from others is a _____.

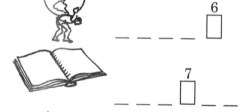

10
_ _ _ [ ] _ _

The first giants created by the marriage of Gaia and Uranus. Today, the word refers to persons or things of large size, strength, or power. A giant ship that sank almost 80 years ago is the _____.

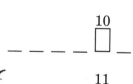

11
_ _ _ _ [ ] _

The god of sleep. A related modern word is:

_____

©1991 by The Center for Applied Research in Education

Literature Analysis and Appreciation with Children's Books

Marshall, James, retold and illustrated by. *Red Riding Hood.* **New York: Dial, 1987.** Granny is most disturbed about having her reading interrupted, and her granddaughter promises "never to talk to strangers again."

Directions

1. Introduce the book by telling students that Granny has a "most unusual reason" for being mad at the wolf.

2. Read and discuss the book with students, including the humor of both the writing and the illustrations.

   Optional: Use context and picture clues for vocabulary understanding of some or all of the following words:

   up to *snuff*

   do not *tarry*

   such *charming* manners

   feeling *poorly*

   escort you

   lurking about

   Red Riding Hood was *distressed*

3. Conduct the completion of the activity sheet as follows:

   A. Reinforce concepts by:

      1. asking students to describe particular people, places, and things that each character especially liked

      2. reviewing with students Granny's appreciation of books and reading

      3. reinforcing, in a positive and light manner, the theme of choice of friends being important

   B. Students write answers independently, in pairs, or with the whole group, depending on the level and purpose.

Related Books *Little Red Riding Hood,* retold and illustrated by Trina Schart Hyman (Holiday, 1983); and *Once Upon a Time* . . . from the Reading Is Fundamental organization, article by Hyman titled: "Little Red Riding Hood."

Extended Activities

1. "Reading in Unusual Places": Granny tried to read inside the wolf. Discuss unusual places where students like to read. Find unusual places to read in the classroom and have a "Read-In."

2. "Red Riding Hood's Book Basket": Familiar books are put inside a basket. Students secretly select one to describe the plot or characters for. Other students identify the book.

Additional Activity "How to Have the Right Friends, A Play": Students role play, or stage a play or puppet show about stranger awareness.

Circle the things
the characters liked:
Red Riding Hood
liked 1. Granny;
2. the deep,
dark woods;
3. to be kind.

Granny liked
1. the wolf;
2. custard;
3. reading.

The wolf liked
1. eating;
2. sleeping;
3. the hunter.

Complete the sentence: When Granny was
inside the wolf, it was so dark that she couldn't

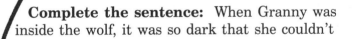

Fill in the missing words for Red Riding Hood's new book
called: *How to Have the Right Friends.*

1. Be kind to the _____ you
    already have!

2. Make new friends by _____

    _____ .

3. If a stranger tries to talk to you when you are

    walking, keep on _____ .

4. You never know if a stranger will act like the

     wolf.

Carle, Eric. *A House for Hermit Crab*. Saxonville, MA: Picture Book Studio, 1987. The true habits of the hermit crab are shown in this modern-day fable when one crab copes with growth, change, and friendships.

Materials

1. Crayons, colored pencils, or other coloring materials to color the sea animals; scissors; glue.

2. *Optional*: Large photographs of the hermit crab and other sea animals, for use after reading the book. Good sources: *Where the Waves Break: Life at the Edge of the Sea*, by Anita Malnig, Carolrhoda, 1985; *Eyewitness Books: Seashore*, by Steve Parker, Knopf, 1989; and *Creatures of the Sea*, by John Christopher, Fine/Atheneum, 1989.

Directions

1. Introduce the book by pointing out the information about hermit crabs adjacent to the title page.

2. Next, read and enjoy the story with the students.

3. When finished, elaborate on the story's concepts and themes.

   A. Define and discuss the meaning of a *fable*.

   - A fable is a story that teaches a lesson about something that happens in someone's life.

   - The characters are usually animals that act like people.

   - Ask students to share this story's lesson.

   B. Share the author information and background information about the sea creatures. (Use the resources suggested above.) Point out the special relationship between the hermit crab and the sea anemone, called *symbiosis*.

   C. Ask students to share their experiences about changes and trying new things.

4. Complete the activity sheet with students as follows:

   A. Follow the directions on the sheet.

   B. Help students compose two- to four-word descriptions of the sea animals. *Optional*: write ideas on transparency as a model.

   C. Discuss additional themes—being a friend (as well as having one), safety, beauty, helpfulness.

   D. Students *lightly* color the animals, leaving as much of the writing showing as possible.

   E. Students glue the objects so that writing is still visible. *Optional*: create a "seascape" with the cut-outs on construction paper (instead of placing objects on the crab).

Extended Activities

1. "Hermit and Company": Students make puppets and tell the original story or create their own adaptation.

2. Students write a group sequel to the story, using additional sea animals—barnacles, clownfish, and so forth.

PART I:
Write what Hermit Crab did in the story. Then tell what the other animals did to help.

PART II:
Lightly color the animals. Cut out and paste on Hermit Crab.

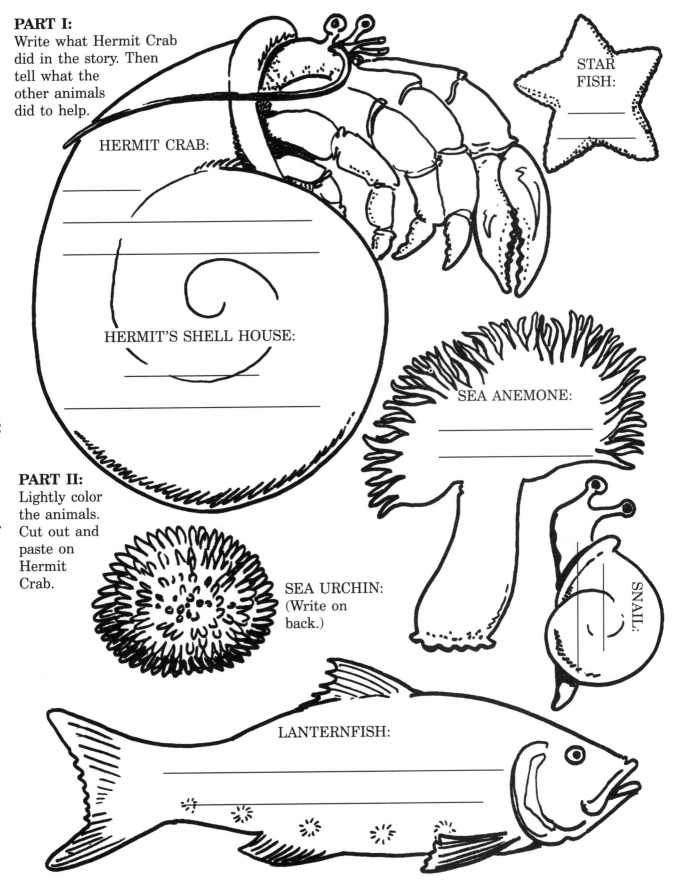

STAR FISH:
_____

HERMIT CRAB:
_____
_____
_____

HERMIT'S SHELL HOUSE:
_____
_____

SEA ANEMONE:
_____
_____

SNAIL:

SEA URCHIN:
(Write on back.)

LANTERNFISH:
_____
_____

Lear, Edward. *The Owl and the Pussy-Cat.* Illustrated by Paul Galdone. New York: Clarion, 1987. Lear's classic nonsense poem with Galdone's fanciful design and features. Other illustrators include Lorinda Bryan Cauley.

Directions

1. Introduce the book by:
   A. presenting the cover and asking students to give their ideas about the humor of a friendship between an owl and a cat
   B. telling them that Edward Lear wrote this poem—and all of his others—as "pure fun" or "utter nonsense."

2. Read the poem to students, focusing on the following:
   A. Ask students to listen for the "utter nonsense" of the characters and happenings that create the humor and charm.
   B. Relate that Edward Lear was an English poet and landscape artist who wrote the poem in 1871.
   C. Point out unfamiliar terms, such as:
      • *Bong-tree—Bong* is from *bung* which means cork or other stopper
      • *runcible spoon*—(Lear's own term, coined especially for this poem, and included ever after in the dictionary) a utensil like a fork, with three wide prongs
   D. Tell students that later they'll hear about Lear's own interests in love and marriage, and cats!

3. After reading and sharing the whimsical incongruencies, point out the following about Edward Lear's life: He loved animals and, some of the time, he liked love and marriage. After many years, he asked his long-time friend to marry him. She said, "No!" after such a long wait. This all happened about the time Lear wrote *The Owl and the Pussy-Cat.* He spent the rest of his life with his cat.

4. Complete the activity sheet as follows:
   A. Depending on the age and level of the students, students work independently, in pairs, or as a large group. For young students, group work is recommended, using a transparency of the page as a model.
   B. Students evaluate and compare ideas.
      Optional: students mount the page on a cut-out heart and decorate as a Valentine.

Additional Book *The Complete Nonsense of Edward Lear,* collected and introduced by Holbrook Jackson, Dover, 1951.

Extended Activities

1. Students dramatize the story, using puppets.
2. Students choose two other incongruous animal characters to write their own story about.

Directions:
Think of how
this poem is "fun
and nonsense" as you
write your ideas.

1. What reason could the Owl and the
   Pussy-Cat have had for taking honey—other
   than needing food? _____

   _____

2. Write one nice thing Owl said about Pussy: _____

   _____

   Write one nice thing Pussy said about Owl: _____

   _____

3. Why is it funny that they sailed for more than a year to

   find a ring? _____

   _____

4. How is the Pussy character like a real cat? _____

   _____

5. Write two more things that happened that make this a

   humorous love story: A. _____

   _____

B. _____

6. What would Pussy have done if Owl had been too scared to marry her?
   Write on the back.

Perrault, Charles. Retold by Amy Ehrlich. *Cinderella*. Illustrated by Susan Jeffers. New York: Dial, 1985. Exquisite illustrations highly compliment the retelling.

Note: Other translations or retellings with the same content as the activity sheet can be used.

Materials

1. One copy of the activity sheet for each student on pink or white (heavy) paper
2. White or pink (the opposite color from above) 9-by-12-inch construction paper
3. Crayons or felt pens, heart-decorating materials

Directions

1. Read and discuss the selected version.
2. Teach or reinforce both the term and concept of *generalization*.
   A. Define the term: A *generalization* is a general idea or conclusion based on known facts.
   B. Give the following examples:
      (1) • The dog tipped over the garbage can and ate out of it.
          • The dog kept sniffing the dry dogfood bag.
          • The dog licked its empty food dish.
          What general idea, or conclusion, can you get from those facts? *The dog was hungry.*
      (2) • The prince thought Cinderella's gown and face were lovely.
          • All the guests at the ball admired her pretty clothes and looks.
          What general idea, or conclusion, can you get about how she looked? *She looked beautiful.*
   C. Supplement with other generalizations, as needed.
3. Students complete the activity sheet writing either as a whole group, with partners, or individually, depending on the skill level.
4. Students complete the puzzle by carefully cutting out the pieces, fitting them together to form a heart, and gluing the pieces onto the background paper. *Optional*: decorate as a Valentine.

Additional Activity "Sensational Synonyms"

1. Make up an activity sheet using both lists, or only list I. Optional: write on an overhead.

I	II
tease	gentle
cry	ball
party dresses	mock
stopped	murmur
whisper	ceased
fine dinner	weep
dance	gowns

kind	banquet
unhappiness	finest
clean	ragged
torn	scrub
best	misery

2. Students either match up the synonyms from the lists, or write their own synonyms for the words in list I.

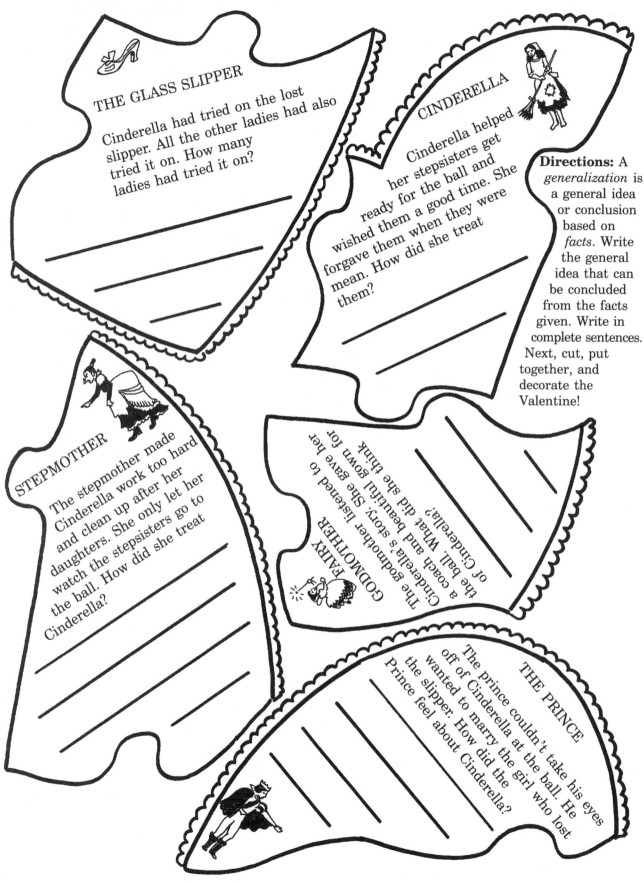

THE GLASS SLIPPER

Cinderella had tried on the lost slipper. All the other ladies had also tried it on. How many ladies had tried it on?

_____

_____

_____

CINDERELLA

Cinderella helped her stepsisters get ready for the ball and wished them a good time. She forgave them when they were mean. How did she treat them?

_____

_____

_____

Directions: A *generalization* is a general idea or conclusion based on *facts*. Write the general idea that can be concluded from the facts given. Write in complete sentences. Next, cut, put together, and decorate the Valentine!

STEPMOTHER

The stepmother made Cinderella work too hard and clean up after her daughters. She only let her watch the stepsisters go to the ball. How did she treat Cinderella?

_____

_____

_____

FAIRY GODMOTHER

The godmother listened to Cinderella's story. She gave her a coach and beautiful gown for the ball. What did she think of Cinderella?

_____

_____

_____

THE PRINCE

The prince couldn't take his eyes off of Cinderella at the ball. He wanted to marry the girl who lost the slipper. How did the Prince feel about Cinderella?

_____

_____

_____

Gerrard, Roy. *Sir Cedric.* **New York: Farrar, Straus and Giroux, 1984.** Sir Cedric, the brave knight, receives more than honor when he battles Black Ned. Satirical comedy poking good-natured fun at chivalry.

Optional Materials

1. Books and pictures about knights, castles, and the Middle Ages.
2. Related Books: Random House All-About Books: *Knights and Castles,* by Jonathan Rutland, 1976; *A Tournament of Knights* by Joe Lasker, Harper, 1989.

Directions

1. Introduce the book by showing the cover and asking students to share their knowledge about knights.

2. Present additional information if possible or summarize with the following:

   Armored knights on horseback, living during the Middle Ages from 500 A.D. to 1500 A.D., were both admired and feared. Since Europe was divided into many kingdoms, and since the kings quarreled, knights were called on to help the kings fight their enemies. As a reward, the knights were given land. They had to build castles to also defend themselves against the king's enemies! They were expected to be honest and kind, and to be good soldiers.

3. Read the book to students, enjoying the satirical comment on bravery and goodness, and the finely balanced watercolor paintings.

   A. After reading, discuss and point out:

   (1) how bravery, politeness, and modesty (implies a becoming shyness and proper behavior) are made fun of in a happy, appealing way

   (2) how exaggeration—in both the rhyming story and the illustrations (horse, etc.)—creates humor. Equally important is understatement—the small people characters with heads normal, bodies small.

   (3) typical fairy tale themes or motifs

   B. Ask students these questions:

   (1) What could be some reasons that Roy Gerrard (who received a *New York Times* award for this book for "Best Illustrated Book of the Year") exaggerated the characters? Types of exaggeration? Why?

   (2) How are Sir Cedric and Matilda like people you know?

4. Review the concept of *character trait:*
   A. Definition: how a character acts or behaves or is thought of by others
   B. Give examples for Sir Cedric and in general (bold, kind, mean, clever, truthful, selfish)

5. Reread the story to find character traits of Sir Cedric. Make a list of at least fifteen traits as a group, or have each student write his own list.

6. Students complete the activity sheet by following directions given. Additional directions for Part II:
   A. If students have difficulty with the fortunes, provide the same format as in the example: Your _____ will _____.
   B. More examples of fortunes:
      • Your popularity will earn you a lifetime supply of cucumber sandwiches.
      • Your friendliness will gain you invitations to all of Black Ned's parties.

Additional Activity   "The Likes of Larger (or Smaller) Than Life":

1. *Optional*: Peruse Roy Gerrard's *The Favershams* with students, noting the oversized and undersized objects.

2. Students draw an object or a part of an object that is either oversized or undersized in relation to the rest of the picture.

3. Students write a short story about what is happening in their pictures.

Name _____

PART I: A. Select one of the four shapes below. B. Lightly outline that shape in the middle of the paper. C. Write 15 or more character traits for Sir Cedric inside the shape, FOLLOWING THE SHAPE'S OUTLINE. Repeat traits to fill up the inside of the shape.

PART II: Since Sir Cedric was "brave for his country, and kind to Matilda," he deserves some "good luck." Matilda has just given him fortune cookies to open. Write three good fortunes for Sir Cedric. Example: "Your kindness will lead to a long and healthy life."

A. _____

B. _____

C. _____   _____

_____   _____

Story Selection and Appreciation

Lobel, Arnold. *Fables.* **New York: Harper & Row, 1980.** Short, original fables with inviting animal characters.

Directions

1. Select several fables with the most likely appeal and read them to the students. Examples that other groups have liked are: "The Ducks and the Fox," "The Ostrich in Love," "The Camel Dances," "The Bad Kangaroo," "The Elephant and His Son."

2. Discuss the fables in terms of the following elements:

   A. What is a *fable?*

   A short story that teaches a lesson, often with animal characters who are personified (act like people).

   B. *Characters*

      1. Their Actions

         Examples: Bad Kangaroo—throwing spitballs and setting off firecrackers; the Camel—practices her ballet routines without stopping;

      2. Personification

         Kangaroo—likes to play tricks, just like some people; Camel—has the ambition to do something well for others to watch, just like most kids and adults like to be recognized;

      3. Humor and Exaggeration

         The animals perform human actions, whereas normally the animals' instincts would tell them not to throw spitballs or try to perfect the five basic ballet positions.

   C. *Plot*—what happens in the story, the problem and its solution. Examples:
      • Kangaroo: Principal comes to see parents and finds them doing the same thing as their son.
      • Camel: She finds out she is not graceful enough to dance for an audience, but learns to be content with dancing for herself.

   D. *Moral* or lesson

      What should be understood or can be learned from the fable? How does it apply to you or to people you know?

3. Ask each student to select a favorite fable, after verbally answering the questions below.

   A. Which character(s) did the most interesting or exciting things?

   B. What did the character(s) do?

   C. Why did the character(s) do it?

   D. Which fable had the most meaning to you? Think about the experiences that you, your family, and your friends have.

4. Distribute the certificates. Tell students to complete the two statements using their answers to the above questions. Sample answers:
   • "I like this fable because it's funny when kangaroo paws can set off firecrackers. It's also humorous that the kangaroos didn't know they were being bad."
   • "I like the lesson or moral ("The Camel Dances") because it shows you that if you like what you do, it doesn't matter what other people think."

   Students complete the certificate by drawing the face of the main character inside the ribbon and decorating.

2–6

CERTIFICATE OF AWARD

This award is given to the fable

_____

for being a favorite fable.

I like this fable because _____

_____

_____

I like the lesson or moral because _____

_____

_____

Signed _____

McGovern, Ann. *The Secret Soldier*. New York: Four Winds Press, reissued, 1987. Paper copies available from Scholastic. The brief biography of Deborah Sampson, a young woman who disguised herself as a man to fight with the Continental Army during the Revolutionary War.

Optional but Recommended Materials

1. Background information and pictures about life before and during the Revolutionary War.

2. Feathers or thin ends of tree branches for making a quill pen. Tempera paint, white paper. See 2C, "A Family Again."

Directions

1. Introduce the book by asking students to describe a situation when someone has disguised himself (Halloween, a play, etc.) enough so that he couldn't be identified. Tell students that *The Secret Soldier* is the story of a young woman named Deborah Sampson who managed to keep her disguise as a man a secret—for an unbelievable amount of time—so she could fight in the Revolutionary War.

2. Read and discuss the book with students as follows:

   A. If multiple copies are available, combine oral reading by the teacher and students with silent reading by the students.

   B. *Optional, but recommended for older students*: students write questions (and their answers) about the story as it is being read. Later, questions can be exchanged among students for answering. Suggested question formats:

   What would happen if . . . ?

   What happened when . . . ?

   Why did _____ do/say . . . ?

   If you were _____, what would you do when . . . ?

   List names, terms, and places for students to use in questions.

   C. Questions and activities to guide the discussion are:

   "Sent Away"*

   (p. 16, end): Summarize what happened to Deborah.

   "A Family Again":

   (p. 18): What could be some reasons people didn't think reading was important for girls?

   (p. 18): How do you teach someone to read? Students are in pairs with one student as Deborah teaching one of the Thomas boys how to read. Use feather or stick, tempera, and white paper for writing letters and words. Brainstorm steps for teaching (letter names, sounds, blending sounds). Other option: pair students with primary-age students to teach the young students new words.

   (p. 20): How is living with a family different than being a member of it? What did Deborah like most about living with the Thomas family?

*Pages are for hardcover edition.

"Free—To Do What?"

(p. 30): How would Deborah set up a class, with twenty students from the ages of six to eighteen? Students are in groups of three or four to brainstorm how reading, writing, math, and social studies could be taught.

(p. 31): If Deborah lived today, what are some daring things she might choose to do?

"The Fortune Teller" (p. 34): Will her mother know her? Why or why not?

"Discovery" (p. 50): Why didn't Dr. Binney give Deborah away?

"Adventure Again" (p. 62, end): What else, beside the adventure, became important to Deborah during her time as a soldier?

Describe other women who have become heroes.

3. Complete the activity sheet using directions on the sheet and the following:

A. Part I, answers:

WHO? DEBORAH SAMPSON; WHAT? JOINED ARMY AS CONTINENTAL SOLDIER; WHEN? AT TWENTY-ONE; WHERE? BOSTON; WHY? ADVENTURE; HOW? DISGUISED AS A MAN.

B. Part II:

(1) Students write the WORDS for their code on another sheet *first*.

(2) Next, the code numbers are identified from the numbers used at the top of the activity sheet and recorded on lines that say "NUMBERS."

(3) Articles and other short words—*a, the, was*—can be written on a line with the longer ones.

(4) Sample sentences: Deborah was hurt badly. Deborah was a teacher.

C. Part III: Example features to add include a hat, mustache, beard, glasses.

Related Book   *A Different Twist,* by Elizabeth Levy, Scholastic 1986.

Additional Activity   Students disguise themselves for identification by classmates.

I. This book is a *biography*. A biography is the story of a person's life written by another person. It usually tells *who, what, when, where, how,* and *why* about the person's life. Figure out the secret code below, and use it to discover the secrets of Deborah Sampson.

A	B	C	D	E	F	G	H	I	J	K	L	M	N	O	P	Q	R	S	T	U	V	W	X	Y	Z
26	24	22	20	18	16	14	12	10	8	6	4	2	1	3	5	7	9	11	13	15	17	19	21	23	25

WHO?   20, 18, 24, 3, 9, 26, 12   11, 26, 2, 5, 11, 3, 1

_____   _____

WHAT?   8, 3, 10, 1, 18, 20   26, 9, 2, 23   26, 11

_____   _____   _____

22, 3, 1, 13, 10, 1, 18, 1, 13, 26, 4   11, 3, 4, 20, 10, 18, 9

_____   _____

WHEN?   26, 13   13, 19, 18, 1, 13, 23   3, 1, 18

_____   _____   _____

WHERE?   24, 3, 11, 13, 3, 1   Why?   26, 20, 17, 18, 1, 13, 15, 9, 18

_____   _____

HOW?   20, 10, 11, 14, 15, 10, 11, 18, 20   26, 11,   26   2, 26, 1

_____   _____   ____   _____

II. Using the numbers for the alphabet above, write a three or four word secret message for a partner to figure out. Think of a phrase or sentence from the story. You write *only* the numbers. Write one word per line.

III. Disguise the girl's face with objects or features for a male soldier. Include a mustache, beard, etc.

Word 1
NUMBERS _____

Letters _____
(Do not write on this line when making code.)

Word 2
NUMBERS _____

Letters _____

Word 3
NUMBERS _____

Letters _____

Word 4
NUMBERS _____

Letters _____

Smith, Doris Buchanan. *A Taste of Blackberries.* **New York: Harper, 1973.** Since Jamie liked to tease and act, it was difficult to tell if he was acting when he fell to the ground after one bee sting. Tasteful treatment of coping with the sudden death of a best friend.

Note about the activity sheet   Duplicate so that character traits in the blackberries are clearly readable.

Regarding review notes on back cover   It is recommended that students not read these notes, so as to retain plot anticipation and suspense.

Directions

1. Show students the cover of the book and discuss the experiences of planning a summer of fun with a good friend.
2. Read the book to students using alternatives to teacher's oral reading. Students read partially or totally independently, or the teacher orally reads selected parts to group.
   A. At the beginning of the book, point out that the unnamed narrator is Jamie's best friend.
   B. Discuss the important points of character and plot as the chapters are read. Include the following:
      • Character traits of Jamie and the narrator—how each *acts* and *behaves*.
      • After chapter 2: Why do you think Jamie accepted the ride?
      • After chapter 3: What does the narrator believe about what happened to Jamie?
      • After Chapter 4: Point out that the narrator is going through the process of acceptance of and grieving for a friend's death. What are some reasons it was hard for the narrator to accept the fact that Jamie was dead?
      • After Chapter 5: Why do you cry for yourself when a person or animal dies?
      • After Chapter 6: Why do you think the narrator couldn't let things be the same (eating and playing, for example) until after the funeral?
      • After Chapter 7: Describe similar feelings you've had when a person or animal close to you has died.
      • After Chapter 8: Why was going to see Jamie's mother helpful to both the narrator and Jamie's mother? Why was going up the street to play "the right thing to do" after talking to Jamie's mother? Point out that the story began with Jamie and the narrator finding out that the blackberries weren't quite ripe. At the end, the narrator completed the activity, fulfilling a promise to Jamie and to himself.
   C. Discuss the stages or phases the narrator went through to accept Jamie's death.
   D. Additional questions about coping with death:
      • What are some helpful things that a person can do to get over someone's death?
      • Why is going back to normal things again important?

3. Present or review the concept of *character traits:*

A. Definition: how a character *acts* or *behaves.*

B. Examples:

Red Riding Hood—friendly, caring, generous, honest

the Wolf—sly, dishonest, greedy

4. Activity sheet completion:

A. Part I:

(1) Display and define the following character traits contained on the activity sheet:

Tease—someone who annoys in a playful way

Risk-Taker—someone who does something that could be harmful or dangerous

Daring—someone who does something to see if he can get away with it

Overdoer—someone who does something "too much" or in excess

Camaraderie—to have a close friendship with someone and to share fun and feelings

(2) Direct students to discriminate carefully to identify the trait each feels best describes the situation.

After students complete Part I, put them in pairs or small or large groups to share and defend their answers. *Note:* there will be differences in answers, depending on the students' backgrounds and experiences.

B. Part II:

(1) Before students work independently, brainstorm a general list of character traits, but include some that could apply to the narrator (careful, serious).

(2) Identify a model trait and experience for the narrator.

C. Point to Parts II and III on the activity sheet.

Additional Activity Students taste blackberries and tell positive character traits of their good friends.

Another Book About Accepting a Friend's Death *On My Honor,* by Marion Dane Bauer, Dell, 1987.

2–8 BLACKBERRIES AND CHARACTERS

A *character trait* tells how a character *acts* or *behaves*. Jamie talked and joked with his friends—he was *friendly*. He decided to help scrape beetles even when he didn't want to—he was *willing*.

PART 1

Below are things that happened in the story that show certain character traits of *Jamie*. Find a trait in the blackberries at the bottom that you think BEST fits each experience. Be prepared to explain your choice. Write choice on the line. Use each trait ONLY ONCE.

_____ Sometimes Jamie didn't know when to quit. He could crawl around barking like a dog all afternoon, even when his friend wanted to do something else.

_____ Jamie took apples from the farmer to prove to himself and his friend that he wasn't afraid.

_____ Jamie liked to make his little sister happy. They took her on the walk to ask the kids to help.

_____ Jamie grabbed his friend's head and pulled him down. They rolled over and *laughed*.

_____ Jamie hitchhiked a ride for the three kids when caught in the thunderstorm. Many kids are afraid to ride with strangers!

_____ Jamie *kidded* that the bees that were too afraid to come out were "Heatherbees."

_____ The boys had a special friendship. They really enjoyed sharing secrets by flashing signals across the street to each other.

PART II

Next, write three character traits of Jamie's friend, the narrator, that are *different* than those for Jamie. Also, give one experience *for each trait* that shows the trait. Write on back. (Don't forget Part III.)

PART III

Explain how picking and tasting blackberries helped the narrator accept Jamie's death (two or three sentences, on back).

Books

1. Select, for group analysis, a high-appeal, high-quality narrative fiction book—either a picture book or a short novel, that:
   - can be read quickly to students
   - has been read to students
   - students have all read independently
2. Student-selected high interest and high quality titles to be independently analyzed later

Materials

Transparency of the activity sheet

Directions

1. Introduce the activity by describing why *you* liked a particular book in terms of the activity sheet components (for example, interesting *characters* depicted by particular traits, exciting *plot* with a satisfying or unusual solution).
2. Review the concepts of *fiction* and *nonfiction,* and *narrative* and *expository* writing.
3. Present the parts of a story as background for the activity sheet:
   A. Present the parts in list form (character, plot, setting, mood, theme, style).
   B. Lead students to identify specific reasons for liking a "good book" as opposed to "it was neat," or "I just liked it."
4. Analyze the selected book as a group:
   A. Use the transparency.
   B. For most groups, distribute copies of the sheet and ask students to copy the information generated.
   C. *Notes:*
      (1) Students are not to give a character's physical description for #3 on the activity sheet.
      (2) Define the terms *protagonist* and *antagonist,* for students.
      (3) *Theme* is a difficult concept for students, but if the themes (e.g., friendship, fear, justice, loyalty, good and evil, rule of law, survival, war and peace), and applications of the themes are connected to the everyday life of the student, and if the concept is repeated over a period of time, a working knowledge will develop for most students.
      (4) *Style* was not included in the activity because of its difficulty for this age group.
5. A "good" book in terms of universality of themes and character depictions: Discuss with students the idea that a good book is "good" for all times and places because of the universal appeal of its themes and character depictions.
6. At a later time, students select and independently analyze a book by completing an additional copy of the outline. Further helps for independent completion:
   A. Generate class lists of possible responses for the various story components, e.g., list of character traits, list of universal themes.
   B. Give students the option of working in pairs (using the same book).

7. Additional descriptors for story parts:

   A. Character: Is the character interesting? How? Why? How has the author created a lifelike, believable character?

   B. Plot: Does the series of events that make up the story line hold your interest?

   C. Setting: Can you picture in your mind where and when the story takes place? Describe the setting.

   D. Mood: Does the author's choice of words set the proper tone for the events that follow?

Additional Activity   Develop a creative writing outline for student use, based on the parts of a story.

2–9 A GOOD STORY—
WHAT ARE THE PARTS?

Name _____

1. TITLE _____

2. AUTHOR _____

3. CHARACTERS:
   Major

   _____ _____ _____ _____

   Minor

   _____ _____ _____ _____

   Character traits describe how a character acts, behaves, or is thought of by others. Examples: friendly, mean, brave, caring, truthful, clever, selfish.

   Name an event that involves one of the main characters: _____

   _____

   _____   Character's
                                                      name   _____

   List three traits that are shown by that character in that event:

   _____   _____   _____

4. Name three to five major events in the order in which they happen (list and number).

   _____

   _____

   _____

   _____

   _____

5. PROTAGONIST: _____   ANTAGONIST: _____

6. The *setting* tells the *time* and *place* of the action. Examples are: *time*—winter, during the day; *place*—Wyoming, at the beach.

   What is the setting?_____

   _____

7. The *mood* is the feeling or attitude the story gives. Examples: joyful, gloomy, satisfied, amused.

   What is the mood?

   _____

The *theme* is the big idea or subject of the story. Examples: love, courage, unselfishness. What are two themes?

_____

_____

**D'Aulaire, Ingri and Edgar Parin D'Aulaire. *D'Aulaires' Book of Greek Myths.*
New York: Doubleday, 1962.** The gods, goddesses, and heroes of ancient Greece come to life with all of their heroic, powerful, mischievous, tricky, and winsome characteristics.

Preferred Materials for the Activity

1. Enough copies of the book for every one to three students; or

2. Duplicated book pages of material, one set for every one to three students, about selected gods. See #3 below for suggested list of gods and summary of the activity. Use index to find pages to duplicate. *Note:* the important information about the gods is contained on one to three pages, except for Zeus, pages 16–20, 24–26, 40–41.

Note: This is a long-term project lasting about three weeks. For teacher background information on mythology, see resources listed at the end of the lesson.

Directions

1. Introduce the book by displaying it and inviting student input about familiar Greek mythological names and terms, such as Zeus, Apollo, and Pandora. Define *myth,* including stories about gods, goddesses, and people who were invented to explain what happened in nature and how people behaved. The stories were thought to be true by the people who told them in the distant past. Use Poseidon and Aphrodite as examples.

2. Review the Table of Contents, pointing out Greece on a map and referring to the ancient map on page 8.

3. Read and discuss pages 9 through 23 with students. Include:

   A. Clarification of concepts and vocabulary (trident, ichor, ambrosia)

   B. List of names, positions, and duties of the "twelve great gods" from pages 22 and 23 for students to review or copy. *Optional:* Present a transparency of the family tree on page 2.

4. Organize the activity "To Tell the Truth: Zeus and His Family" as follows:

   A. Select enough gods—one for every three students—to be featured in the presentation by group members. Recommended list: Zeus, Hera, Hephaestus, Aphrodite, Athena, Poseidon, Apollo, Artemis, Hermes, Hades, Prometheus, Proserpine.

   B. Format of presentations—patterned after the former television show, "To Tell the Truth"—features three persons assuming and presenting information about a god or goddess character, with only *one* telling the "whole truth." The other two, as imposters, present *mostly* truthful information with one or two pieces of false information included.

   C. Write selected gods' names, each name one time on three pieces of paper. Students then draw a name. *Optional:* students trade names as desired.

   D. The three students sharing a common character work together to formulate their presentations.

(1) Students decide who will be the "real" Zeus and who will be the imposters.

(2) They use the key information in the book to write *one to two minute* speeches and make notecards for the presentation.

(3) Each student presents the major points of that character, with the two imposters giving small details of untruth for two or three points.

(4) Begin speeches with established title for that god, e.g., "I am Hera, goddess of marriage and Queen of Olympus."

(5) Optional, but recommended: costumes, or at least one significant prop and article of clothing.

E. Student-audience preparation: Students who compose the audience for a presentation must know the material presented, so as to ascertain who is telling the "whole truth." Therefore, students giving presentations must use only material presented in the book.

5. The presentations

A. Schedule two group presentations per day.

B. After a trio presentation, the audience members each select the "real" god or goddess, in writing. An individual tally sheet kept by students is helpful.

C. Next, the direction is given: "Will the real (__Hera__) please raise her hand."

Note: If student group is small, assign a second god for presentation.

Follow-Up Activities

1. It's Greek to Me, 1–12

2. "Mythology Today": Choose themes from mythology of interest to students today, such as competition vs. cooperation, peer group pressure, love and commitment. Students give examples from the stories that exhibit the theme and discuss today's applications.

Extended Activity   See activity 3–11, Great Greeks' Badges. Badges can be used as rewards.

Additional Materials for Students

• Filmstrip: European Mythology Series, BFA Educational Media

• *The Greek Gods,* by Bernard Evslin et al, Scholastic, 1988

• "By Jove," a mythological game from Aristoplay, Ltd., PO Box 7028, Ann Arbor, MI 48107

• *Unit Ties: Greek and Roman Myths,* a study guide from Learning Links Inc., 11 Wagon Road, Roslyn Heights, NY 11577.

• *Classic Myths to Read Aloud* by William F. Russell, Crown, 1989.

• *Theseus and the Minotaur,* retold and illustrated by Warwick Hutton, McElderry, 1989.

Background Sources for the Teacher

• *The Encyclopedia Britannica*

• *Gods, Demigods & Demons: An Encyclopedia of Greek Mythology,* by Bernard Evslin, Scholastic, 1975.

• *Mighty Myth: A Modern Interpretation of Greek Myths for the Classroom,* by Greta Barclay Lipson, et al., Good Apple, 1982.

Story Analysis; Multilevel Comprehension

Ullman, James Ramsey. *Banner in the Sky.* New York: Harper & Row, 1954.
Young Rudi Matt carries on the dream of his father to reach the summit of the
Citadel, the highest mountain in Switzerland. A compelling drama of determination,
skill, pride, and jealousy that prompts discussions of the value of life itself.

Materials

1. Refreshments for victory celebration: rock candy; cupcakes, decorated as Citadel;
   Mountain Dew® or Swiss Miss®
2. *Optional*: costumes for characters and materials for facsimiles of awards

Directions

1. If multiple copies are available, select parts for oral as well as independent reading.
   Call attention to author's note at the beginning, geographical location of Switzerland
   and the Matterhorn, and the novel's Newbery Honor Award.
2. Proceed through the book as follows:

   A. Teach the necessary vocabulary.

   B. Discuss the major elements of the book: character, plot, setting, theme, point of
   view, and style, as encountered in the reading. Point out the following, with
   students responding either in oral or written form (either as group or independently):

   - *Character and Plot:* Find examples of character and plot detail that "keep the
     reader reading."
   - *Point of View:* Contrast the major characters' point of view about mountain
     climbing, being a guide, and climbing the Citadel at both the beginning and end
     of the book.
   - *Style:* Give examples of choices of words that make Ullman's writing interesting
     and exciting.

   Note: Be prepared for students to seek clarification of details, for example, climbing terms, physical characteristics for and obstacles of the mountain.

   C. Questions for specific chapters include:

   - before Chapters Four and Five: What will be the "trial" and "error"?
   - after Chapter 5: Who should Rudi believe—Captain Winter, who told him "don't
     worry about it," or Uncle Franz, who implied that he had committed an unforgiv-
     able sin? Why?
   - after Chapter 6: Explain what Rudi learned about being a "real" guide.
   - before Chapter 8: What could the "White Fury" be?
   - after Chapter 9: (1) What does it take to do daring things? (2) Whose idea do you
     agree with most, regarding what a real mountaineer is, Teo's or Franz's? Why?
   - chapter 10, page 136: What does Winter expect of Rudi?
   - chapter 11, page 148: Describe the way through to the upper mountain.
   - after Chapter 12: Why does Rudi deserve to be called the son of the great Josef
     Matt?
   - after Chapter 13: What finally caused the guides to let Rudi come?
   - after Chapter 15: Describe what happened in the most exciting event of this
     chapter. Why was it exciting?

- after Chapter 16: Was Rudi right in the choice he made? Why?
- after Chapter 19: (1) Why was Rudi Matt the real conqueror of the Citadel? (2) List character traits for each of the major characters that led to accomplishments for each man. (3) What valuable lessons have you learned from this book about how to live your life?

D. Additional ideas for gleaning information:
- Summarizing
- Student-written questions
- Sequence lists

3. *Class Enactment of the Victory Celebration for the Conquerors of the Citadel*

A. Use the outline of the celebration on the activity-sheet/invitation to determine specific details of the celebration. Suggestions: classroom can become the town square for holding the celebration, students selected to portray honorees, with additional students as the townspeople.

B. Each student completes an invitation and gives to mayor to pass out.

C. Celebration is held, with awards presented and refreshments enjoyed.

Additional Material   Walt Disney film based on *Banner in the Sky: Third Man on the Mountain.*

Directions: *Cutting and folding the invitation* – 1. Cut out the square on the dotted lines. 2. Cut out the outline of the mountain (left corner). 3. Holding the invitation upright, fold the bottom corner to the top corner, matching "points." 4. Next, fold the bottom corner down to the middle crease. 5. Fold the two side triangles to the center.

Completing the writing – 1. Fill in the "When," "Where," "Refreshments," and "R.S.V.P. to:" blanks as decided by your group. 2. Tell what unique contribution each honoree made to the conquering of the Citadel by filling in the blanks.

A VICTORY CELEBRATION

The Conquerors of the Citadel

cut

RUDI MATT will receive a gold-plated model of the Citadel, for: _____

CAPTAIN WINTER will be given a silver-plated model of the Citadel, for: _____

FRANZ LERNER will be presented with the Plaque of Understanding award for: _____

SAXO will be given the Plaque of Determination for: _____

TEO will receive the Plaque of Inspiration for: _____

Refreshments: _____

When: _____

Where: _____

at: _____ (time)

R.S.V.P. to: _____ (name)

Mayor of Kurtal

Writing with Children's Books

3–1 SUBJECTS AND PREDICATES ARE POURING DOWN _____
Parts of a Sentence

Barrett, Judi. *Cloudy with a Chance of Meatballs.* New York: Atheneum, 1978.
The weather in the town of Chewandswallow, where it rains soup and snows mashed potatoes, is delicious—until it takes a turn for the worse.

Directions

1. Read the book to students, enjoying "a downpour of weather humor."

2. Next, reinforce or review the concept of the two parts of a sentence, the *subject* and *predicate.*

   - *Note for younger students:* terms *subject* and *predicate* can be replaced with "*who's doing it*" and "*what is happening.*"

   - *Note for older students:* the terms *complete subject* and *complete predicate* can be used, discussing modifiers, etc.

   A. Display the following sentences from the book:

   "The wind blew in storms of hamburgers."

   "A huge pancake covered the school."

   Tell students that all correct sentences are made up of a subject and a predicate.

   B. Define:

   (1) The *subject* tells *who* or *what* does something.

   Example: *Dogs* eat the meatballs that are left.

   The subject can be more than one word.

   Example: *Black, brown, and white dogs* eat the meatballs that are left.

   Identify the subject in the examples from A above.

   (2) The *predicate* tells what the subject *does.*

   Example: The people *eat.*

   The predicate can be more than one word.

   Example: The people *eat hot dogs.*

   Identify the predicate in the examples from A above.

   C. Ask students to supply possible subjects and predicates:

   __Popcorn__ fall(s) like snow.

   Butter and jam __drips slowly.__

3. Choose one of the three methods of activity sheet completion below, depending on the skill level of the students:

   A. *Beginning stage* of subject/predicate understanding: Complete as a group (transparency of sheet recommended) using one- or two-word subjects and predicates.

   B. *Middle stage* of understanding, where students can generate one- or two-word subjects and predicates on their own: Students complete in pairs or independently.

   C. *Higher stage,* where students have had instruction in modifiers and direct objects: Students complete in pairs or independently, supplying noun and verb modifiers and direct objects.

Extended Activity

For older students. Students make up sentences using weather-related records from the *Guinness Book of World Records,* labeling the complete subject and complete predicate.

Subject: Predicate:

Example: A summer storm in Wyoming/sent three feet of hailstones!

3–1 SUBJECTS AND PREDICATES
ARE POURING DOWN

Name _____

Directions: Write a *subject* (who or what) or a *predicate* (what doing) below.

Subject _____

_____ pour(s) down.

Predicate

Food _____

Subject _____

_____ blow(s) meatballs.

Predicate

The people _____

Predicate

A giant hot dog _____

_____

Subject _____

_____ sneeze(s) from the pepper.

Now write your own sentences! Use ideas about food from the sky. Write only the *subject* on the first part, and the *predicate* on the second part.

Example: SUBJECT: _____Yummy pizza_____

PREDICATE: _____drops down._____

1. _____

2. _____

1. _____

2. _____

3–2 SQUEEZE OUT A RHYME

Rhyming and Word Play; Illustrating

Morrison, Bill. *Squeeze a Sneeze.* **Boston: Houghton Mifflin, 1977.** Witty and wacky rhyming word play that starts the reader creating rhymes.

Materials

1. White paper for drawing, either 5″ × 7″, 8½″ × 11″, or 9″ × 12″, one piece for each student
2. Coloring materials
3. Optional: felt-tip pens

Directions

1. Ask students if they have ever thought of "squeezing a sneeze" or "cooling tea with the wings of a bee." Read and enjoy the book—its zany humor and word play—with students.

2. Next, brainstorm two to three sets of rhyming words, listing at least two words for each set.

   Note: the more words, the more potential for creativity. Examples: locks, rocks, socks, docks; Jello, mellow, cello. Choose words from the sets to form witty sentences.

   Examples: "Put locks on your socks." "Watch Jello play the cello." *Optional*: sketch out illustrations.

3. Next, do one of the following, depending on the age and ability level of the group:

   A. For younger and lower-performing students, brainstorm enough rhyming sets for each student to choose a different set with which to form a sentence. Students form a sentence and then illustrate it. Check that sentences end in a rhyming word.

   B. For older or higher performers, instruct them to create rhyming word groups either with a team, with a partner, or independently. Sentences are then created, with illustrations to follow.

   Note for illustrating: Lightly drawing with pencil before adding permanent lines will give students the option for changing and improving their drawings.

4. *Optional*: Make a class book.

   Note: For securing a class book in addition to giving the student the original to take home, instruct students to complete the writing and drawing with black felt-tip pen. After photocopies are made, students can add color.

Put locks on your socks

Watch Jello play the Cello

Dance with a lion going Hawaiian

Ahlberg, Janet and Allan. *The Jolly Postman.* **Boston: Little, Brown and Company, 1986.** A book of real letters written by well-known fairy tale characters to each other demonstrates and stimulates imagination.

Materials

Regular white paper, regular or legal-sized envelopes, one for each student.

Note: Make a backup copy of the letters.

Directions

1. Review fairy tales and Mother Goose rhymes associated with the book as needed by students.

   Note: Many students will need more pre-teaching than anticipated.

2. Read the book to students, enjoying its creativity and humor.

   Note: The humor of the letters to Cinderella and to the Wolf is directed to older students. If available, read letters from familiar characters in Beatrix Potter's book, *Affectionately Yours.*

   Alternative: Read the book to students after student letters are written. This will promote utilization of students' own ideas rather than the book's.

3. Write a group story from one fairy-tale character to another. Suggestions:

   • From Peter Rabbit to Mr. MacGregor: "Are the cabbages ready yet?"

   • From Snow White to the Seven Dwarfs: "I'm so happy with the prince, but I miss you all so much."

   • From Rapunzel to Sleeping Beauty: "Could you take my place in the tower for awhile? I need some sleep!"

   Optional: Address an envelope, decorate it, and create a postmark and stamp.

4. For older or higher-performing students: Prepare them to write individual letters:

   A. Brainstorm characters to use (Big Bad Wolf to Three Pigs, Mary Had A Little Lamb to Bo Peep, etc.).

   Notes: (1) Students may need to review stories! (2) Asking students to write from one character to another character in the *same story* will simplify the process.

   B. Brainstorm purposes for writing the letters (to inform about a problem, to invite to a party, to request information, to ask a favor, apologize).

   C. Instruct students to draft their letter, envelope, illustration, stamp, and postmark in pencil, adding felt-tip pens and color later.

   D. When letters are complete, but before color is added, make a photocopy for a class book(s).

Related Book *Stringbean's Trip to the Shining Sea,* by Vera B. Williams, Greenwillow, 1988.

Silverstein, Shel. *Where the Sidewalk Ends.* New York: Harper & Row, 1974. "What's in the Sack," page 111. Everyone wants to know what's in the traveler's sack—but that's not the real question, says the traveler.

Materials Needed for Teacher

Sack and object (examples: stuffed animal, candy bar, book) for carrying while reciting the poem.

Note: disguise object by wrapping it in newspaper, etc.

Directions

1. Recite the poem using the props.

2. Next, students try to guess what is in the sack either by asking questions which can be answered by *yes* or *no,* or through being given clues from the activity sheet statements. The floor is open to guesses after everyone has had a chance to ask a question. After a wrong guess, students must ask five more questions before attempting another guess.

3. Prepare students for the activity sheet completion by modeling the process:

   A. Group selects an object.

   B. Write clues together to establish criteria for "good clues," i.e., how to give a clue without giving away the answer.

   C. Brainstorm types of descriptive words. Practice making the comparisons close.

   D. Brainstorm ways of disguising statements that tell what the object can do. For example, for *key:* A "twist of the wrist" will help it work.

4. Additional notes for completing the activity sheet:

   A. One of the goals of the activity is for students to enjoy the describing process. Therefore, help students keep their efforts uncomplicated by telling them to give the descriptions of how the object *usually* is (if it varies) and to give *approximations* for size, shape, etc.

   B. Another goal is for the object to be identifiable at the end of the clue-giving. Therefore, instruct students to provide an "almost give-away" for clue 9, "I like it because . . ."

   C. If students have difficulty thinking of descriptive words, brainstorm words and phrases for the additional sample objects as a group.

   D. For younger students: Ask them to select an object to describe that they can fit into a sack and can bring to school. The emphasis on concreteness will make describing the objects easier.

   E. Teachers have found "other ways to describe it" (clue 8) to be an enlightening clue.

   F. Sample objects for students to describe: a balloon, spaghetti, a teddy bear, dollar bill, vitamin C.

Extended Activities

1. "What About Me?": In keeping with the theme of the traveler's plea for someone to ask questions about him personally, a student conducts a personal interview of someone else in the group to learn more about that person. Use the questions from the poem, for example, "When is your birthday?" "Do you play Monopoly?" Additional possible

questions: "What games do you like?" "What's your favorite dessert/animal/music/ sport . . . ?"

2. "You Name It": Place actual objects, or their names written on paper, in a sack. Students select an object to describe for the group to identify.

3. "Math . . . Bag It": Students write math (or other subject) problems for others to solve. Problems are put in a sack, drawn out by different students, and solved.

What
could be in *your* sack? Think
of an object, alive or not alive, that
you do have or want to have a lot of fun with.
Use words that won't give the object away, but that
will give others clues to guessing. When you're finished,
read your clues so others can guess.

1. It is/is not, alive. (Circle one)

2. It is larger than a _____ and smaller than a _____.
    (Make large and small as close as possible.)

3. It is heavier than a _____ and lighter than a _____. (Make
    heavy and light as close as possible.)

4. Its shape is _____. (round, square, oval, long and skinny, etc.) If shape
    is different when it's doing different things, write: "Its shape is _____
    when it is _____."

5. Its color(s) is/are _____.

6. It's made out of _____.

7. It can (What can it do, or what can you do with it?) _____
    _____.

8. Other ways to describe it: _____
    _____
    _____

9. I like it because _____
    _____

10. It's more fun than _____

    Bonus: Describe your object in a *simile* sentence. A
    simile is a comparison of two objects in which the word
    like or *as* is used: "It is (the cat's fur) *as soft as snow.*"

    It is as _____ as (a) _____.

    WHAT IS IT??? (**Hide** its
    name in the mouse
    at the right)

> **Lasker, Joe.** *A Tournament of Knights.* **New York: Crowell, 1986.** Justin, a brave young knight about to fight his first tournament, learns that courage is only one of the characteristics of a duel.

Materials

1. Short newspaper sports articles—event-report-style as opposed to a feature about a person—with two contenders having competed for a top prize (for example, boxing, wrestling). Select either three articles or enough for each pair of students. (See 3 below.) Articles should answer: who, when, where, what, and why about the event.

2. Bulletin board display area with caption: "Knightly News Bulletin."
   Optional: Background information about life in the Middle Ages and knighthood. See "Related Books" at conclusion.

Directions

1. Conduct the reading of the book as follows:
   A. Read "A Note to the Reader" as an introduction.
   B. During and after the reading of the story, define terms listed in the glossary.
   C. Point out the armor parts as given on the back cover.
   D. Point out the important reason each man fought in the important duel.

2. Informally discuss the duel between Justin and Sir Rolf in the context of the "Five *W*s" of giving information—who, when, what, where, why.

3. Prepare students for writing their own news account of Justin's duel.
   A. Conduct an analysis of the gathered newspaper articles for the "Five *W*s. Complete two or three articles as a group. *Optional*: Assign pairs of students to complete an analysis and share with another pair of students or with the class.
   B. Discuss the following points of writing style in relation to the newspaper articles:
      • adding background information about the persons and the event
      • describing the play-by-play account of the duel
      • using direct quotes from the contestants
      • beginning with important information (who, what, and when) and ending with a summary in the form of a "punchline."

4. Set the stage for the independent writing by telling students:
   A. you are a sports reporter for the (nonexistant) newspaper, the "Knightly News Bulletin."
   B. you will get to give the exciting account of what happened between Justin and Sir Rolf.

5. Students each write an article, using the Five *W*s and information from 3 above.

6. Display articles on bulletin board.

Other Activities With Middle Age Themes   2–5, Cedric the Fortunate Character, 6–4, A Feast to Remember, 6–5, A Day at The Castle.

Related Books   *Sir Cedric,* by Roy Gerrard, Farrar, Straus & Giroux, 1986; *Saint George & the Dragon,* retold by Margaret Hodges, Little, 1984; *The Middle Ages,* by Giovanni Caselli, Bedrick Books, 1988.

Additional Activity   Students design a poster as an advertisement for a second duel.

Steptoe, John. *Mufaro's Beautiful Daughters.* **New York: Lothrop, Lee & Shepard, 1987.** An African tale in which kindness wins over pride and greed. Stunning illustrations enrich a meaningful story.

Directions

1. Introduce the "good guy"/"bad guy" story motif that will occur in this tale, with a role-playing situation:

   A. One student plays a kind, considerate, loving person.

   B. A second student plays a spoiled, jealous, bad-tempered person.

   C. Situation: Both have been invited to participate in a talent contest.

   D. Role-play: What do the "good guy" and the "bad guy" say about who has the most talent, who is the best-looking, who will win?

   Note: set up the situation for students by asking: what talent? why is it good? Model appropriate responses for each role-player.

2. Introduce the book by:

   A. noting *protagonist* and *antagonist* character roles

   B. sharing information from the introductory note

   C. displaying character names and roles

   D. telling students to notice the rich illustrations where the characters show strong individuality and where colors are used to bring out feelings.

3. Read the book to students. (*Note:* this book is good for oral reading by older students, especially if the story is familiar.) Discuss the following:

   A. the *story structure* of protagonist/antagonist and test or goal

   B. the structure of other fairy tales, such as Cinderella

   C. *character traits* and other descriptive words for the two character types

   Examples: Nyasha—pleased to serve, kind, sang sweetly; Manyara—bad-tempered, clever, teaser.

   Note that the author uses these attributes as a way of projecting feeling, emotion, value, and point of view.

   D. *themes* (big, important ideas)—pride, love, unselfishness, and so forth

   E. *the illustrations*—Point out the characters' faces; notice the author's use of rich, warm tones on the characters' faces, use of lighting, and the bursts of color throughout the book.

4. Preparation for the activity sheet:

   A. Students assume the role of Manyara, recalling her goal of becoming queen. (*Optional*: students note roles of good and bad characters on TV shows and tell how they would play those roles, as practice for assuming roles.)

   B. Task: Write a persuasive letter. Each student, as Manyara, writes a letter to the King to persuade him to choose her as queen.

   C. Students develop a "think sheet" by brainstorming words and phrases that make Manyara appear more appealing than Nyasha or any other girl. Include exaggerations:

   • Ways I (Manyara) am beautiful: _____

   Examples: dark brown hair, golden skin, stylish clothes

- My other attributes—personality traits, things I can do and like:
  _____

    Examples: clever, strong, entertain well, like to decorate palaces
- Nyasha's personal traits that I could use to make myself look better
  _____

    Examples: kind, gentle, caring, considerate
- Things that Nyasha does that might seem strange to many people
  _____

    Examples: talks to a snake, spends more time in the garden than in front of the mirror to make herself attractive

    Note: Make sure students stop short of making exaggerations unbelievable.

D. Students develop an outline of key points they will make in the letter.

   (1) Before students work independently, brainstorm as a group the kind of housing, food, clothing, entertainment, education, and social engagements appropriate for the setting.

   (2) Point out:
   - This persuasive letter is based more on feelings and emotions than on reason and true facts.
   - This letter is written before the trip to the city, so Manyara doesn't know that Nyoka is really the King.
   - The letter should be set in the time and place of the story.
   - The letter is complete when writer believes he/she has convinced the King to select Manyara as queen.

E. Students write their letters to the King.

   Notes: Since the writer's role for this task is to assume the character of Manyara, both boys and girls should be equally successful.

   Encourage students to use additional paper as needed.

   Students should make sure the reason for writing the letter is clear to the receiver, whether stated or implied.

Additional Activities

1. Drama: "Mufaro . . . As A Play" (Works well and students love it!):
   Students perform roles as a play, with simple costumes and scenery. Students write additional parts or roles, as needed to accommodate more people.

2. Social Studies: "A View of Africa Today"
   Students explore six regions of modern Africa (not including Zimbabwe) through the eyes of photographer/writer John Chiasson, in *African Journey*, Bradbury, 1987.

Name _____

Directions: Write a letter AS MANYARA, telling why you should be queen.

_____

_____

_____

_____

_____

_____

_____

_____

_____

_____

_____

_____

_____

_____

_____

_____

_____

_____

_____

de Regniers, Beatrice Schenk, selected by. *Sing a Song of Popcorn.* **New York: Scholastic, 1988.** Four appealing limericks on pages 110–111 from a collection of 128 poems that are illustrated by nine Caldecott artists.

Related Books

The Complete Nonsense of Edward Lear, Dover; *The Complete Nonsense Book by Edward Lear,* Amereon.

Note: Use with middle-performing fourth graders and up.

Directions

1. Read and enjoy the poems with students. Point out that Peru is a country in South America and Leeds is a city in England.

2. Ask students to identify the characteristics of a limerick. Supplement with needed parts from the following definition: a nonsense poem with five lines, in which the first, second, and fifth lines have three feet (each foot has two unaccented and one accented syllable) and rhyme, and the third and fourth lines have two feet (two accented syllables) and rhyme. The poetry form was made popular by Edward Lear.

3. Write one of the limericks on the overhead or chalkboard and point out the above distinguishing features.

4. Next, write a group limerick based on a familiar children's book.

   A. Begin by listing a character and at least five character descriptions, traits, or actions, *rhyming with the character's name.* Example: Story—*Jack and the Beanstalk;* character—Jack; character traits/actions—Jack, knack, backpack, whack, track, rack.

   B. Now list other characters and one-word actions from the story, pairing listed words with a new rhyming word. Examples: giant, client; beanstalk, talk; goose, loose; egg, leg; chased, traced.

   C. Construct a limerick using ideas from the generated lists.

   Example: There once was a big boy named Jack,
   Who wanted to steal a backpack.
   He climbed to the giant,
   But the giant had a client.
   So Jack left and never came back.

5. Next, instruct students to select a book, nursery rhyme, or another familiar character or topic (examples: pet, sports hero, or famous person) and write a limerick.

   A. Students write a "think sheet," where they follow steps A and B from 4 above. *Note:* This step is necessary. Watch for students who try to skip the pre-writing and then say "I can't think of anything to write."

   B. Next, students write their limerick from the ideas they generated. *Optional:* Students write a second limerick.

   C. Students copy their limerick on drawing paper and illustrate.

6. Enjoy other poetry from the book "for poetry's sake."

Spier, Peter. *People.* **New York: Doubleday, 1980.** We are alike, but also are unique, different individuals.—Isn't it wonderful!

Note: This is a reinforcement or review and application lesson for capitalization

Directions

1. Introduce *People* by telling students:
   A. there are 5 billion different, unique, individuals on this earth; and
   B. it would take 95 years just to count one billion of us! (Counting detailed in David M. Schwartz's *How Much Is a Million?* Scholastic, 1987)

2. Enjoy the book with students, expanding discussion of topics of interest. Examples: games, foods. Optional: Explore records for games (longest and shortest) foods (top-selling candy, largest cake), and other topics in a recent edition of *The Guinness Book of World Records.*

3. Preparation for completing the activity sheet:
   A. Reinforce and review concepts contained on the sheet as needed.
   B. Carefully read directions with the students.
   C. Point out: *Peter Spier* is the author and is a proper noun. Some words in the book are capitalized and usually would not be, because they are titles or picture captions. *Optional*: Discuss and ask students to label the common and proper nouns in Part I.
   D. Depending on student level, complete activity as a group, in pairs, or independently.
   E. Bonus sentences to capitalize:
      The state of _____ is named after king george II of great britain. benjamin franklin invented the _____ _____ that keeps people warm in january.

Extended Activity Students make up their own sentences—from the book or from *The Guinness Book of World Records*—for a partner to capitalize correctly.

Answer Key to Activity Sheet

I. 1. Peter Spier; 3. John F. Kennedy; 4. Japan; 5. Thanksgiving Day; 7. France; 9. Mount Everest.

II. 1. Columbus Avenue is named after Christopher Columbus.
    2. The steam engine was invented by James Watt, an inventor from Scotland.
    3. In Sweden, the people celebrate St. Lucia's Day in December.
    4. Three religions are Christianity, Judaism, and Hinduism.
    5. The holiday, Valentine's Day, comes from Saint Valentine.

III. 1. "Snails are great to eat," said the Frenchman.
     2. I explained, "Many people would like to be rich."
     3. The tennis player said, "Losing makes me cry."
     4. "Don't you think it's great that my friends and I are all different?" asked the student.
     5. "I'm good at catching balls," said the juggler.

Directions: Cross out each small letter where a capital is needed. Write the capital letter above.

I. CAPITALIZING PROPER NOUNS

A *proper noun* is the name of a specific person, place, or thing. Begin each proper noun with a capital letter.

1. peter spier
2. holidays
3. john f. kennedy

4. japan
5. thanksgiving day
6. president

7. france
8. gods
9. mount everest

II. CAPITALIZING PROPER NAMES, SPECIFIC PLACES, AND THINGS

Capitalize the names of specific people, places, holidays, and religions.

1. columbus avenue is named after christopher columbus.

2. The steam engine was invented by james watt, an inventor from scotland.

3. In sweden, the people celebrate st. lucia's day in december.

4. Three religions are christianity, judaism, and hinduism.

5. The holiday, valentine's day, comes from saint valentine.

III. CAPITALIZING DIRECT QUOTATIONS

A direct quotation is the exact words someone has said. Begin each direct quote with a capital letter.

1. "snails are great to eat," said the Frenchman.

2. I explained, "many people would like to be rich."

3. The tennis player said, "losing makes me cry."

4. "don't you think it's great that my friends and I are all different?" asked the student.

5. "i'm good at catching balls," said the juggler.

Barrett, Judi. *Cloudy With a Chance of Meatballs*. New York: Atheneum, 1978.
The weather in the town of Chewandswallow, where it rains soup and snows mashed potatoes, is delicious—until it takes a turn for the worse.

Directions

1. Introduce the book by asking students to share their dreams of eating all the donuts and ice cream they want to. Reveal that in the town of Chewandswallow, storms blew in more hotdogs and ice cream than people could eat!

2. Read the book to students and enjoy!

3. Preparation for completing the activity sheet:

   A. Review the concepts of and rules for *common and proper nouns, singular and plural nouns,* and *singular and plural possession.* (See the activity sheet.)

   B. Notes:

   • The rule for a singular noun ending in *y* preceded by a consonant (*french fry* to *french fries*) has been omitted.

   • The rule for nouns ending in *f fe* (*knife* to *knives*) has also been omitted.

   • For section II, Singular and Plural Nouns, point out that *potatoes* and *tomatoes* are exceptions to the rule for plurals of singular nouns ending in *o*.

   • For section III, Singular and Plural Possession, point out the following: Both the person, place, or thing that "owns" something and the person, place, or thing that is "owned," are nouns.

Extended Activity   Students have a "Noun Bee" with two teams, using common and proper nouns. Team members give proper nouns to supplied common ones. Example: city— Seattle.

Answer Key to Activity Sheet

  I. 1. Chewandswallow (P), street, Main Street (P), stores, houses, trees, gardens, school, people

   2. hamburgers, Rex's Restaurant (P), sky

   3. weather report, Friday (P), KING television station (P), menu, breakfast, lunch, dinner

   4. Ralph's Roofless Restaurant (P), Frazzle's Frankfurters (P), bun

 II. 1. plates, cups, glasses, spoons, forks

   2. Lunches, pieces, cheeses, beans

   3. peas, potatoes, clouds

   4. pancakes, donuts, tomatoes, sandwiches, pies, pickles

III. 1. Department's

   2. children's

   3. people's, animals'

3–9 CLOUDY WITH A CHANCE OF NOUNS

Name _____

I. COMMON AND PROPER NOUNS

A *common noun* names general groups of persons, places, or things. A *proper noun* names a specific person, place, or thing. Proper nouns are often made up of more than one word.

Directions: Underline all of the nouns. Write a *P* above the proper nouns.

1. Chewandswallow had a street called Main Street, which was lined with stores, houses, trees, gardens, a school, and three-hundred people.
2. The hamburgers didn't come from Rex's Restaurant; they came from the sky!
3. The weather report for Friday, January 24, given on KING television station, gave a menu for breakfast, lunch, and dinner.
4. Ralph's Roofless Restaurant featured Frazzle's Frankfurters already in the bun.

II. SINGULAR AND PLURAL NOUNS

To make the *plural* of most nouns, add *s*. If the singular noun ends in *s*, *sh*, *ch*, *x*, or *z*, add *es* to make it plural.

Directions: Write the plural of each of the nouns. Rewrite the whole word.

1. The people carried their plate _____ , cup _____ , glass _____ , spoon _____ , and fork _____ when they went outside.
2. Lunch _____ of piece _____ of cheese _____ , and baked bean _____ could be eaten.
3. Periods of pea _____ and baked potato _____ can be followed by a clearing with cloud _____ of whipped cream in the west.
4. When the weather took a turn for the worse, pancake _____ , donut _____ , tomato _____ , sandwich _____ , cherry pie _____ , and pickle _____ were huge and came down in large amounts.

III. SINGULAR AND PLURAL POSSESSION

To make a singular noun show *possession*, add an apostrophe and *s*.

When a plural noun ends in *s*, add an apostrophe after the *s* to show it "owns" something. If a plural noun does not end in *s*, first add an apostrophe and then an *s* after the apostrophe.

Directions: Make each noun with a blank after it show possession. Rewrite the whole word.

1. The Sanitation Department _____ job was very big.
2. The children _____ school was covered with a huge pancake.
3. The people _____ sandwich boats held up very well, but all the animals _____ feet got stuck in the bread.

Sharmat, Marjorie Weinman. *The 329th Friend.* **New York: Four Winds, 1979.**
Emery Raccoon discovers that he is his own best friend.

Materials

1. Refreshments for "Punctuation Party": red or black licorice lace, at least one foot per student, or gummi snakes (squiggles), at least three per student.

2. One piece 8½″ × 11″ white paper per student.

3. One 9″ × 12″ piece of plastic wrap per student.

4. Optional masks: construction paper, face paint, etc., for a selected character in the story.

Objective of Lesson and Activity: This is a *review* and *application* lesson of the basic punctuation rules.

Directions

1. Read and enjoy the book with students, or summarize its basic content.

2. Plan the party:

   A. Plan the logistics—the date and the treats—with students. (See sections I and II of the activity sheet.)

   B. Record that information—*without* the punctuation—on the chalkboard or overhead.

3. Review the punctuation rules on the activity sheet by carefully reading through them with students, and discussing. Additional information to point out:

   A. Using Periods, Question Marks

   - Review the definitions of the four kinds of sentences

   - Note that abbreviations for *metric* units of measurement do not have a period at the end, but that abbreviations in the English (or standard) measurement system do.

   B. Using Quotation Marks

   - Review the possibilities for punctuation marks *after* the speaker's words—comma, question mark, and so forth.

   - Review the need for a comma when the speaker's name comes before the quotation.

4. Complete the activity sheet as follows:

   A. Students work independently, if skill level is high. Otherwise, they work in pairs or as a whole group.

   B. Many students find it difficult to use several rules at a time, so coaching or group work may be necessary, even if not anticipated. For example, tell students "Section I, sentence 1 needs *four* punctuation marks."

   C. *Optional*: Assign points for each correct mark.

5. Conduct the Punctuation Party as follows:

   A. Students each write one or two sentences of their own—without punctuation marks—on the 8½″ by 11″ paper, large enough to allow for (cut) licorice or gummi snakes to be inserted for the punctuation marks. Require students to use at least three of the following marks: period, question mark, exclamation point, comma, apostrophe, quotation marks.

B. Pass out lengths of licorice or snakes for students to cut to appropriate size (or cut the candy in advance). Also, pass out the cut plastic wrap.

C. Students place the plastic wrap over the paper, and then lay on the appropriate punctuation with the candy.

D. Next, students trade sentences around the group several times, and punctuate each other's sentences.

E. Add other treats for the party, and eat!

F. *Optional*: Select a student to be Emery Raccoon, students wear chosen character masks, and act out the story.

Answer Key to Activity Sheet

   I. 1. Please come to the party at E. J. Raccoon's on (will vary) afternoon!

      2. Three cheers for the delicious, exciting treats!

      3. A punctuation party feeds both your brain and your stomach.

      4. Will I gain an oz. or a lb. at the party?

  II. Answers will vary.

III. 1. Emery's punctuation party is for the guests who punctuate correctly.

      2. I'll sit at the spiders' table with the children's mother, Barbara.

      3. The goats' names are Zachary and Whackery.

 IV. 1. "The eggs taste fine with ketchup," said (will vary).

      2. "Who is my 329th friend?" asked (will vary).

      3. Emery said, "Please pass the (will vary)."

Directions: Write the details for the party and the correct punctuation for all sentences.

I. USING A PERIOD, QUESTION MARK AND EXCLAMATION POINT

Use the following rules for correct punctuation: For *declarative* and most *imperative* sentences, use a period. For *interrogative* sentences, use a question mark. For *exclamatory* sentences, use an exclamation point.

Use a period after initials and abbreviations including abbreviations for units of *English* measurement.

1. Please come to the party at E J Raccoon's on _____ afternoon
   (day abbreviation)
2. Three cheers for the delicious exciting treats
3. A punctuation party feeds both your brain and your stomach
4. Will I gain an oz or a lb at the party.

II. USE A COMMA

Use the following rule for correct punctuation: Use a common to separate the day of the month from the year, for a series, and between city and state.

1. The date for the party is _____ _____ _____.
   (month)   (date)   (year)

2. Items for the party include _____ _____ and _____.

3. The party is in _____ _____.
   (city)   (state)

III. USING AN APOSTROPHE FOR POSSESSION

Use the following rules for correct punctuation:
For the possessive of a *singular* noun, add an apostrophe and an *s*.
For a *plural* noun that does not end in *s*, add an apostrophe and an *s*.
For a plural noun that *ends* in *s*, add an apostrophe.

1. Emerys punctuation party is for the guests who punctuate correctly.
2. I'll sit at the spiders table with the children mother, Barbara.
3. The goats names are Zachary and Whackery.

IV. USING QUOTATION MARKS

Use the following rules for punctuation:
Place quotation marks before and after every direct quote.
Place commas, periods, or question marks where needed.

1. The eggs taste fine with ketchup said _____

2. Who is my 329th friend asked _____

3. Emery said Please pass the _____

© 1991 by The Center for Applied Research in Education

Presenting Character Information

D'Aulaire, Ingri and Edgar Parin D'Aulaire. *D'Aulaires' Book of Greek Myths.* New York: Doubleday, 1962. The gods, goddesses, and heroes of ancient Greece come to life with all of their heroic, powerful, mischievous, tricky, and winsome characteristics.

Materials

Activity Sheet Duplicate enough copies of the sheet, black copies preferable, for at least one badge per student.

Other Materials for Badges

1. Yellow 9″ × 12″ construction paper, cut into quarters, one quarter for each student; compasses for students to draw a circle 3½ inches in diameter onto the paper, or provide circle patterns.
2. Pastel blue or green 9″ × 12″ construction paper (light enough to be written on), one quarter sheet for each student, to become the ribbon for the badge.
3. Felt pens and crayons, scissors, glue.

Books If students are to independently gather information about a selected god, either secure multiple copies of the book or duplicate the pages to be studied. (See #2 below.) Otherwise, read the appropriate pages to students. To streamline the activity, select from pictured characters, thus limiting the amount of information to be read or duplicated.

Directions

1. Introduce students to mythology and the book by completing steps 1 and 2 from activity 2–10, To Tell The Truth. See also background sources for students and teacher at the end of that lesson.
2. The Activity: Reading, Making a Badge For, and Summarizing Information About Selected Characters from Mythology:
   A. Assign or let students choose a particular pictured god or goddess to study. (Note for groups that have already completed the activity "To Tell the Truth": Students select a different character.)
   B. Read the key information for identified gods to students, or pass out books or duplicated pages for independent reading.
   C. Students write six important points distinguishing the character, including character descriptions, traits, actions, and deeds.
      • notes should be *brief*—two- to four-word phrases.
      • Example: Hera—Queen of Olympus, goddess of marriage, very jealous wife, has golden apple, sent gadfly to chase Io, had servant named Argus.
   D. Students complete badges by:
      (1) cutting out circle from yellow paper and the blue "ribbons." *Note:* Ribbons need to be large to accommodate the writing of the six important points.
      (2) following directions on the activity sheet.
   E. Students wear their badges and present the information to the class.

Alternative Activity   Students make bookmarks instead of badges, writing "good book" slogans for the characters. Examples: Hephaestus: "Fire up with a good book," Poseidon: " 'Sea' what you can learn in books," Hades: "Brighten up your world with a great book."

Extended Activity   "Which Greek Am I?" For ten or more players.

1. Teacher selects a badge (a different one than the student has worked on) and pins a different one to each student's back.
2. Students ask each other five questions that can only be answered "yes" or "no."
3. After five questions, a guess as to the identity of the god the student is wearing can be made. If wrong, five more questions must be asked. *Note:*   the questions (a) "Am I a brother or sister of Zeus?" (b) "Am I a child of Zeus?" (c) "Am I a god or goddess?" (d) "Does my name begin with _____?" (e) "Am I immortal?" may only be asked after the fourth question.

   Encourage students to refer to the book for information as needed, before answering "yes" or "no."

Additional Activity   Write limericks for the characters from Greek mythology. "There once was a strong man named Zeus, Who had a prize golden goose . . ."

Directions for Badge: Glue picture circle to yellow circle and attach ribbon. Write six character points on the ribbon. Color the character. Decorate badge with symbols depicting the god or goddess. Example: Aphrodite—heart, arrows, cushion of foam.

Listening, Speaking, and Nonverbal Communication With Children's Books

Cole, Joanna. *Large As Life Animals*. New York: Alfred Knopf, 1990. Life-sized paintings with brief but high-interest text, giving the characteristics of various small nocturnal and daytime animals. Included are the greater Indian fruit bat and the fennec. NOTE: The original edition of the book, *Large As Life: Nighttime Animals*, was used for this lesson. Select the nocturnal animals from the new edition.

Directions

1. Introduce the book by giving an example of the surprising and interesting information available.
   A. Ask students what size they think most bats are, then, show the picture of the greater Indian fruit bat
   B. Show the picture of and give information about the royal antelope
   C. Explain that all of these pictures of nocturnal, or active-at-night, animals are actual size!
2. Read and discuss the book.
   A. Point out to students that the paintings are intended to convey realistic features of the animals
   B. Tell students to listen carefully to the interesting information, so as to be able to recall it later for an activity
   C. *Optional*: Read additional information in "Nature Notes" at the back of the book.
3. Complete the activity sheet.
   A. Use the activity sheet as a review of the characteristics that distinguish each of these animals.
   B. Students complete the sheet as a large group, small group, or individually, depending on the age and performance level of the group.
   C. For younger and/or lower-performing students:
      (1) List animal names on the board to assist in identification and spelling.
      (2) Read clues to students and give them "think time."
      (3) *Optional*: Write correct answers on a transparency.

Extended Activity for Older Students   "Who Am I? Part II"

1. Write clues for six to ten of the animals from the "Nature Notes." Three examples are:
   • Greater Indian Fruit Bat: "I quarrel and yawn with my friends before going to sleep in our camp. I am also called a flying fox, because I have a foxlike head."
   • Chinchilla: "Each of my soft hairs is divided into about twenty even finer hairs. I get scared easily and give a loud cry before I run for my den."
   • Giant Toad: "I eat any live food that I can swallow. If the animal isn't dead when I swallow it, I will puff myself up and suffocate it."
2. Read information from "Nature Notes" to students.
3. Organize students into small groups and distribute a copy of the clues to each group.
4. Students decide on a group answer identifying each animal from the clues given. The first team with all the correct answers wins.

Additional Activity   "Drawing From Life"

1. For younger students: Students choose an animal from the book to draw life-sized. *Variation*: students bring and draw simple objects, life-sized. Examples: doll, teddy bear, small toy.
2. For older students: Students draw an animal of their choice (not from book) life-sized, either from dimensions given in an encyclopedia, etc., or from a live model, such as a cat or dog.

Answer Key to Activity Sheet

1. greater Indian fruit bat
2. royal antelope
3. brown hare
4. giant toad
5. western European hedgehog
6. fennec
7. lesser mouse lemur
8. wood mouse
9. chinchilla
10. elf owl

Directions: Think about the clues and write the name of each animal.

1. I fly through the night eating fruit and spitting out the seeds. My wings are five feet wide.

   I am the _____.

2. I am only as big as a rabbit. I can have pencil-thin legs and hooves that fit on a fifty-cent coin.

   I am the _____.

3. I'm the size of a dog, but I can jump very high—maybe over a horse!

   I am the _____.

4. I am very large. I poison enemies that try to bite me through my warty skin.

   I am the _____.

5. I love milk, but in the wild I have to eat slugs and insects. I protect myself by becoming a "ball of prickles."

   I am the _____.

6. I'm proud of my large ears which can even hear insects underground.

   I am the _____.

7. Sometimes I even eat flowers. I'm the monkey's cousin, not a mouse!

   I am the _____.

8. I jump like a kangaroo, and the moonlight is too bright for me.

   I am the _____.

9. My fur is very warm, soft, and thick. It's so thick fleas can't live in it!

   I am the _____.

10. I can turn my head almost all the way around. When I'm first born, I can fit on a postage stamp.

    I am the _____.

Snyder, Dianne. *The Boy of the Three-Year Nap*. Boston: Houghton Mifflin, 1988. Taro, the lazy son of a Japanese seamstress, who spends his life taking naps and eating, finds out that laziness doesn't pay—or does it?

Directions

1. Read and enjoy this Japanese folktale with the students. Review the definition of a folktale. Point out the energetic, colorful brush line paintings, noticeably influenced by Japanese artists. These both depict and complement the humorous and dramatic elements of the text.

2. Play the game: "Follow the (Nap) Leader." (Similar to: "The Rhythm Game.")

   A. Students sit in a circle (*desks preferable,* because of providing more room for gestures).

   B. One person is "it" and leaves the room.

   C. A student is selected to be the "Nap Leader."

   D. After the student who is "it" comes back in, the Nap Leader makes nap-like gestures (folding hands over ear, yawning, bowing head), for the rest of the group to discretely follow and imitate.

   E. The one who is "it" tries to figure out who the Nap Leader is through:

      (1) three guesses

      (2) must move eye focus around circle to all students

      (3) must make guess about every ten to fifteen seconds

      (4) if guesses correctly, Nap Leader becomes "it." Variance: If the Nap Leaders tend to give themselves away in order to be "it," alter rules and select other students to be "it."

      (5) two options for third incorrect guess: person continues to be "it" or another person is chosen.

   F. Game continues as above, adding new gestures to keep interesting. *Grades 2 and 3:* See activity 6–2, Napping and Living in Japan and America.

Additional Activity   The four or five major scenes of the story are set up with "mannequins," or students posing as story characters. The dialogue is then given by other students.

Charlip, Remy; Mary Beth; and George Ancona. *Handtalk.* **New York: Macmillan, 1974.** This book presents the basics of two kinds of sign language, finger spelling and signing.

Related Books by the Same Authors

Handtalk Zoo, Four Winds, 1989.

Handtalk Birthday, Macmillan, 1987. Depicts a deaf girl's celebration of her birthday.

Recommended Material

1. Large chart of American Sign Language Alphabet or transparency or enlargement of the two alphabet pages from the book.
2. If available, transparency or enlargement of the two number pages from *Handtalk Birthday.*

Important Note: Practice performing the alphabet and words contained in the lesson and on the activity sheet until they can be accurately demonstrated to students. Also practice the numbers one through ten, either from the book, *Handtalk Birthday,* or from the activity sheet.

Directions

1. Introduce the book, *Handtalk,* and the concept:
   A. Show the book and elicit student knowledge about sign language. Note that this is a new and interesting way to communicate!
   B. Sign the following words:
      • *big* and *hello* (or *laugh* and *read*) from the back of the book. Ask for identification of the words.
      • Next, sign *eat* and *love* from the pages listed alphabetically.
2. Present the book content:
   A. Begin by showing the finger spelling alphabet pages inside the front cover. Refer to large chart, if available. Form the letters *A, B, C,* with students.
   B. Point out important information from the introduction, including:
      • *Finger spelling* is forming words, letter by letter, with the fingers of one hand.
      • *Signing* is making a picture or sign with one or two hands for each word or idea. Show inside back cover.
   C. Practice forming the alphabet symbols with students through modeling. Supplement with large chart or front of book.
   D. Present the book pages, up to but not including the signing pages.
3. Present the activity sheet:
   A. Practice finger spelling with students, using the symbols at the top of the activity sheet.
   B. Students complete Part I independently, in pairs, or as a group.
   C. Present the signing pages at the back of the book.

   D. Students complete Part II of the activity sheet.

   E. Present the book, *Handtalk Birthday,* if available, and then complete Part III. Otherwise, teach recognition of the numbers one through ten from teacher demonstration and completion of Part III of the activity sheet.

Additional Activities

   1. Conduct a "Finger Spelling Alphabet Word Bee," or a "Signing Word Bee."
   2. Perform *Handtalk Birthday* as a play.

Answer Key to Activity Sheet

   I. butter, eat, love, kiss

  II. name, kite, read

 III. one, two, eight, nine, ten, six, three, four, five, seven

Name _____

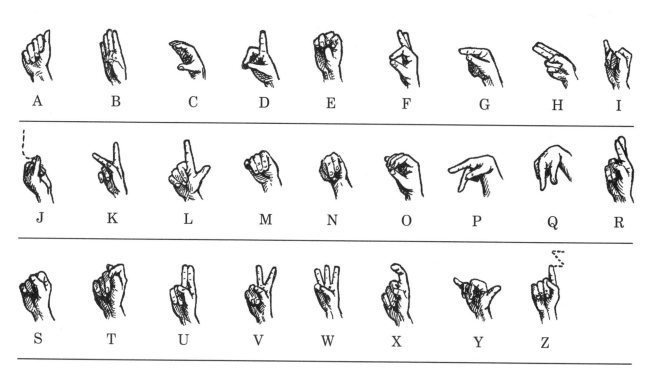

A   B   C   D   E   F   G   H   I

J   K   L   M   N   O   P   Q   R

S   T   U   V   W   X   Y   Z

PART I Directions: Write the letters for each word given in finger spelling.

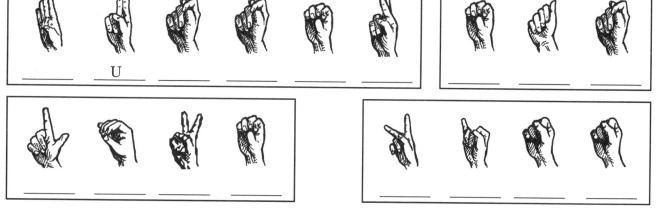

____ ____ ____ ____ ____ ____   ____ ____ ____

        U

____ ____ ____ ____   ____ ____ ____ ____

PART II Directions: Write the words given in sign language (one symbol for each word).

_____   _____   _____

PART III Directions: Write the number for each symbol.

____ ____ ____ ____ ____ ____ ____ ____ ____ ____

Asking Specific Questions About Line and Color

A selected book that features a main character or object that is relatively easy to draw shape and line for. Examples: *The Owl and the Pussy-Cat,* by Edward Lear, illustrated by Galdone, Warne, 1988; *Buffalo Woman* (buffalo, page before last) by Paul Goble, Macmillan, 1986; *The News About Dinosaurs* (cover illustration) by Patricia Lauber, Bradbury Press, 1989; *Fables,* "The Camel Dances," by Arnold Lobel, Harper Junior, 1983.

Materials

1. White 9-by-12-inch drawing paper, one sheet per student.
2. Coloring materials (felt-tip pens, crayons).

Directions

1. Read selected book to students and discuss.
2. Select the object that all students will draw.
3. Teach basic drawing techniques as needed for selected object:
   A. Point out the details of shape, line, and color.
   B. Students lightly sketch the object with pencil, imitating the artist in terms of shape and line as closely as possible. Illustration is displayed for students to look at.
   C. Note that the game below is based on the idea that even though students try to imitate the illustrator's use of the above design elements, individual differences will occur. The object of the game is for students to closely discriminate differences in the drawings.

   Recommended for younger students: Students outline the basic parts of the shape (head, body, tail, etc.) with fingers on the paper (for accurate placement) before using pencil.

   D. Students add color to object, imitating the artist as closely as possible. *Note:* Bold color makes it easier for students to discriminate the details. Names are written on the back. No background objects are drawn.
4. Play the game, "Which Drawing Is It?"
   A. For the first game, choose six or seven drawings with moderate differences in shape, line, and color. Display them for student scrutiny.
   B. Teacher selects one drawing to be identified, or "it."
   C. Students ask questions that can only be answered "yes" or "no," and that concern the art features of shape, line, and color.
   - Game format is similar to Twenty Questions.
   - The questioners try to group characteristics and eliminate similarities.
   - Sample questions for the camel from *Fables:*
     "Is the camel's head down?"
     "Does the tail point upward?"
     "Does the hat have a black and white ribbon?"

D. After six or seven students have each asked a question, an identification can be made. If wrong, questioning continues with at least two more questions.

E. Subsequent games can feature student chosen picture to be identified and student question fielder. Continue to display different pictures.

Extended Activity

Students write their questions on a card. Card is read by the person on their right.

Speaking, Writing, Appreciating Rhymes

Choose an available Mother Goose book that includes the rhymes: "There was a crooked man," and "Peter Piper picked a peck of pickled peppers." *The Random House Book of Mother Goose* (selected by Arnold Lobel, Random House, 1986) and *The Glorious Mother Goose* (compiled by Cooper Edens, Macmillan, 1988) are good choices.

Materials

1. For "Crooked Man," a pair of binoculars; two masking tape lines made on the floor, one straight and one "crooked," each approximately 12 feet long.

2. A stopwatch. Practice the "Peter Piper" tongue twister until you can say it accurately, as fast as possible.

Directions

1. Let students enjoy trying to walk the straight and crooked lines. Students walk first with "normal vision" and then with the opposite end of the binoculars held up to eyes (so that objects appear farther away). Encourage reactions to differences in difficulty between the two lines, with and without the binoculars.

2. Now recite and enjoy the rhyme, "There was a crooked man" with students.

3. Next, since the purpose of this activity is to promote the sophisticated enjoyment of Mother Goose for older children, brainstorm:

   A. synonyms for the adjective *crooked,* including several meanings (slanted, bent, dishonest, jagged, deformed, askew).

   B. persons, places, and things that would be "more fun" if crooked!

4. Recite "Peter Piper picked . . ." for students, challenging them to a contest, for repeating it correctly in the least amount of time. Set the contest for later, giving time for practice.

5. Write a group tongue twister patterned after Peter Piper, using the following format:

   (Cackling Katie) (cautioned) (kilometers) (of) (caroling) (cats) .
        names   verb   amount   adjective   noun, object

   ____ (Kilometers) of (caroling) (cats) (cackling Katie) (cautioned).
       amount   adjective noun, object   names   verb

6. Next, brainstorm "amounts" words, such as acres, billion, several, bushel, as possibilities for writing the tongue twister. Students write and illustrate their own tongue twisters. (How about "Crooked Peppers"?)

7. *Optional:* Include student-written tongue twisters in the reciting contest.

Additional Source for Tongue Twisters *Tongue Twisters,* by Charles Keller, Simon & Schuster, 1989.

Lobel, Arnold. *Fables.* **New York: Harper & Row, 1980.** Short, original fables with inviting animal characters.

Directions

1. Read and discuss the following fables: "The Hen and the Apple Tree," "The Bad Kangaroo," "The Camel Dances," "The Pig at the Candy Store," and "The Mouse at the Seashore."

2. Reinforce the definition of *character description* and *character trait.* Use examples from "The Hen and the Apple Tree."

   A. A *character* is who or what the story is about.

   B. A character's *description* is what the character *looks like. Example*: the wolf: furry, pointed ears, tail.

   C. A character's *traits* tell how a character *acts or behaves. Examples*: the wolf: sly, hungry, mean, foolish; the hen: smart, brave, clever, quick-thinking.

3. Play the "Fables Characters Relay Game" as follows:

   A. Divide students into two teams.

   B. Give the key rules:

   • Each student has seven seconds to give a character description or trait.

   • The team loses a point if someone on the team talks out of turn.

   • If a description or trait is not correct or appropriate, player gets one more chance, with five seconds to give an answer.

   • Character descriptions or traits meaning the same as one already given may be used.

   • No points are awarded for a word already used.

   C. Start with "The Hen and the Apple Tree" and the character, hen.

   D. Write the team names and the character name on a transparency or the chalkboard. Record the descriptions and traits under the correct team as given. (Students can then scan the lists before giving an answer.)

   E. After at least five descriptions or traits have been given from each team for the hen, start a list for the wolf. Next proceed to "The Bad Kangaroo," then "The Camel . . . ," etc., with one character for each fable.

   F. Score-keeping: The student making the point records it on the chalkboard.

   G. Proceed until all team members have had ample turns, or the stories are completed.

   H. Other fable possibilities: "The Poor Old Dog," "The Ostrich in Love."

Cole, Joanna. *Large as Life Animals*. New York: Alfred Knopf, 1990. Life-sized paintings with brief but high-interest text, giving the characteristics of various small nocturnal and daytime animals. Included are the greater Indian fruit bat and the fennec. NOTE: The original edition of the book, *Large As Life: Nighttime Animals*, was used for this lesson. Select the nocturnal animals from the new edition.

Directions

1. Introduce the book by giving examples of the surprising and interesting information available.

   A. Ask students what size they think most bats are

   B. Show the picture of the greater Indian fruit bat

   C. Show picture and give information about the royal antelope

   D. Explain that all of these nocturnal, or active-at-night animals, are actual size!

2. Read and discuss the book.

   A. Point out that the paintings are intended to convey realistic features of the animals.

   B. Advise students to listen carefully to the interesting information, so as to be able to recall it later for the game.

   C. *Optional*: Discuss additional information in "Nature Notes" at the back of the book.

3. Play the game, "Draw It, Say It!"

   A. Review concepts as needed to facilitate success of the game.

   B. Play game:

      (1) Form students into two (or more) teams.

      (2) Review the categories of cards with students (person, place, thing; object; difficult)

      (3) Students randomly select a playing card as their turn comes.

      (4) The student who is "it" draws a picture of the object on the chalkboard or paper.

      (5) The other team members call out objects, with a time limit set for responding (one to two minutes).

      (6) Objects not identified go back into the draw.

   C. For larger groups, or more individual turns, make more cards. Examples for additional objects: flea (chinchilla), extra big ears (fennec), prickly ball (hedgehog), flowers (mouse lemur).

Additional Activity

"To Tell the Truth" (For students who have not already completed the extended activity for activity 4–1, Large As Life: "Who Am I?")

Materials Needed

One or more copies of the book pages, "Nature Notes"

Directions

1. Read the information contained in "Nature Notes" to the students.

2. Organize students into groups of three, with each group selecting or being assigned to a particular animal.

3. Students in a group write descriptions of the animal, using the information in "Nature Notes" with *one* student using all truthful and accurate information and the other two including one or two small details that are untrue or false. Suggested description beginning: "I am the (brown hare). I _____."

4. The information by each group of three students is presented to the large group as a speech. Individuals in the large group vote on who is telling the "whole truth," and is the "real" animal.

   (*Note:* Either make the book available to the large group for reviewing information ahead of the presentations, or duplicate copies of the information.) Optional: Students make appropriate animal masks for their presentation.

5. See activity 2–10, To Tell the Truth: Zeus and His Family, for the same activity format.

4–7 LARGE AS LIFE: DRAW IT, SAY IT!

Directions: Copy and cut apart as cards.

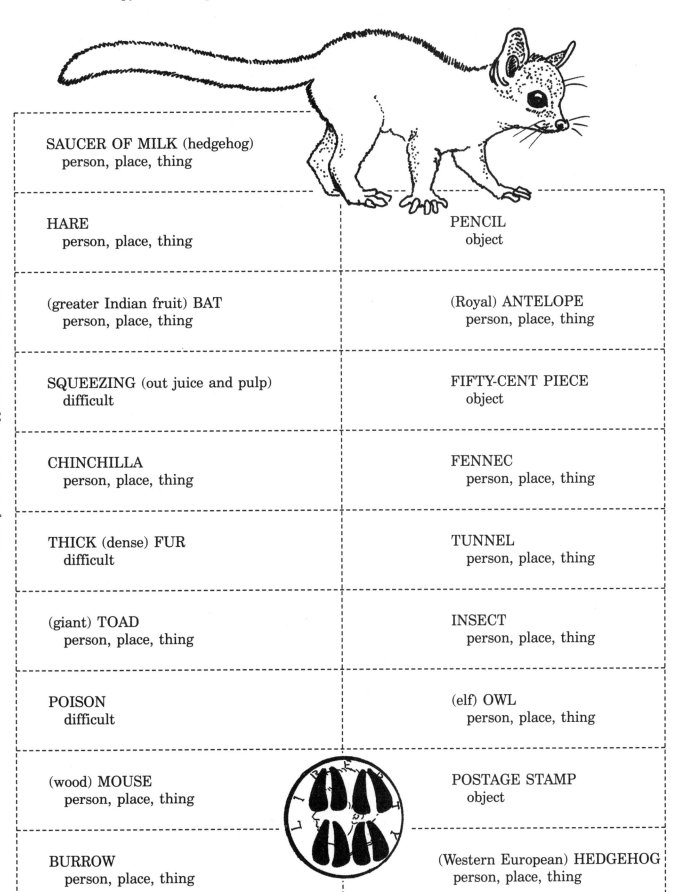

SAUCER OF MILK (hedgehog)
person, place, thing

HARE
person, place, thing

PENCIL
object

(greater Indian fruit) BAT
person, place, thing

(Royal) ANTELOPE
person, place, thing

SQUEEZING (out juice and pulp)
difficult

FIFTY-CENT PIECE
object

CHINCHILLA
person, place, thing

FENNEC
person, place, thing

THICK (dense) FUR
difficult

TUNNEL
person, place, thing

(giant) TOAD
person, place, thing

INSECT
person, place, thing

POISON
difficult

(elf) OWL
person, place, thing

(wood) MOUSE
person, place, thing

POSTAGE STAMP
object

BURROW
person, place, thing

(Western European) HEDGEHOG
person, place, thing

Lilly, Kenneth. *Kenneth Lilly's Animals.* **Text by Joyce Pope. New York: Lothrop, Lee & Shepard, 1988.** Magnificent, realistic illustrations and lively, readable text depicting wild animals from six habitats around the world.

Materials

1. Three desks or small tables, three bells or other objects that have distinguishing sounds
2. Overhead projector and transparency of activity sheet
3. Calculator

Directions

1. Read about and discuss all of the animals from the six habitats that are contained in the activity. See activity 9–10, Artistic Animals, for background and points of discussion about the art.

   A. Point out the information contained in the questions.

   B. Reinforce concepts and information.

2. Play the game, "Animal Money Adventures"

   A. Select two students to be scorekeepers, one to write the money amounts earned by team members on the chalkboard or paper, and one to add amounts on a calculator. *Optional*: "referee" to determine which "contestant" rang the bell first.

   B. Divide the rest of the group into three teams. Each team of students will represent one game-show contestant, with each student on a team taking turns. Determine the contestant order, and which team starts.

   C. A student is given a statement below, according to the dollar amount. Student responds with "What is (answer)." Teach, reinforce, and practice the correct procedure for responses in the game! *Note:* For most students, do not require the "What is" part of the answer for the first game.

   D. Set up facilities and contestants in the following manner:

   (1) Gameboard (transparency of activity sheet) is displayed on overhead.

   (2) Position the three desks somewhat apart from each other, but where they can be easily seen for identifying the first one to ring the bell.

   E. Playing the Game:

   (1) Starting contestant selects one of the six habitats and a dollar amount. *Note:* The increase in question difficulty with increase in dollar amounts is not highly significant in this game.

   (2) Teacher reads the appropriate statement from those below. Cross out that dollar amount in the appropriate category on the transparency. If the correct animal is given, the dollar amount is recorded by the scorekeeper.

(3) If the answer is incorrect, or if no response is given, the two other contestants are given a chance to answer. If neither responds, the correct answer is revealed. To break a tie, the teacher selects another statement from the same habitat to read.

(4) Contestants continue to choose from amounts not crossed out.

(5) The winning team is the one with the largest dollar amount.

(6) The game can be played again, either with the same or different statements.

3. Statements for the Game:

Hot Forests

$100: They lie in water during hot weather.
   Answer: What is a tiger?

$400: They eat at 6 A.M., rest at 10:00 A.M. and make nests of branches at dusk.
   Answer: What is a gorilla?

$600: Babies stay with their group until they are at least 10 years old!
   Answer: What is an (Indian) elephant?

$1000: It uses its teeth to comb its soft, wooly fur.
   Answer: What is a (slender) loris?

Cool Forests

$100: This animal has been called "the one who does not drink."
   Answer: koala.

$400: Its method of protection carries for 3 miles.
   Answer: skunk.

$600: Food is found by smell, rather than remembering where it is buried.
   Answer: (gray) squirrel.

$1000: A brood can eat more than 1 million ants by the time they leave the nest.
   Answer: (green) woodpecker.

Seas and Rivers

$100: The female lays between 10,000 and 20,000 eggs.
   Answer: bullfrog.

$400: They are greatly feared because they often swim into shallow water.
   Answer: (great white) shark.

$600: The baby is small enough to fit into a person's hand. The mother weighs as much as three people!
   Answer: (green) turtle.

$1000: Each of these animals greets another with specific clicking sounds.
   Answer: (sperm) whale.

Grasslands

$100: The fastest moving animal in the world!
   Answer: cheetah.

$400: They can tell each other apart because of the different fur pattern each has.
　　　Answer: zebras.

$600: Males have neck-wrestling matches.
　　　Answer: giraffes.

$1000: A baby can swim before it can walk.
　　　Answer: hippopotamus.

Deserts

$100: Once the water is gone from its body, it must drink a lot of water quickly.
　　　Answer: camel.

$400: It can dig so fast that it disappears "like magic" under ground.
　　　Answer: fennec.

$600: It loves to be active during the day when it's very hot.
　　　Answer: thorny devil.

$1000: It can survive indefinitely without drinking.
　　　Answer: Merriam's kangaroo rat.

Mountains

$100: This animal is the symbol of the World Wildlife Fund.
　　　Answer: giant panda.

$400: This animal is not dangerous to livestock, as many people think.
　　　Answer: spectacled bear.

$600: This animal keeps the same mate for life.
　　　Answer: golden eagle.

$1000: It cannot smell its food at all—uses only sight.
　　　Answer: Andean condor.

Bonus Round (optional)

Use the following or another statement:

These animals are totally protected by law. They have received money and worldwide attention. But they are still one of the world's rarest and most endangered animals. Answer: giant panda.

Let students choose how much they want to wager in the bonus round.

Extended Activities

1. Students generate additional questions to present to each other.
2. Students work in cooperative groups studying the specific habitats and generating more questions and answers.

Hot Forests

$100

$400

$600

$1000

Cool Forests

$100

$400

$600

$1000

Seas and Rivers

$100

$400

$600

$1000

Grasslands

$100

$400

$600

$1000

Deserts

$100

$400

$600

$1000

Mountains

$100

$400

$600

$1000

Mathematics With Children's Books

Barrett, Judi. *Cloudy With a Chance of Meatballs.* New York: Atheneum, 1981.
The weather in the town of Chewandswallow, where it rains soup and snows mashed potatoes, is delicious—until it takes a turn for the worse.

Note: Decide whether the problems are to be solved by the students with addition, multiplication, or a combination of both. Prepare problem numbers to be filled in by teacher before duplicating for younger or lower-performers, or for the students to fill in later. Gear problems to the *application level* of the students.

Directions

1. Read the book to students, enjoying the creativity and humor.
2. Review the rules and steps for adding and multiplying.
3. Complete the activity sheet.
    A. Depending on the level of the students, problems can be completed:
       - by the whole group, using transparency of activity sheet in addition to student sheets
       - partially by whole group participation and partially with student pairs or independently
       - independently
    B. Carefully read through the problems with students before solving.
    C. Students work the problems in the blank areas.

Follow-Up Activity   Students contribute ideas for additional problems, and/or students supply numbers for the problems. Problems can then be solved by groups or individuals.

Additional Activity   Art and Storytelling—"It's Raining Down . . ."

1. Students, in groups or individually, create their own story about other objects that could rain down from the sky.
2. Students make the objects using paint, crayons, felt-tip pens, etc. Attach props using string to a railroad board "cloud" or a large hat.
3. Everyone tells stories with the props "raining down" to the class.

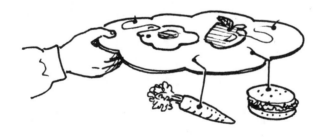

5–1 CLOUDY WITH A CHANCE OF ADDING OR MULTIPLYING

Name _____

Directions: Use this rule for the problems below. "If you want to know how many in all, *add* (or *multiply*) the numbers together."

1. The kids liked the hamburgers to come down! _____ hamburgers came down each hour. They came down for _____ hours. How many hamburgers came down in all?

_____

2. Lots of maple syrup ran down the big pancake. _____ gallons ran down each hour. It ran for _____ hours. How many gallons ran in all?

_____

3. The truck had to clean up the food. It made _____ trips each day. It made trips for _____ days. How many trips in all?

_____

4. The kids had to eat lots of sandwiches! One kid ate _____ each day. He did it for _____ days. How many sandwiches did he eat in all?

_____

5. Life was delicious until spaghetti tied up the town. _____ pounds fell each day. It fell for _____ days. How many pounds fell in all?

_____

Mahy, Margaret. *The Boy Who Was Followed Home.* **New York: Dial, 1975.** A growing number of hippos follow Robert. The "solution" has a surprise permanency to the problem!

Materials

1. Newspaper strips, one for each child, cut about 3″ wide. Second grade: two pages (one folded); third grade: four pages (two folded). Students will make string paper hippos.
2. Scissors for every one or two students.
3. Also, one die for each pair of students to complete step 5 on the worksheet.

Before duplicating the activity sheet: Determine the level of the students' addition and subtraction skills and supply appropriate numbers for the problems.

Directions

1. Read and enjoy the story with the students! Point out the humor and vitality of the classic Kellogg illustrations. Also make note of the climactic point; that the pill contained an ingredient that attracted giraffes.
2. Reinforce addition and subtraction concepts appropriate to the activity sheet. Also review the story problem formats used, noting key words for determining the correct operation.
3. Complete the activity sheet.
   A. Students solve the first five problems, as a group, in pairs, or independently. The second blank for the answer is for the *label*. Students work with a partner for step 5.
   B. Make the string paper hippos.
      (1) Students fold the newspaper *twice* (into eight or sixteen equal sections).

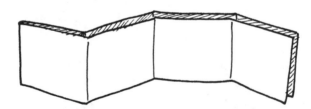

      (2) Students *carefully* cut out the sixth hippo from the activity sheet.
      (3) The cut hippo is glued to the "front" of the closed newspaper.

(4) Next, students cut around the hippo at the top and bottom of the newspaper only. Folds on the sides of the newspaper *must not be cut*, or the sections will come apart! (Sections with two 8s can then be taped together.)

(5) Students combine all their hippo strings and count them, recording the grand total of new hippos.

4. *Game: "How Many Hippos Can Get Onto the Lawn?"*

   A. Two lines are drawn across the floor—one is the starting line and one is the finish line.

   B. One student—Robert—is "it" and stands ahead of the finish line with his/her back to the group.

   C. Other students—the hippos—all stand at the starting line.

   D. Object of game: Get to the finish line—onto the grass—without Robert catching you. If caught, student goes back to the starting line.

   E. Robert turns around quickly x times (determine how many). The hippos who get onto the grass are the winners.

Additional Activity   Speaking and Writing—"Those Gigantic Giraffes, What to Do?"

1. Since Robert was "very pleased" to see the giraffes, he probably wanted to keep them. But what about Robert's father?

2. Brainstorm: Robert's father's reactions, what Robert would probably like to do with the giraffes, how many giraffes might come, what Robert could do.

3. Write a group letter to Robert, suggesting plans for and solutions to the new visitors' arrival.

5–2 HIPPO HAPPENINGS

Directions: Find out if you should ADD or SUBTRACT to get the answers to the problems about the hippos. Write the answer and label it. You can work the problem in the empty space.

1. If there were

_____ hippos one

day and _____ more came the next, how many hippos *in all?*

_____ hippos

2. There were _____ hippos

in all. If _____ went to school with Robert, how many were *left* at home?

_____   _____

3. The hippos all came to Grandpa's birthday

party. There were _____ pieces of cake. If only

_____ pieces were eaten, how many were *left?*

_____   _____

4. If the 27 hippos each

got _____ dishes of ice cream, how many dishes were eaten *in all?*

_____   _____

5. Write the name of your favorite animal here:

_____

Pretend you ate a magic pill that will bring that animal to your house. Roll the die 4 times to see how many will come in all. WRITE THE NUMBERS:
Did you get more animals than your partner?
YES   NO

_____
_____
_____
+ _____
TOTAL: _____

6. Follow directions for the string hippos.

How many *in all?*

CUT ⟶

_____   _____

Books and characters selected by teacher, students, or both.

Materials Needed

1. One or two puzzles (below) per student, enlarged, if possible, on heavy, light-colored paper.
2. Nine-by-twelve-inch white paper, one sheet per student.

Directions

1. Teach, reinforce, or review the shape names contained in the tangram puzzle. For older or higher-performers, point out the significance of the angles.

2. Students each cut out ONE enlarged puzzle and experiment with creating an object or a character. Examples: cat, candle, tower. For younger students: Give several examples, and discuss.

3. *Optional (for older students):* Students make a shape and then outline it by tracing around the shape (instruct students how to hold each piece as it is traced). Have other students work the new puzzles.

4. Students think of a book character name or book title for their object. Paste object onto white paper and write its name or title. For younger or lower-performers: Brainstorm possible book characters and titles.

THE TORTOISE
AND THE
HARE

CLASS
CLOWN

SOCKS

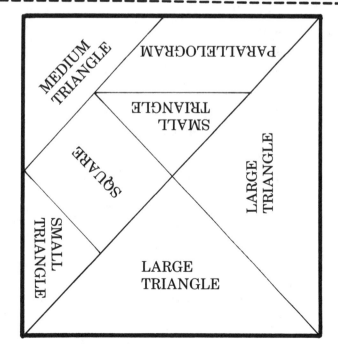

A TANGRAM PUZZLE is a Chinese puzzle made by cutting a square into five triangles, a square and a parallelogram. These pieces are used to form various figures and designs.

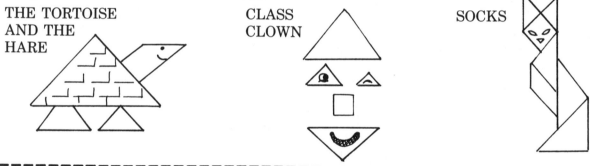

Mean, Median, Mode; Graphing

Bayer, Jane. *A, My Name Is Alice*. **New York: Dial, 1984.** Ball-bouncing rhymes and Steven Kellogg illustrations that "sell humor from *A* to *Z*."

Materials Needed

1. Two pieces of one inch squared graph paper per student
2. Glue, scissors, plain white paper

Directions

1. Read and enjoy the book with students, focusing on the first five letters. Tell students that they will find out three new and interesting ways that names can be important.
2. List the nine names given in the illustration for students to copy. Tell them to:
   A. Write the names in alphabetical order on one piece of graph paper, one letter per square (paper placed horizontally).
   B. Use the first column for writing the number of letters in each name, and write the numbers.

3. Finding the *mean*, or *average*:

   To find the average number of letters in a word, tell students to:

   A. Cut off all of the letters at the ends of the lines that are needed to give the same number of letters to all or most of the lines.

   Students cut off and put aside.

   Teacher demonstrates with a model.

   B. Next, place the cut and uncut letters on a piece of plain paper. (It doesn't matter beside which word the "extra letters" are placed.) Glue down.

C. Count the number of letters in each row.

What is the *mean* or *average*? It is a little less than six, because all the names evened out to be six letters long except one.

Students label mean on paper.

Tell students that the mean is the number that can be substituted for each of the given numbers and still give the same sum. Demonstrate:

$$4+8+7+4+6+6+4+9+5 = 53$$
$$6+6+6+6+6+6+6+6+5 = 53$$

Students line up the cut numbers as originally on the graph and add them. Also, add, substituting with sixes.

4. Finding the *median*:

Tell students to:

A. Put the cut numbers in numerical order.

B. Find the center, or middle, number. This is the *median*. The median in this example is 6.

C. Write numbers on back of the white sheet and label.

$$\boxed{4}\boxed{4}\ \boxed{4}\ \boxed{5}\ \boxed{6}\boxed{6}\boxed{7}\ \boxed{8}\boxed{9}$$

5. Finding the *mode*:

Tell students to:

A. Write the numbers from 1 to 9 across the bottom of the second piece of graph paper.

B. Glue numbers onto the paper above the written numbers, as shown in the illustration. Look for the number which occurs most often. This is the *mode*. The mode is 4. Label.

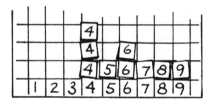

Materials

1. Catalogs, where sections can be cut out, that feature items of high student interest and knowledge. Catalogs with good possibilities: regular department stores (such as J.C. Penney); discount department stores; specialty and holiday item books; other option: newspaper ads.
2. One legal-sized envelope for each student.
3. Small strips of paper for students to write estimates on.

Directions

1. Read or refer to one or more of the following books or poems: *A Chair for My Mother* (Greenwillow, 1982) and *Something Special for Me* (Morrow, 1986), both by Vera B. Williams; *Where the Sidewalk Ends* (Harper, 1974) by Shel Silverstein, "Smart," and "For Sale." These focus on earning, purchasing, or selling.

2. Instruct students to find in a catalog and to *carefully* cut out:

   A. The picture of an item from their "wish list" that costs $100 or less and that other students would recognize.

   B. The description of the item with its price.

3. Next, students glue the item picture—top part only—to the front of the envelope. The item description and price is glued under the picture, so that it can only be seen when the item picture is lifted up. See illustration below. Note: Students should be careful not to let other students see the item price.

4. Now, students take turns reading their item descriptions to the class. Each class member then writes an estimate of the price and gives it (with their name on it) to the presenting student. Estimates are kept in the student's envelope. In addition to the item description, students give the following information to the class:

   A. whether item is from a regular or discount catalog, name of catalog

   B. whether item is on sale

5. After all presentations and estimates have been given, each student screens the given estimates to find the estimate closest to the actual price and the highest and the lowest estimates. These figures are written on the back of the envelope and the winners announced to the group. *Optional*: Award prizes for the closest estimate(s).

6. Discuss the factors that bring estimating expertise with students, including:

   • experience and familiarity with item
   • interest in particular catalog and items
   • particular store
   • accurate and detailed description of the item
   • experience with estimating

Barrett, Judi. *Cloudy With a Chance of Meatballs.* **New York: Atheneum, 1981.**
The weather in Chewandswallow is delicious—until it takes a turn for the worse.

Teacher Preparation

Decide on appropriate numbers for the activity sheet problems.

1. Gear problem difficulty to computation ability.
2. Decide whether to use problems that yield remainders.
3. *Optional*: Supply the numbers before duplicating for low-performing groups.

Optional Materials Manipulatives for hands-on experience with the division process, such as macaroni, Cheerios™, raisins, pieces of tagboard.

Directions

1. After reading and discussing the book, point out that even in Chewandswallow the food was divided and shared by the people and animals.
   A. Present the following situation: *twenty* ice cream cones fell *altogether*. If *five* kids wanted to eat all *twenty*, how many did *each* get? _____

   Optional: Distribute the manipulatives, ask students to draw five circles to represent the five kids and then to distribute the twenty objects among the five kids.

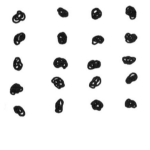

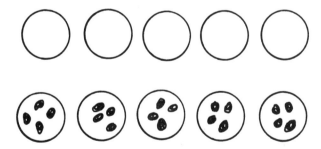

   B. Present the following rule for division: "If you know for all and you want to know for one or part of the whole, divide! Divide the *part* you know into the *whole* (all), to get the other *part*." "The twenty objects are divided among the five kids, which means that the five (kids) goes into the twenty."

$$\begin{array}{r} 4 \text{ cones each } (\textit{other part}) \\ \text{5 kids (known part)} \overline{)\ 20 \text{ cones } (\textit{whole})} \end{array}$$

Optional: Give term names:

$$\overset{\text{``quotient''}}{\text{``divisor''} \overline{\smash{)}\, \text{``dividend''}}}$$

C. Give other examples as needed:

- *Five* fish wanted to eat all *thirty* rolls. How many did *each* eat?
- Six dogs wanted to eat all twenty-four lamb chops. How many did each eat?
- In seven days, twenty-eight people were washed away by the soda flood. How many were washed away each day?

2. Students complete the activity sheet.
   A. Problems are completed independently by students, or in pairs, or as a group, depending on the skill level. Use manipulatives, if needed.
   B. Problems are worked on a separate sheet of paper. Students *number* the problems and *circle* the answers to assure correct transfer of information to the activity sheet.
   C. Optional difficulty control for bonus problem: "Use numbers higher (or lower) than _____."

Extended Activity   "More Store(y) Food Problems": Students are formed into groups of two to four. They either:

A. supply numbers for the above or other problems; or
B. write their own problems in sentence form and illustrate with symbols.

5–6   CLOUDY WITH A CHANCE OF DIVISION

Directions: If you know for all and you want to know for one or part of the whole, divide! Divide the part into the whole to find the other part. Solve the problems below using this rule. Label.

1. A storm of hamburgers blew in. If _____ boys wanted to eat all _____ hamburgers, how many did *each* eat?

_____ _____
         (label)

2. The school was closed and the kids couldn't take their tests.
If school were closed for _____ weeks, and they missed _____ tests all together, how many did they miss *each* week?

_____ _____

3. If the Sanitation Department cleaned the streets for _____ days, and they made _____ trips all together, how many trips did they make *each* day?

_____ _____

4. If _____ kids ate _____ cream cheese sandwiches all together, how many did *each* eat?

_____

_____

BONUS: WRITE YOUR OWN PROBLEM!

If _____ kids ate _____ donuts all together, how many did *each* eat?

_____ _____

Pasta Press
Noodles Hit the Streets

5. Life was delicious until the weather took a turn for the worse. If spaghetti snarled traffic for _____ days, and _____ pounds came down all together, how many pounds came down *each* day?

_____ _____

BONUS: WRITE YOUR OWN PROBLEM!

If a tomato tornado blew for _____ days, and _____ kids were carried away, how many were carried away *each* day?

_____ _____

Bayer, Jane. *A, My Name Is Alice*. New York: Dial, 1984. Ball-bouncing rhyme featuring animal characters, with art created by Steven Kellogg, that sells "humor and fun from A to Z."

Directions

1. Read and discuss the book, especially pointing out the letters and items from the activity sheet: *G*—giggles; *K*—kisses; *I*—ice cream; *Q*—question marks; *T*—teeth from the saber-toothed tiger.

2. Reinforce or review the concept of rounding to the nearest hundredths place or dollar: When rounding to the nearest dollar, look at the number to the right of the decimal point. If it is 5 or more, round up to the next dollar.

   Give examples around the theme of the "*B*" page, if needed:

   If a balloon costs $1.98 and was rounded to the nearest dollar, it would cost $2.00.

   Review the concept of adding rounded numbers.

3. Play the game:

   A. Pass out one copy of the activity sheet to each student, even though the game is played with partners. Two games is a normal amount to play.

   B. Select students with comparable skills as partners.

   C. Teach and reinforce the game rules from the activity sheet.

   D. Emphasize the following rules to students:

      1. The idea of the game is to stop your partner as well as to win yourself.

      2. Make sure your partner says and adds the items out loud, to check on accuracy.

      3. You may not buy only one of any item—if that's all you buy.

4. During the first game, watch lower-performing students for understanding and accuracy. Typically, the first game will be a learning process for everyone, and some students will win without much provocation.

5. After the first game, ask students to share strategies they developed both for winning and for blocking opponents.

6. Play a second game so that students can use what they have learned.

   Note: For some students, the challenge will be in blocking their opponent to the finish and calling the game a draw.

For completion of the activity with lower performers: Round off the dollar amounts as a group before the game is started, or limit rows to four by four or three by three.

Extending the Game

1. Give students a blank game sheet and ask them to rearrange the amounts on their own. Each one will be different.

2. Add a teacher-directed game, like Bingo, where the teacher tells the students what to buy.

3. Try a variety of strategies for winning, for example:

   • one in any corner

   • vertical only

   • horizontal only

   • center spot only

Directions: This game is similar to tic-tac-toe. 1. Buy two or three things—you may buy more than one of the *same* item. 2. Round the price to the nearest dollar. Mark your estimated cost with a *K* (for kiss) or *G* (for giggle)—choose one. 3. Four marks in a row—up, down, or diagonal—wins!

WISH LIST

Note: Partners SAY and ADD items *out loud* for accuracy check. Try to keep your partner from winning. You may not buy just one of one item.

$6	$21	$11	$28	$60
$15	$7	$48	$40	$22
$23	$16	$47	$19	$9
$24	$10	$14	$27	$44
$12	$8	$13	$26	$43

Schwartz, David M. *How Much Is a Million?* New York: Lothrop, Lee & Shepard, 1985. Concepts, examples, and the numbers for a million, billion, and trillion—with humor and accuracy.

Materials

1. One two-pound bag of popcorn kernels.

2. At least one title of students' favorite full-length book (see last part of activity sheet).

3. *Optional*: Visual of 1 million stars, through reproduction of one of the stars pages, seventy times. Tape together and laminate or use self-adhesive paper. Present with millions concepts in book.

Note: Peruse "A Note from the Author" at the back of the book before presenting the book to students.

Directions

1. Reinforce and review the reading and writing of numbers up to one million as needed by students.

2. Introduce the book by asking students to estimate the following:

   A. How many children's heads of hair would it take to equal 1 million individual strands of hair? (Each child has approximately 75,000 hairs.) Answer: 13 children.

   B. How many pages of a typical dictionary contain 1 million individual *letters*? (Each page contains approximately 3,500 letters.) Answer: about 300 pages.

   C. How many pages of stars (show one of the pages from the book containing over 14,000 stars) make 1 million stars? Answer: 70 pages.

3. Present the book content through one million or further, stopping for students to estimate before the answer amount for each "If . . ." statement is given.

4. Present the activity sheet as a concrete, fun method of understanding actual quantities of a million, as opposed to a test of student understanding of math operations and story problems. Choose the completion option which best matches the students' competency level: Students complete most of the items independently or with partners or students complete the activity as a whole group, with a large amount of teacher direction.

   A. Note about counting 1 million popcorn kernels: Distribute kernels to each student and add the individual results.

   B. Note about counting 1 million words:

      (1) Either select one book for the whole group to evaluate, or if skills permit, instruct individual students to select their own books.

      (2) Students count the number of words per line and multiply by the number of lines per page.

      (3) Students multiply the number of words per page by the number of pages in the book.

Related Activity   5–10, Large Numbers World Search

Answer Key to Activity Sheet

1. 111 days
2. 59 days
3. over 3 school years

4–9. Answers will vary.

5–8 DAYS, POPCORN, AND WORDS TO ONE MILLION

Name _____

Directions: Find out how many millions are in: schooldays of counting, popcorn, and words in books by solving the problems below.

COUNTING TO 1 MILLION IN SCHOOL

1. It takes 555 *hours* to count to one million. If the schoolday is 5 hours long (not including lunch and breaks), and you counted all 5 hours each day, how many days would it take you to count to

   one million? _____ days

2. If there are about 170 schooldays in the school year and you spent 111 days (5 hours a day) counting to 1 million, how many days would there be left for "readin' and writin' and other

   'rithmetic"? _____ days

3. If you counted for 1 *hour* each day, it would take 555 days to count to 1 million!
   Bonus question: About how many school years would it take to reach 1 million, counting 1 hour per day for 170 days?

   _____ school years

COUNTING 1 MILLION POPCORN KERNELS

4. Estimate the number of popcorn kernels in the bag of popcorn

   and write the number here: _____ kernels

5. Count (with a partner or group) the actual number of kernels

   and write that number: _____ kernels

6. If there are _____ kernels in the bag (copy from above), how

   many bags would you need to have 1 million kernels? _____ bags

COUNTING ONE MILLION WORDS

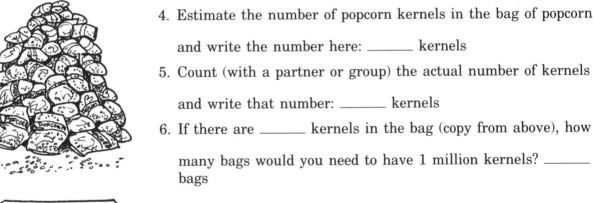

7. A favorite book has about 200 300 400 (circle one) words per page.

   Title: _____

   _____

8. If there are _____ words per page, how many words are there

   all together in the book? _____ words

9. How many books of this title would it take to equal 1,000,000

   words? _____ books

5–9 HARE, TORTOISE, AND FRIENDS TO THE FINISH! _____
Problem Solving: Making a Drawing

Stevens, Janet, adapted and illustrated by. *The Tortoise and the Hare.* **New York: Holiday House, 1984.** Tortoise eats right, works out, and jogs over the finish line, while watching Hare in his pink jogging shorts try to catch up.

Directions

1. Read and enjoy the fable with students.

2. Present the following sample problems to students on the chalkboard or overhead, brainstorming strategies for solving the problems on the activity sheet. Alternatively, place students in groups to brainstorm.

   A. In the first race, Hare and Tortoise raced.

      Tortoise finished 2 minutes *before* Hare.

      Hare finished 2 minutes *after* Tortoise.

      Who came in first? _____ Second? _____

   A Suggested Strategy: Draw a "raceline" using a centimeter ruler to mark off the minutes. Write animals' initials above the positions, starting with the first animal at zero.

   For even more concreteness: Students place objects representing Hare and Tortoise, or colors to indicate the animals, on a raceline in correct positions.

   B. In another race, Hare, Tortoise, and Chicken raced.

      Hare finished 2 minutes *after* Chicken
      Hare finished 3 minutes *before* Tortoise
      Tortoise finished 5 minutes *after* Chicken

      Who came in first? _____ Second? _____ Third? _____

      Repeat the strategy used above.
      Discuss other strategies students develop for solving the problems.

   C. For students needing additional practice, present other problems similar to 2 and 3 on the activity sheet.

3. Completing the activity sheet:

   A. Students solve the problems independently, in pairs or small groups, or as a total group, depending on the purpose and student level. Point out in problem 4: "Tortoise finished 3 minutes before Raccoon."

   B. Most students will need to draw racelines to solve the problems, even though many will indicate that they've "figured it out in their head."

   C. Extension of the activity sheet:
      Students write their own problems with these directions:

      • Choose three book characters.

      • Copy problem 1, but use book character names.

      • Exchange problems with a friend and solve.

Additional Activity "A Real Tortoise and Hare Race"

1. Obtain a live tortoise and rabbit (or turtle and guinea pig, insect, etc.). Discuss the movement of animals and why different kinds move differently. Look at the legs and feet.
2. Set a race course.
3. Students predict which animal will win, why, and in what amount of time.
4. After the race, determine whether the predictions matched the results. Also ask how the results matched the story.

See also Activity 1–3, The Big Antonyms and Synonyms Race.

Answer Key To Activity Sheet

1. Chicken, Hare, Tortoise
2. Tortoise, Raccoon, Hare, Chicken
3. Chicken, Hare, Raccoon, Tortoise
4. Frog, Hare, Tortoise, Chicken, Raccoon

5—9 HARE, TORTOISE, AND FRIENDS TO THE FINISH!

Name _____

DIRECTIONS: In the book, Tortoise won the race. Now, his friends are racing, too! Figure out who wins each race, and who places second, third, etc.

1. In the second race, Hare, Tortoise, and Chicken raced:
   Hare finished 1 minute *after* Chicken.
   Hare finished 2 minutes *before* Tortoise.
   Tortoise finished 3 minutes *after* Chicken.

   Who came in first? _____ Who came in second? _____

   Who came in third? _____

Draw raceline here:

2. In the third race, Hare, Tortoise, Chicken, and Raccoon raced:
   Tortoise finished 3 minutes *before* Hare.
   Chicken finished 2 minutes *after* Hare.
   Raccoon finished 1 minute *before* Hare.
   Raccoon finished 2 minutes *after* Tortoise.

   Who came in first? _____ Who came in second? _____ third? _____

   fourth? _____

Raceline:

3. In the fourth race, Hare, Tortoise, Chicken, and Raccoon raced:
   Chicken finished 2 minutes *before* Hare.
   Tortoise finished 3 minutes *after* Hare.
   Raccoon finished 2 minutes *after* Hare.
   Raccoon finished 1 minute *before* Tortoise.

   First? _____ Second? _____ Third? _____ Fourth? _____

BONUS

4. In the fifth race, Hare, Tortoise, Chicken, Raccoon, and Frog raced:
   Hare finished 1 minute *after* Frog.
   Hare finished 2 minutes *before* Chicken.
   Raccoon finished 4 minutes *after* Hare.
   Tortoise finished 3 minutes *before* Raccoon.

   First? _____ Second? _____ Third? _____ Fourth? _____

   Fifth? _____

© 1991 by The Center for Applied Research in Education

Large Numbers: Estimating, Rounding

Schwartz, David M. *How Much Is a Million?* **New York: Lothrop, Lee & Shepard, 1985.** Concepts, examples and the numbers for a million, billion, and trillion—with humor and accuracy!

Spier, Peter. *People.* **New York: Doubleday, 1980.** We are alike, but we are also unique, different individuals. "Isn't it wonderful."

***Guinness Book of World Records,* 1989 edition. New York: Bantam, 1989.**

Teacher Preparation

Plan place value to be rounded for Part II, 7 and 8 on the activity sheet.

Directions

1. Read, summarize or refer to the above books and their interesting large-number facts and ideas. Ask students: "Why are large-number facts—and records won—so interesting?"

2. Present the following attention-getting large number records and facts:

   - Longest word: 182 letters. A Greek word for meat stew.
   - Longest sentence in the world: 1,300 words, in *Absalom, Absalom!*, a novel by William Faulkner.
   - Longest Monopoly® game: 660 hours.
   - The number of smells that noses recognize: up to 1,000 different smells.
   - Country with the largest population: China, with 1 billion people. There are 5 billion people on earth. China has one-fifth of the world's population. There are 250,000,000 people in the U.S. Although the land size is about the same for both countries, we have one-quarter of the population that China has.
   - Most numerous creatures on earth: sea worms, with 40 septillion.

3. Review, in visual form, large number concepts and the numerals, through billions, as needed by the group. Suggestion: extend numeral display from the title page of *How Much Is a Million*, and then compare 1 million stars, ½ million, ¼ million, ⅛ million, and one page of stars = 14,000.

4. Present the activity sheet. Complete as follows:

   A. Students point to the place value chart at the top and name the number periods.

   B. Students give *oral* estimates for the facts and records in Part I. Point to Part I, question 1. Students make an estimate and then record correct answer on the chart as it is read.

   Note: Background and comparison information is included to give a basis for the oral estimates.

   C. Facts and records for Part I:

      (1) *The number of pages in the largest dictionary* (This dictionary has 12 volumes, with about 1,300 pages per volume.) Answer: *Oxford English Dictionary*, 14,487 pages

      (2) *The largest amount of coins made per day* (Done in the U.S. Mint, with approximately 2.75 million coins made per hour, with one eight-hour shift per day.) Answer: 22 million coins

      (3) *The number of chickens in the world* (The most abundant domesticated bird of all) Answer: about 6 billion, 500 million, according to the *Guinness Book* (That's about 1.4 chickens for every person in the world!)

(4) *The number of TV sets in the U.S.* (There are approximately 93 million households in the US.) Answer: about 100 million TV sets

(5) *The number of stars in the Milky Way Galaxy* (Galaxies are giant clouds of stars grouped together. There are 88 different constellations, with varying numbers of stars in each.) Answer: 120 billion stars

(6) *The number of cans of Coca-Cola® sold worldwide in one day, or 24-hour period* (Approximately 12 million are sold each hour.) Answer: 280 million cans. In one month, the amount sold would make 3 chains around the moon!

(7) *The number of cells in a newborn baby* (There are 50 trillion cells in an adult.) Answer: 26 billion cells

(8) *The number of thunderstorms in the world in one year.* Answer: about 16 million thunderstorms

D. Complete Part II as follows:

(1) Emphasize the CAPITALIZED words in problems 3, 4, and 5.

(2) Review rounding off procedures as appropriate for completing problems 6 through 8.

(3) Students work problems independently, in pairs, or as a group.

Sources for facts *The Second Kids' World Almanac of Records and Facts,* by Margo McLoone-Basta & Alice Siegel, Pharos Books, 1987; *The Usborne Book of Facts and Lists,* EDC, 1987 edition.

Extended Activity Ask students to contribute a list of "most wanted facts or information," such as how many ice cream cones eaten in the US each year, or how many kids in school in the world. Then assign students to find as many answers as possible in the three "Records" books cited. Alternative: students find and contribute interesting items of information.

5–10 LARGE NUMBERS WORLD SEARCH

Name _____

Directions: On a search throughout the world, many large numbers—the largest or the most of something—were found to be "amazing but true."

Part I: Write the correct numbers told to you in the chart below.

Part II: Write answers to the statements and questions below. Do your computations on the back or another paper.

Part I

1. Pages in largest dictionary
2. Largest amount of coins made per day
3. Number of chickens in the world
4. Number of TV sets in U.S.
5. Stars in Milky Way galaxy
6. Cans of Coca-Cola® sold worldwide in one day
7. Cells in newborn baby
8. Number of thunderstorms in the world each year

	BILLIONS			MILLIONS			THOUSANDS			UNITS		
	100	10	1	100	10	1	100	10	1	100	10	1
1.												
2.												
3.												
4.												
5.												
6.												
7.												
8.												

Part II

1. Write the population for your city or town below:

_____

people

2. There are about two hundred fifty million people in the U.S. Write number below:

_____

3. You have about 75,000 hairs on your head. How many hairs do YOU AND 13 friends have altogether?

_____

4. The world has 5 billion people. Two billion are kids. How many MORE adults?

_____

5. Each person speaks about 4,000 words a day. How many in a YEAR?

6. American teens eat 1,817 pounds of food per year. Round that to the nearest *hundred*:

_____

7. The highest mountain peak in the world—Mt. Everest—is 29,028 feet high. Round to nearest

_____ place.

8. The sun is 92,960,000 miles from earth. Round to nearest

_____

_____

Social Studies With Children's Books

> **Goble, Paul.** *Buffalo Woman.* **New York: Bradbury, 1984.** A young hunter's love for a buffalo in the form of a beautiful maiden requires that he become a buffalo to remain with her.

Materials

1. Transparency of the activity sheet.
2. Scissors, glue.
   Optional—activity sheet duplicated on manila paper; pictures of buffalo and Indians on the plains.

Directions

1. Read the story to the students and enjoy the illustrations that show many colorful details of tribal life on the Great Plains.

   Point out the following plot details:

   A. The brave young hunter became *very happy* when he gave up being a person so that he could be with his wife and son. *Note:* Explain his joyful transformation as not a sacrifice, or many students will have difficulty accepting this as a positive event.

   B. The Buffalo Nation gave meat to the People so that they could have good food to eat.

   C. Basic and unique needs, beliefs, and understandings of native American culture, such as bravery in hunting for food, tracks on the ground to find people and animals, and mutual acceptance of each person in a tribe.

2. Extend the understanding of the contribution of the buffalo to the Indians of the Great Plains with the activity sheet:

   A. Present the activity sheet on a transparency and discuss the meaning of the objects to the right of the Buffalo Woman. Tell students that when the Indians and the buffalo roamed the plains together not so long ago, the buffalo provided the people with food, shelter, clothing, and other items. The objects and their meanings:

   • shank (back leg) of meat—Buffalo meat was the Indian's main food. It could be roasted, dried to make jerky, or pounded with berries and suet to make pemmican.

   • tepee—Buffalo skins were scraped, dried, greased with buffalo brains, liver and fat, and stretched and dried, then decorated.

   • robe—Buffalo hides (skins) with fur kept the people warm in winter.

   • rug—Hides were used as blankets and for sitting on.

   • moccasins—Hides were used for foot covering.

   • Buffalo Nation and People become related—Love of hunter for the maiden and the buffalo giving of their flesh make *sharing* a happy experience.

   • whip—Made of buffalo hair and skin, used for capturing buffalo.

   • fire—Dry buffalo manure was used as fuel for cooking and heat.

   • spoon—Buffalo bones and horns were used to make spoons, cups, knives, and other utensils.

B. Students complete the activity sheet as follows:

(1) Carefully cut out the Buffalo Woman and all the objects.

(2) Glue the objects onto the top part of the coat. Label.

(3) Fill in the answers at the bottom.

Other Books About Native Americans   The long list of other wonderful books by Paul Goble; Byrd Baylor's *And It Is Still That Way*; Longfellow's *Hiawatha's Childhood*, illustrated by Errol Le Cain and also *Hiawatha* illustrated by Susan Jeffers; Bill Martin Jr.'s *Knots on a Counting Rope*, Holt, 1990; John Steptoe's *The Story of Jumping Mouse*, Lothrop, 1984.

See also Activity 4–4, Which Drawing Is it?

6–1 THE BUFFALO SHARED THEIR BEST

Name _____

Directions: 1. *Carefully* cut out the Buffalo Woman and the food, clothing, shelter, and other objects the buffalo gave to help the Indian people. 2. Paste the objects onto the woman's robe. 3. Write the name of each. 4. Complete the sentences at the bottom.

©1991 by The Center for Applied Research in Education

1. The young hunter felt the buffalo robe become a _____ of _____ .

2. The young man became a buffalo because he _____ his _____ and _____ .

3. In return, the Buffalo People gave _____ for people to _____ .

Snyder, Dianne. *The Boy of the Three-Year Nap.* Boston: Houghton Mifflin Company, 1988. Taro, the lazy son of a Japanese seamstress, who spends his life taking naps and eating, finds out that laziness doesn't pay—or does it?

Materials

1. Enlarge and duplicate the outline of the American and Japanese houses on 9-by-12-inch light-colored construction paper or tagboard, one outline of each per student. Pink paper for the Japanese house, and yellow for the American makes identification easy. *Optional*: Students draw own outline on construction paper.

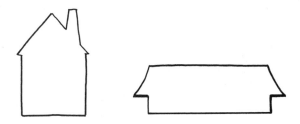

2. scissors, glue. *Optional*: crayons, other coloring materials.
3. *Optional*: Pictures and other materials depicting Japanese life and culture.

Directions

1. Before reading the story, point out that this is a well-known Japanese folk tale that has been told by storytellers traveling throughout Japan.
2. After the story is read to students, ask them to describe the characters and give traits (how they act). Discuss the meaning and humor of the plot. Also point out:
   - ceramic container on pillow—similar to a stove, for keeping warm
   - *ujigami*—is an imaginary god that people usually can't see
   - Japanese custom from times past—Families of young people choose a bride or groom for their children (usually with children's consent, now), and the husband-to-be provides a house for the bride-to-be.
3. Next, discuss how the customs of everyday living in Japan—in this story—are *different* from everyday living in America today. Point out differences in:
   - housing, and the name of a business in Japanese on a sign outside the door of the house (when there is a business at the house)
   - eating, clothing, furniture
   - wedding attire

   Also, discuss similarities of the two cultures.
4. Complete the activity sheet: Read and reinforce directions on the activity sheet with students.

Other Books About Japanese Customs and Culture Ina R. Friedman's *How My Parents Learned to Eat* (Houghton-Mifflin, 1984); Claude Clement's *The Painter and the Wild Swans* (Doubleday, 1990); Sumiko Yagawa's *The Crane Wife*, translation from the Japanese by Katherine Paterson (Morrow, 1987); Taro Yashima's *Crow Boy* (Penguin, 1987), *The Village Tree* (Penguin, 1987), and *Umbrella* (Penguin, 1977); Keith Baker's *The Magic Fan* (Harcourt Brace Jovanovich, 1989).

Name _____

Directions: 1. Cut out the Japanese and American houses. 2. Carefully cut out the objects below and place them on the correct house. Write what they are. 3. Write a paragraph on the back of each house. For the Japanese house, write: "The important thing about Japanese life is

_____." American: "The important thing about American life is _____."

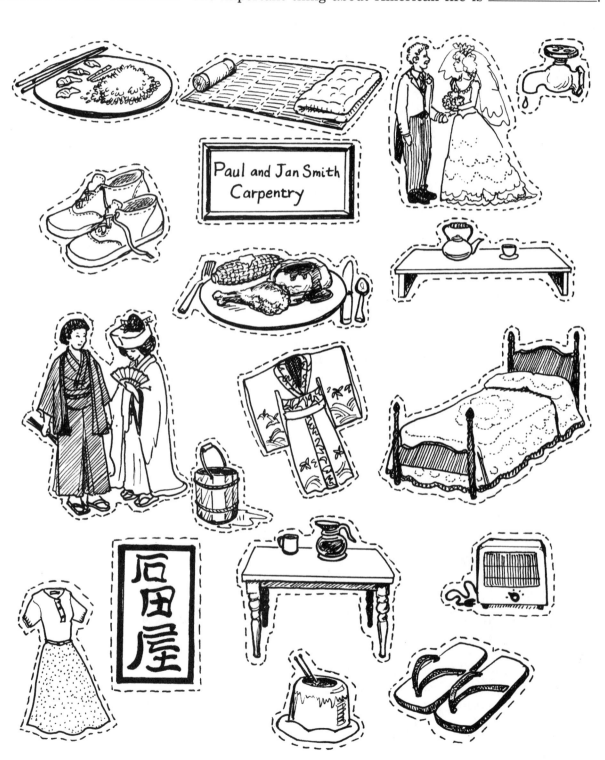

History: Early Exploration, Biography

Gerrard, Roy. *Sir Francis Drake: His Daring Deeds.* New York: Farrar, Straus, Giroux, 1986. Drake's battles with the Spaniards, told from an Englishman's point of view.

Optional, but Recommended Materials

Background information about and pictures of Sir Francis Drake.

Directions

1. Present relevant and interesting information about Drake before reading the book to students. Include the material at the top left of the activity sheet.

2. As the book is read and discussed, point out:

   A. Vocabulary and terms, such as *fathomed, lionhearted*, and *circumnavigated*.

   B. Significance of *knighting*—gives an honorary, nonhereditary rank (next to baronet) to someone for achievement or service to the country. The honor entitles one to use "Sir" before the given name.

   C. Concept of this book as a *biography*.

3. After reading, ask students:

   A. How is this book different from reading about Drake in a history or social studies book?

   B. Why did the story show Drake only as a brave hero? Point out that the Spanish would tell the story a different way—that Drake's deeds were not always honorable.

4. Complete the activity sheet:

   A. Students complete Part I either independently or with a partner. *Optional*: give a time limit (three minutes suggested) or declare the first team or individual to complete list, with correct/appropriate answers, the winner. Possible words:

save:	brave
gold:	bold, scold
chase:	race, ace
fired:	admired, hired
daring:	caring, glaring
sped:	led
caught:	fought, taught
knighted:	sighted

   B. Review pertinent information from the book and on the coat of arms, with students, before they write the speech for Part II.

   C. Plan a celebration, with a student being chosen to play the part of Sir Francis, while the other students read their speeches applauding his heroic deeds. *Optional*: Serve food and wear simple costumes to the celebration.

Extended Activity   Discuss the concept of author's point of view, noting that Roy Gerrard wrote this rhyming biography from his understanding and opinions of what happened, as an Englishman. Find information about and discuss how the Spanish tell "the other side of the story."

Additional Activity

"_____, His/Her Daring, _____, Deeds": Students write rhyming couplets about their life—interesting, fun, brave, or humorous "deeds" they have performed or been part of.

You are living in Sir Francis Drake's time. You have been a sailor on his ship. Now that he has returned to England, the queen is having a big celebration in his honor.

You have been asked to give a speech, telling of his heroic deeds. You know him well. (You could be older than 10 years.) First summarize what he did, and then tell why you like him as a person. *Use at least five words from the lists in Part I.*

Sir Francis Drake, who lived from 1540 to 1596, was a smart English sailor who liked adventure. He became rich and famous for fighting the Spanish both at sea and on land. He took their gold and sank their ships, but was good to the prisoners. He went to Mexico, Panama, South America, and all around the world! Queen Elizabeth I honored Drake by knighting him.

Spain and England were fighting because they both wanted land and riches in America. The queen sent Sir Francis to Cadiz, Spain to defeat the Spanish. Then the Spanish Armada came to English waters and was defeated.

Write a word beside each word below that has to do with the *brave* or *heroic* things that happened. The word must RHYME with the given word. Example:

dived: ___survived___

save: _____

gold: _____

chase: _____

fired: _____

daring: _____

sped: _____

caught: _____

knighted: _____

Aliki. *A Medieval Feast.* **New York: Crowell, 1983.** The preparation and celebration of a feast at an English manor house—fit for the king who *is* coming to visit!

Materials

1. Shoebox with lid for each student. (Department stores might supply these.)
2. Activity sheet duplicated onto white tagboard or other heavy paper. (A diorama will be made with the box and activity sheet's figures.)
3. Construction paper, crayons or felt-tip pens, scissors, and glue.

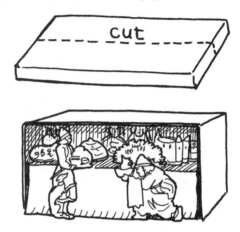

Background Resources for Teacher and Students   *The Middle Ages*, by Giovanni Caselli, Bedrick, 1988; *The Days of Knights and Castles*, by Pierre Miquel, Silver Burdett 1986; *Looking Into the Middle Ages*, by Huck Scarry, Harper, 1984.

Directions

1. Present the book's cover to students and ask them to tell about the biggest or fanciest meal they have attended (wedding, Thanksgiving, etc.).
2. Present the following summary of information about the Middle Ages:

    This story takes place in England at a time when noble families lived in castles. Kings traveled throughout the land and stayed with the lords who helped defend the kingdom. Life was much different than it is today. Armies in plated armour and colorful shields rode away on horseback, and only noble children went to school to learn to read and write. This time period is called the Middle Ages and lasted from about 500 A.D. to 1500 A.D.

3. Read the book to students.
4. Next, include the following in a discussion:
    A. the social and cultural importance of the food-related ceremonies and practices
    B. a comparison of modern customs and practices to those of the Middle Ages, noting that each age and culture has its specialties, but that some modern customs originated in that time period
    Point out these specifics from the story:
    • difference between king's castle (first one) and lord's manor house
    • the two classes, rich and poor, with serfs being different than slaves
    • cockentrice roasted—today we roast pig, deer, etc.

- information from inside the back cover, including the idea that live blackbirds were baked into pies (Relate to "Sing a Song of Sixpence.")
- Pudding de swan neck and other puddings where live jugglers jump out—today people jump out of modern day "cakes."

C. Review the function and importance of the activity sheet figures:
   platter of vegetables and fruits, cockentrice, pie with blackbirds, king and queen, panter with trencher, ewerer with scented water and towel, pudding de swan neck, pastry castle, marzipan king and queen called a *subtletey.*

D. Emphasize that medieval cooking and feasting were *arts*, with entertainment and ceremony a high priority! *Optional:* provide a taste of marzipan candy (obtained from supermarket specialty section or deli).

5. Reinforce and review concepts associated with the activity sheet figures as needed.

6. Additional directions for completing the diorama:

   A. Make sure cutting of objects is done carefully.

   B. List names of objects for students to copy.

   C. *Optional:* Students read and evaluate a partner's information from the back of the figures, before they are glued. *Note:* Figures should be glued so that information can still be read.

   D. Students decorate box with construction paper: back wall, "tablecloth," etc.

7. Students display dioramas and tell what they enjoyed most about the project.

Other Activities With Medieval Themes   2–5, Cedric the Fortunate Character; 3–5, Knightly News; 6–5, A Day at the Castle

Related Books   *Saint George & the Dragon*, retold by Margaret Hodges (Little, 1984); *Sir Cedric*, by Roy Gerrard (Farrar, Straus & Giroux, 1986); *A Tournament of Knights*, by Joe Lasker (Harper, 1989); *Castle* by David Macaulay (Houghton-Mifflin, 1977).

Extended Activity   Plan a feast similar to the one in the book.

6–4 A FEAST TO REMEMBER

Name _____

(Save this top.)

Directions: 1. Carefully cut out each figure. Color according to book. 2. Write the name of the object on the back. Next, in a phrase or sentence, write what the person or object did that was important (or what it was used for). 3. Cut the shoe box lid in half, *lengthwise*. Place half of lid inside box as the table. Bend tabs, arrange objects and glue.

Fleischman, Sid. *THE WHIPPING BOY*. New York: Greenwillow, 1986. Newbery-winning novel about a spoiled prince and his whipping boy. The two boys run away and are caught by two ruffians who confuse their identities.

Note: This is a follow-up activity to The Whipping Boy—A Winner, 1–11.

Materials Needed for the Game

1. Black copies (recommended) of the activity sheet for every two students.
2. Game markers: gummy bears in assorted colors (recommended).
3. One die for each pair of students.
4. One package of licorice rope for "whip" (square 2).
5. Two or three bird feathers, with fat end cut, for quill pen; OR ends of tree branches, sharpened, for wood-nib pen. Also, red tempera paint (fairly thick), or ink; and paper for writing message (square 6).
6. *Guinness Book of World Records*, at least two copies of a recent edition. *Optional*: enlarge and copy page on "Castles and Forts" (squares 17 and 21).
7. About six beanbags for juggling (square 20).
8. Recommended: pictures of life of the nobility in the Middle Ages, including interests of children, such as clothing, games, food.
   Sources: *A Medieval Feast*, by Aliki (Harper, 1986) and *The Middle Ages*, by Giovanni Caselli (Bedrick, 1988). (Can be used for discussion and reference during game.)

Directions

1. Organize materials for the specific game squares in separate areas of the room.
2. Establish game rules with students: (use sample gameboards or transparency).
   A. Read through game rules on gameboard with the group.
   B. Give these additional instructions and helps:
      • Tell students not to overlook the written answer asked for at square 1.
      • Brainstorm the style of shirt and hat for square 4.
      • Brainstorm foods young people in the Middle Ages *could* choose.
      • For square 16: repeat alphabet *without looking*.
      • Students find answers to squares 17 and 21 in *Guinness Book* article.
      • Brainstorm items that might be found in a castle dungeon for squares 24 and 25. (Students draw items for *both* numbers).
      • Blanks are filled in only once, but activities are repeated if a player lands on that space more than once.
      Point out that all the ideas, activities, and objects show life for a king's child during the Middle Ages.
3. Select pairs of students, distribute markers, etc., and point out where materials for completing the activities are located. The game lasts about twenty to thirty minutes.

You are invited to spend a day with Jemmy and the Prince at the castle! Play game with a partner. Castle Game Rules: (1.) Roll to start. (2.) Roll a 1 to play. (3.) Use 1 to 4. (4.) To win, land on 26, with all blanks (with *'s) filled in. Fill in blanks once. Wait for player to finish a turn. The second and fourth rows move from right to left.

5. Lose one turn to get through secret passage. Come out at #11.

6. With your partner, write a three word message from the prince to the king.

16. Tutor says: Repeat the alphabet *backwards* (from M to A).

17. The largest ancient castle had an *area* of: 5 18 1½ acres (circle one) one football field is over 1 acre. Go to # 20.

26. Fun with the king is to: _____ Oops! The king is running away!

4. With ___ partner draw shirt and hat.

7. Q. What animal would HYN Billy look like if he took a bath? A. A little bear. Take Billy back to the moat for a bath.

15. The pet monkey is hiding!

Q. When does a monkey hide in a grape? A. When it's an ape.

18. Cutwater hides a whip in the straw. Go back #14 to look for it.

3. Q. How is a star and Jemmy's cage the same? A. they both contain R-A-T-S!

8. LUNCH MENU:
1. _____
2. _____
3. _____

14. Z V N

Sleep in the straw for two turns.

19. A trick to play on the king is: _____

24. **25.** *With your partner*, draw five objects that you'd find in a dungeon.

2. Roll the die. Multiply the number by 3. Answer: ___ Hear partner "howl" as you "whip" him that many times.

9. Clap for the tight-rope walker. Go to #12.

13.

20. Juggle two or three balls for 1 minute.

23. Go back to #19 to tell the king about a favorite book.

1. Jemmy swims the moat looking for: _____

10. Give Capt. Nips a tour for one turn. He liked:
1. _____
2. _____
3. _____

11. Everyone plays: *BATTLEDORE!* A modern game like it is: _____

12.

21. The largest inhabited castle is called: _____ Castle.

22. A book I love is: _____

Munro, Roxie. *The Inside-Outside Book of Washington, D.C.* New York: E.P. Dutton, 1987. An artist for *The New Yorker* artistically and architecturally creates the unique atmosphere of both the inside and outside of Washington, D.C.'s most famous buildings.

Directions

1. Introduce the book by showing students the front and back cover, and inviting them to share their information and interests about the White House and Washington, D.C. Ask students where the White House is viewed from. Point out the outside view of the Washington Monument and then the two inside views. Tell students that an illustrator named Roxie Munro, who illustrates for *The New Yorker* magazine, drew the most interesting and famous buildings in Washington, D.C. from an outside and inside view (perspective) for us to enjoy.

2. Present selected or all parts of the book (including those from the activity sheet), thoroughly discussing the information about each building given at the back. Reinforce and review information contained on the activity sheet.

3. Specifically discuss the following elements of design for each building contained on the activity sheet: shape, line, space, color. Include concepts featured in the activity. Reinforce art descriptions given on the activity sheet. Note that art descriptions given on the activity sheet emphasize descriptions of the actual book art, as opposed to the art contained on the sheet.

4. Pass out the activity sheet and scissors. Carefully instruct for cutting and folding. Demonstrate! Folds need to be accurate if the questions are to be readable. Follow directions on the activity sheet. *Note:* show students the drawing or a sample of the finished "fortune container." Many will recognize the design. Then demonstrate the process of completing the activity with a student partner.

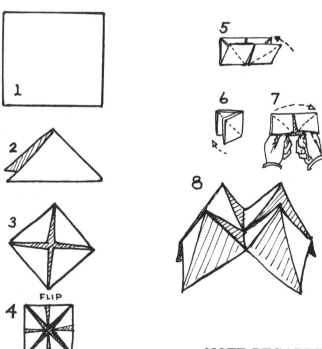

NOTE REGARDING FOLDS: In all steps, writing faces out.

5. Students follow directions for completing the activity as given on the sheet. Give these additional directions to students:

A. Work in pairs, taking turns giving answers.

B. Answer questions A through D and 1 through 4 *orally*. (The closest picture to letters A., B., C., D., is the answer.)

C. Each partner writes answers to 5 through 8 on his own fortune paper.

D. Give your partner a star for a correct answer and an *X* for an incorrect one.

E. Flip back and forth between the letters and numbers, one flip for each letter in the first name of the building.

NOTE REGARDING FOLDS: In all steps, writing faces out.

Additional Books by Roxie Munro *The Inside-Outside Book of New York City* (Putnam, 1985) and *The Inside-Outside Book of London* (Dutton, 1989).

Additional Activity Art and Writing, "A View from a Personal Point of View." Students choose an outside or inside view of one of the buildings or scenes from any of Munro's books (some of the inside views in the New York City book offer an easier task for the less-experienced student) and draw the scene. Next, students describe in writing what is seen from that particular view. Students list at least three objects, with at least two descriptive words for each. Example:

From inside the Statue of Liberty,
I see calm, blue water; one chugging, smoking, red tugboat;
two low-flying silver planes; and a group of high, medium, and
low brown buildings.

Answer Key to Activity Sheet

1. Library of Congress, 80 million, 532

2. money and stamps (or invitations)

3. Air and Space Museum

4. 32

5. 31 billion, 1,500

6. A. print; B. cut; C. check for flaws; D. print seals, serial numbers; E. cut again

7. 17

8. 18

6–6 D.C. FORTUNES (Save this paper)   Name _____

Directions for making fortune container: 1. Carefully, cut on the dotted line. 2. Fold the square paper in half twice, corner to corner. 3. Open it, then fold all four corners in to meet exactly in the center. 4. Flip this over, and again fold the four corners to the center, creasing the folds well. 5.–6. Fold this in half two times, so you have a small square. 7. Open the square, put your thumb and fingers under the four flaps, and pinch the center part together. 8. Now you are ready to "flip for your fortune!"

Both partners do questions 1 through 4 and A through D (two tries for getting them right). Flip between the numbers and the letters by spelling the first name of a building. Next, choose a number or letter. Later, write answers to 5–8.

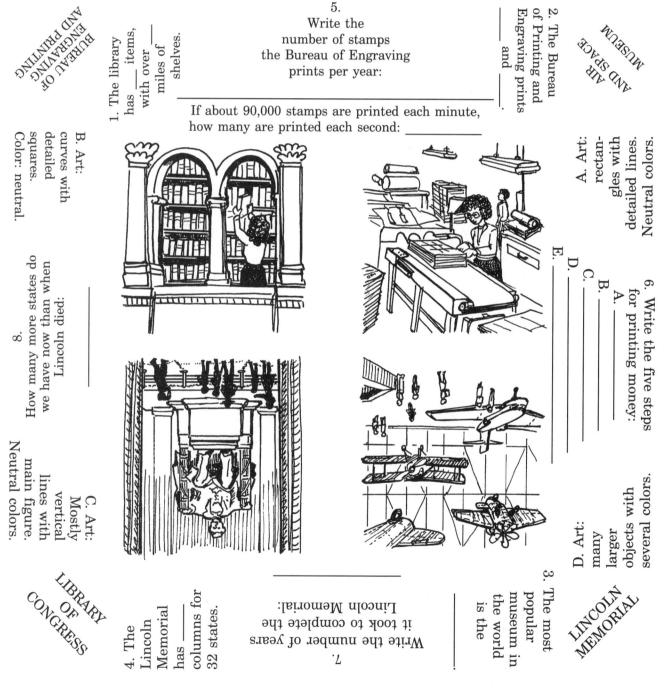

BUREAU OF ENGRAVING AND PRINTING

1. The library has ___ items, with over ___ miles of shelves.

B. Art: curves with detailed squares. Color: neutral.

8. How many more states do we have now than when Lincoln died: ___

C. Art: Mostly vertical lines with main figure. Neutral colors.

LIBRARY OF CONGRESS

4. The Lincoln Memorial has ___ columns for 32 states.

7. Write the number of years it took to complete the Lincoln Memorial: ___

5. Write the number of stamps the Bureau of Engraving prints per year:

___

If about 90,000 stamps are printed each minute, how many are printed each second: ___

2. The Bureau of Printing and Engraving prints ___ and ___.

AIR SPACE AND MUSEUM

A. Art: rectangles with detailed lines. Neutral colors.

E.
D.
C.
B.
A.

6. Write the five steps for printing money:

D. Art: many larger objects with several colors.

3. The most popular museum in the world is the ___

LINCOLN MEMORIAL

Freedman, Russell. *Children of the Wild West.* **New York: Clarion, 1983.** Actual historical photographs and informative text chronicling the American West from 1840 to the early 1900's.

Supplemental Recommended Titles   Kalman, Bobbie. *Early Schools,* Crabtree, 1982; Caney, Steven. *Steven Caney's Kids' America.* Workman, 1978.

Optional Materials

Memorabilia from everyday pioneer life during the mid-1800's through the early 1900's, (including school-related items), as available personally from students and the community.

Directions

1. Read the following parts of *Children of the Wild West* to students and discuss:
    A. Read or summarize information from chapters 1, 2, and 3.
    B. Read chapter 5, "Frontier Schools." Discuss:
        • Similarities and differences between pioneer and modern schools
        • Why children of all ages and grades were in one room
        • Why textbooks and other materials were scarce
        • Why many teachers were so young, their training so minimal, and their pay so low

2. Present the idea of a "Pioneer School Day" to students. Note: Plans below allow for a full day. Modify for a half day or less.

    A. Brainstorm ideas and possible activities. Suggestions: Students choose a grade (from 1–8) to be in; feature a dunce cap and chair; conduct reading and math from books of the time; have a spelling bee; write on slates; bring lunch in a tin box, with appropriate food; conduct class without electricity; sit on benches or hard chairs.
    B. Supplement brainstorming with information from other sources:
        • Recommended sources above (several chapters in Caney's book contain helpful information), or other titles
        • Family or community members

C. Possible topics for exploration:

- How (materials and lesson plans) students were taught reading, writing (any creative writing or just handwriting?), arithmetic, geography and history
- What did students in one grade do while the teacher was instructing students in another grade?
- Discipline
- Recess and games
- Student responsibilities at school and at home
- Clothing
- Transportation
- Food

D. Information can be gathered either through whole group participation or through cooperative groups of two or more.

3. Set up a plan for the anticipated day:

A. Develop a schedule. Example:

(1) Children bring, wear, and describe memorabilia (Period clothes are usually a lot of fun.)

(2) Reading lesson with the different grade levels (Students not being instructed help other students or complete yesterday's reading assignment.)

(3) Recess with appropriate games and activities

(4) Math lesson with same structure as reading lesson

(5) Spelling bee

(6) Stories and music (Example: Write and sing verses for heroes from the past—Daniel Boone, Johnny Appleseed—to the tune of "Sweet Betsy From Pike")

B. Plan for role-playing some typical situations and interruptions: misbehavior, students being called home to plow the field, animals entering the classroom.

C. Assign roles and jobs to students.

4. On the day of "A Pioneer School Day":

A. Enjoy!

B. Summarize and evaluate. Possible topics: what was liked most, most important thing learned, what made you feel like a pioneer, what would have been harder or easier about going to school in pioneer times.

Related Books *If You Traveled West in a Covered Wagon*, by Ellen Levine, Scholastic, 1986; *Sarah, Plain and Tall*, by Patricia MacLachlan, Harper, 1985; *Iva Dunnit and the Big Wind*, by Carol Purdy, Dial, 1985; *All-of-a-Kind Family*, by Sydney Taylor, Dell, 1985; *Farmer Boy* (Harper, 1953), *Little Town on the Prairie* (Harper, 1953), and others in the series by Laura Ingalls Wilder.

Additional Activities

1. Further topics to explore:

A. Teacher qualifications and hiring practices

B. Why frontier towns decided to hire teachers—to teach basic skills, to babysit, to discipline?

    C. What parts of pioneer life showed good repeated use of everyday items or fit our modern ideas about recycling? Examples: tin lunch pails, slates.

2. A Pioneer Treasure:

    A. Students explore customs and lore about pioneer daily life, choosing an item or object to make a facsimile, model, or production of. Examples: patchwork pillow, old-fashioned sponge cake, model of cabin.

    B. Students share with group.

Swan, Robert. *Destination: Antarctica*. New York: Scholastic, 1988. British explorer Robert Swan and two others trek 900 miles over treacherous, icy terrain, tracing the footsteps of early explorer Robert Scott to the South Pole.

Directions

1. Locate Antarctica on a map or globe and orally give students the following true-and-false quiz, to provide background and interest. Give answers later.

   <u>T</u> Antarctica is the coldest and most deserted area on earth.

   <u>F</u> It is the same size as the United States.

   <u>T</u> Most of its land is buried beneath one-mile-thick ice and snow.

   <u>T</u> This ice has more *fresh* water than the entire rest of the world.

   <u>F</u> A lot of snow falls during the winter.

   <u>T</u> The temperature averages below 0°F.

2. Next, present the following information, along with the correct quiz answers. Supplement with pictures and additional information as desired.

   The continent of Antarctica has high mountains and the wind can blow up to 200 miles per hour, which is twice as strong as a hurricane! The land mass is as large as North America and Europe together. Not much snow falls, but when it does, it turns to ice right away. Because most of Antarctica is covered with ice, and because winter temperatures can be −100°F, most plants, animals, and people cannot live there. However, research stations have been built for scientists to study the climate, wildlife, rocks, and ice.

3. Read the book to students and discuss its important points, including concepts contained in the activity. Sample points for clarification and discussion:

   A. Why did Robert Swan and his partners follow Scott's exact route, without help from the outside world and technology?

   B. What does Swan mean when he says that in Antarctica, it will "cost you" if you forget to concentrate?

   C. Explain how the men lived up to the expectations of Tennyson's quote: "To strive, to seek . . ."

4. Review concepts and vocabulary to complete the crossword puzzle as needed by the group.

5. Students complete the puzzle independently, in pairs, or in small groups. Highly recommended for most groups: Display puzzle answers in random order, for students to refer to or write in the letters *p* and *c* for the word *particles* and the *h* and *u* for the word *exhausted*.

Extended Activities

1. Social studies: "Admirable Adventures"

   Students read *Destination* . . . as part of an adventure series, for example, in conjunction with the *National Geographic* article, "Sailing in Jason's Wake," September, 1985, or other real life adventures such as seen on a TV adventure series.

2. Reading: "Exciting Exploration Records"

   Students read about travel and exploration records to the North and South Poles in *The Guinness Book of World Records*, "Human Achievements."

Additional Activity   Students write their own "adventures wanted" advertisement for a similar or a different adventure.

Answer Key to Activity Sheet

ACROSS	DOWN
2. PROGRESS	1. FOOTSTEPS
4. BORED	3. PEOPLE
8. PARTICLES	5. DAYDREAMED
10. JOURNEY	6. PLAN
12. CAVE	7. OUNCE
13. EXHAUSTED	9. NINE
15. NOTHING	11. RADIOS
16. MISTAKE	14. MONTHS

6–8 ANTARCTIC CROSSWORD

Name _____

Directions: Fill in the puzzle below with words or ideas from the book.

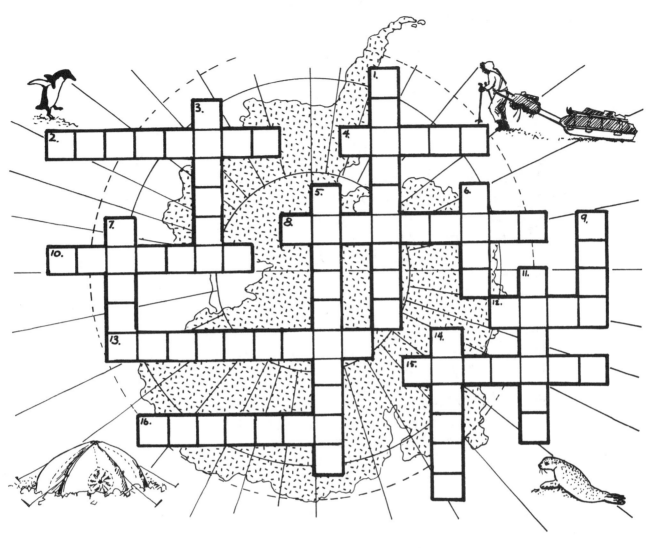

ACROSS CLUES

2. The Beardmore Glacier was a welcome sight because it showed the _____ the explorers had already made.
4. The climbers were hungry all the time and often _____.
8. It was hard to see and hear when the wind blew spinning _____ of frozen snow.
10. Brave people were needed for the hazardous _____.
12. The Ross Ice Shelf had crevasses and snow crusts that could _____ in from the men's weight.
13. The men became _____ from the long days of walking.
15. It would be the South Pole or _____.
16. In Antarctica, the smallest _____ can mean defeat or death.

DOWN CLUES

1. "In the _____ of Scott," was their goal.
3. The explorers were disappointed that they met other _____.
5. The men _____ about nicer conditions.
6. When the Southern Quest sank, a different _____ had to be made.
7. Every _____ of weight was important.
9. The climbers lived in a small hut for _____ months.
11. Without the help of animals, machines, or _____, they walked to the Pole.
14. There was no sunlight for over two _____.

Spier, Peter. *We the People.* **New York: Doubleday, 1987.** American diversity and unity are presented in detailed illustrations, celebrating the concepts of the Preamble, as well as the Constitution itself.

Optional Materials

Activity sheet duplicated on pastel shades of pink, white, and blue.

Directions

1. Provide background for and introduction to the book with the following:

   A. Ask students what it would be like if:

   - someone stole from your home and there were no police to call
   - you were told by the government which church to go to, how often you could move, or which books you could read
   - you couldn't get letters and packages through the mail, or harmful food and drugs were allowed to be sold in stores

   Make up additional questions dealing with concepts contained in the Preamble

   B. Tell students that in our country, the United States of America, "We the People," can do a lot of things we want to, when we want to, and where we want to, because a long time ago, in 1787, and in 1791 with the addition of the Bill of Rights, our leaders made rules that guaranteed us the freedom to make choices for our health and happiness. Because of these rules, our government is prohibited or limited from interferring with a person's life, liberty, and property.

   C. Next, tell students that the rules are part of a document called the Constitution. George Washington and Benjamin Franklin were among the famous people who helped write it. Madison, Hamilton, and Jay wrote The Federalist Papers to persuade the states to ratify the Constitution. *Optional*: give more background surrounding the writing and signing of the Constitution as desired, from the front of this book or related titles.

   D. Explain that Peter Spier has drawn the illustrations for this book to remember and to honor the laws of freedom that make our country so great. The words are from the Preamble (or beginning) of the Constitution and give the basic ideas of our government. Mr. Spier's pictures, however, show specific ideas of what the Constitution really means.

2. Complete the reading of the book and the activity sheet as follows:

   A. Read and discuss the book in sections, using each phrase as a separate section. Note: Seat students close to the book, or circulate.

   B. Complete the writing after each section is discussed. Writing can be completed by the group, in pairs, or individually.

   C. Framework for discussion and writing:

   (1) Ask questions and develop answers that reveal how students can work together in their classroom, school, home, and country to promote leadership qualities, fair rules, peace and tranquility, protection from harm, happy living, and the chance to make choices. For example:

   - Which classroom rules show fairness?

- Which groups and organizations help keep us safe and healthy?
- What are other words that mean "liberty"?

(2) Point out the diversity and individuality that our Constitution allows each one of us and groups of us.

(3) Encourage originality and diversity of written answers. Note: If students verbalize their answers before writing, efficiency of words will be increased.

3. *Optional*: create a red, white, and blue bulletin board display with student papers.

Related Book   *A More Perfect Union: The Story of Our Constitution*, by Betsy and Giulio Maestro; Lothrop, Lee & Shepard, 1987.

Additional Activities

1. Writing: "The Most Important Thing about . . . (freedom, government, laws, a constitution, making choices, etc.) is _____ ." Students write a paragraph or two about one of above or other topics.

2. Social studies: "A Classroom Constitution"

   Students develop a set of rules for class meetings, the daily schedule, or another aspect of classroom life with consideration for individual freedom and responsibility.

Name _____

We the People

Directions: Write short answers, using small writing.

Two things we need to be defended from are _____
_____
_____

People have different _____
_____
That is good because _____
_____

Two ways we are helped to be healthy and happy (our general welfare) are
_____
_____
_____

We can work together well by (two ways) _____
_____
_____
_____

Liberty is wonderful because _____
_____
_____

Justice means _____
_____
_____

Our Constitution is the best for all of us because
_____
_____
_____

Having peace or tranquility is _____
_____
_____

Science With Children's Books

Wexler, Jerome. *Flowers, Fruits, Seeds.* Englewood Cliffs, NJ: Prentice-Hall, 1987. Highly appealing, full-color photographs with short but informative text depicting the cycle of a plant from flower to fruit to seed to flower.

Optional Materials

Transparency of the activity sheet. See #5 below.

Directions

1. Introduce the book by asking students to identify the three pictures on the cover, and telling them that each of the pictures shows a special part of a plant that has a special reason for growing.

2. Set the framework for book concepts by identifying, using a colored-chalk drawn example, the three parts of a plant that will be presented:
   * the flower—the blossom part that produces the fruit
   * the fruit—the part that contains the seed
   * the seed—the part that starts the new plant

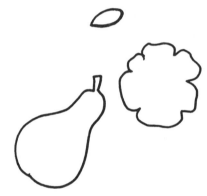

   Ask students to think of some of their favorite flowers, fruits, and seeds, and to watch for them as the book is read.

3. Read the book to students, emphasizing and pointing out:
   * the *purpose* of a flower, a fruit, and a seed
   * the *kinds* of plants that have flowers and other features of flowers
   * the *characteristics* of both fruits and seeds

4. Review the book and reinforce concepts by listing examples of each of the three parts of a plant, including those examples given on the activity sheet. Review the purposes of each of the plant parts. *Note:* Tell students that the part of the tomato that we eat is really the *fruit* part of the plant, even though we call it a vegetable because it's "not sweet."

5. Complete the activity sheet with students as follows:
   A. Students work independently, in pairs, or with the large group, depending on the skill level
   B. *Optional*: Write part or all of the information on a transparency to assist students (highly recommended for younger or lower-performers).

C. Names of the plants for Part II:

    flowers—pussy willow, dandelion (seed also shown), African violet, rose

    fruits—pear, watermelon

    seeds—bean, coconut, corn, acorn

Additional Book   *The Reason for a Flower*, by Ruth Heller, Grosset & Dunlap, 1983.

Extended Activity   "A Classifying Class"

Students cut examples of one, two, or three of the plant parts from magazines and classify according to size, texture, color, etc.

Additional Activities

1. Art: "From Texture To Texture"—Students collect and then describe fruits and seeds with a variety of textures. *Optional*: draw the objects, creating texture on paper. Make a collage.

2. Nutrition, Speaking: "A Seed Tasting Party"—Students taste and describe seeds, such as sunflower, pumpkin, popcorn.

Mostly, *flowers* are here to

_____
_____
_____
_____
_____

Directions: I. Write the reason or purpose for each part of a plant.

Mostly, *seeds* are here to

_____
_____
_____
_____

Mostly, *fruits* are here to

_____
_____
_____
_____
_____

II. Write the *names* of ten plants. Tell whether it is a *flower, fruit,* or *seed.*

Branley, Franklyn M. *What the Moon Is Like*. New York: Thomas Y. Crowell Junior Books, 1986. Details about the moon's surface as described by astronauts.

Note: Other books with basic information about the moon's surface, such as *The Moon*, by Seymour Simon (Macmillan, 1984) can be used.

Materials

1. "Moon rocks" (pebbles) about one square cm, one for each student.
2. Die, one for each pair of students.
3. One copy (black copies preferable) of the activity sheet for each pair.
4. *Optional*: Photographs of the moon taken from space and from its surface; a lunar globe or map; two cake pans or boxes and sand or dirt (see 2C).

Directions

1. Introduce the book to students by asking these questions:
   A. What do you think it would be like to be in a place where it was daylight for two whole weeks and completely dark for two whole weeks?
   B. What would it be like to not have any water or trees or animals?

2. Next, read the book to students, emphasizing the most important and interesting information. Thoroughly discuss the information contained on the game sheet. Point-outs and questions include:
   A. On July 20, 1969, Neil Armstrong and Buzz Aldrin became the first people to walk on the moon.
   B. Pages 16 and 17: What is the hottest temperature in your town? The coldest?
   C. Page 20: Optional Activity—"Footprints, For Now and Forever"
      (1) Using a student's shoe, make a footprint in one of the pans. Label as "The Earth." Add water and wind and observe the erosion that takes place on earth when the ground is disturbed.
      (2) Make a second footprint in the other pan. Label as "The Moon." Observe the non-erosion of the print over several days due to the absence of the water and wind.
   D. Page 22: What would be good about living where everything stayed the same? What wouldn't be so good about it?
   E. Page 27: Describe what you would see standing on the moon, looking at the sky. (List several things.)

3. Reinforce basic concepts from the game sheet. *Optional*: Play "Around the Moon" according to the usual rules used for "Around the World." Students make an orbit around the moon!

4. Students play "Win a Moon Trip" following directions on the sheet. Additional information:
   A. Blanks are filled either as a group before playing the game or during the game by the student landing on a particular number. *Note:* a blank must be correctly filled in before player continues. *Option*: Write answers randomly on the chalkboard for students to copy.

B. Pair students with consideration for reading ability. *Option for low-performing students*: Play the game as a group (individual game sheets optional) using a transparency. To increase the length of the game, students use only numbers 1 and 2 on the die.

Extended Activity "A Heavy Rock Turns Light"—Make a "rock" by crumpling newspaper or grey construction paper. Attach one pound of clay to the bottom of the rock. Students lift the rock, which represents its weight on earth. Next, take away 5/6 of the clay, to represent the rock's weight on the moon. Students lift and compare to its weight on earth.

Directions: (1.) Play with a partner using a "moon rock," as your marker. (2.) Roll 1 to start. (3.) Play with ONLY numbers 1, 2, and 3. (4.) You are taking a trip on the moon, riding in the moon rover and walking. Start at #1. The winner is the first person to get to #31!

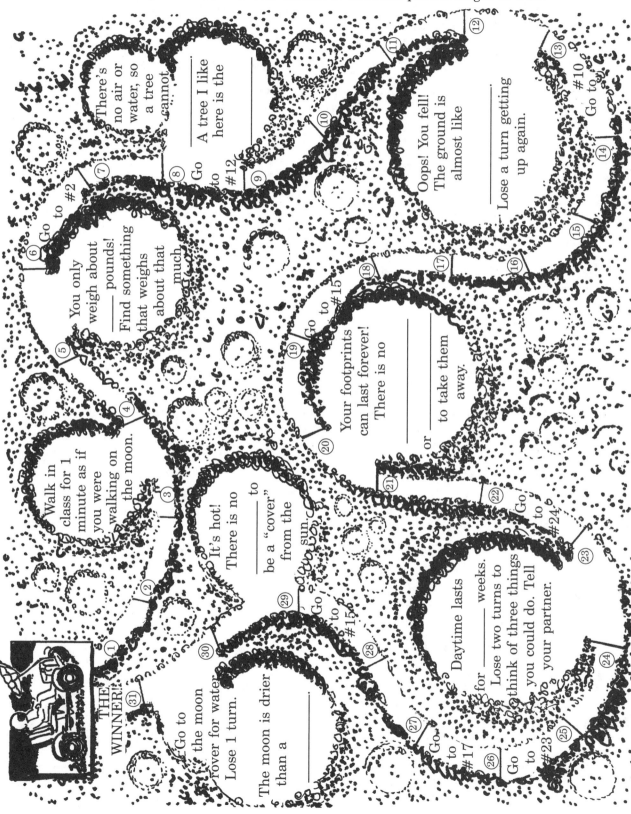

There's no air or water, so a tree cannot _____

Go to #2

A tree I like here is the _____ Go to #12

Oops! You fell! The ground is almost like _____ Lose a turn getting up again.

Go to #10

You only weigh about _____ pounds! Find something that weighs about that much.

Your footprints can last forever! There is no _____ or _____ to take them away.

Go to #15

Walk in class for 1 minute as if you were walking on the moon.

It's hot! There is no _____ to be a "cover" from the _____ sun. Go to #15

Daytime lasts for _____ weeks. Lose two turns to think of three things you could do. Tell your partner.

Go to #24

Go to #17

Go to #23

Go to the moon rover for water. Lose 1 turn.

The moon is drier than a _____

THE WINNER!

Danks, Dr. Hugh. *The Bug Book.* **New York: Workman, 1987.** An excellent child-oriented field guide for catching, identifying, and caring for twenty-six bugs, including grasshoppers and sowbugs.

Optional Recommended Materials

1. Large pictures, live or preserved specimens of some or all of the bugs included in the lesson.
2. Transparency of the activity sheet. See 2 and 3 below.

Directions

1. Introduce the book.
   A. Ask students the following questions:
      - Which insect would be strong enough to lift twenty cars if it were the same size as a person?
      - Which insect, if it were the same size as a person, could jump over a very tall building?
   B. Read and discuss the Table of Contents and the structure of the book with students. Point out:
      - the definition of *bug* on page 7
      - The Bug Chart with the group names and characteristics on pages 8 and 9
      - "Did You Know?" on page 10
   C. Tell students that this activity shows how much fun this book and bug collecting can be!
2. Read and discuss the book with students, and complete Part I of the activity sheet as follows:
   A. *Students fold under* the bottom part of the activity sheet to complete later.
   B. Read the introductory paragraph for the particular bug habitat (e.g., "Look on Leaves").
   C. Next, read the information for a specific bug (one included on the activity sheet). Note that bugs are listed in order of presentation.
   Alternative to reading about each of the eight bugs: Select three to five bugs to read about.
   D. Review highlights of the information.
   E. Choose, with students, the most interesting piece of information to put into a phrase or short sentence. Or, individual students select their own ideas.
   F. Students write the phrase or sentence. *Optional*: Display transparency with model of phrase or sentence.
   G. Follow above steps for each of the eight bugs.
   H. Next, instruct students to complete letter I. *daddy-longlegs*, and J. *grasshopper*, on the back of the paper.
   Note: This activity is excellent practice for summarizing and notetaking.
3. Students complete Part II as directed. *Option for younger students*: Display a colored-in transparency. Older students, fold back the names at the top.
   Note: The hidden bugs include all bugs from Part I (including the daddy-longlegs and the grasshopper).

Additional Book *Bugs*, by Nancy Winslow Parker and Joan Richards Wright, Greenwillow, 1987.

Extended Activity "Bug Poetry"

Enjoy poetry about bugs and other living things from "The Way of Living Things" in *The Random House Book of Poetry for Children*, selected by Jack Prelutsky, Random House, 1983. Examples: "Green Stems," "Hey, Bug!" "Crickets," "A Dragonfly."

Additional Activity "Bug Boasting"—Students write a description of a specific bug, read it to the group, and ask a student to identify the bug.

Answer Key to Activity Sheet Part II

PART I: Write one interesting idea about each bug. PART II: Find and color ten bugs. Write the name near the picture.

A. ladybug _____

B. caterpillar _____

C. diving beetle _____

D. dragonfly _____

E. sowbug _____

F. centipede _____

G. ant _____

H. monarch butterfly _____

Simon, Seymour. *Animal Fact/Animal Fable.* New York: Crown, 1979. Common beliefs about popular animals are given, and then the facts are distinguished from the fables, with the reasons why being noted.

Optional Materials

Transparency of the activity sheet. (See 3.E below.)

Directions

1. Present the book and its cover, and ask students whether it is true that:
   - snakes bite with their tongue?
   - bulls get angry when they see red?
   - raccoons wash their food?
   - crickets tell the temperature with their chirps?

2. Present the Introduction, including the definitions of *fact* and *fable*. Amplify the book definition with the following:

   A. A *fact* is information that is *true*.

      A statement is true if the information is correct.

      A true statement can be proven to be true.

   B. A *fable* states a belief that is *false*.

      It is false if *some* or *all* of the information is not correct.

      A false statement cannot be proven to be true.

   Tell students that they will find out whether the statements about the four animals on the cover are true.

   Note: A working understanding of the concepts of fact and fable is not essential to the success of the activity. A major purpose of the book and the activity is to use the examples to clarify understanding.

3. Read the book to students and complete the activity sheet as follows:

   A. Distribute the activity sheet.

   B. Read the introductory fact or fable statement for the first animal.

   C. Students write *fact* or *fable* (or *true/false*, or for younger students, *yes/no*) on the short line before the number.

   D. Next, the correct answer is read, followed by the explanation or reason. Students change incorrect answers.

   E. Students record the explanation on the two lines, using one idea or sentence. *Optional*, but recommended for younger and/or lower-performing students: Use a transparency, with reason statements generated by the group or teacher and copied by the students.

   F. Continue the above sequence for the other animals. *Note:* Not all of the animals in the book are included on the sheet. *Optional*: Leave some pages for students to peruse on their own.

Note: For older students, see the following activity for additional true/false material: 1–9, Those Sensational Snakes.

Extended Activity "Fable versus Fable" (for older students)

Contrast and discuss with students the differences in meaning between *fable* in Simon's book and in Arnold Lobel's book, *Fables* (Harper, 1983). Cooperative groups could then choose an animal and present information in both contexts.

Additional Activity Writing and Art: "Fancying a Fact or Fable"

Students choose an animal from the book and create a cartoon series. Example: Show what things dogs communicate when they talk with their tails or scenes where cats get out of situations unhurt.

Answer Key to Activity Sheet

1. fable
2. fact
3. fact
4. fable
5. fact
6. fact
7. fable
8. fable

Directions: A *fact* is a belief that is *true*. A *fable* is a belief that is *false*. 1. Write FACT or FABLE on the short line. 2. Write how we know the statement is true or not true.

_____ 1. Bats are blind.

_____

_____

_____ 2. Some bees sting only once.

_____

_____

_____ 3. Some fish can climb trees.

_____

_____

_____ 4. A cat has nine lives.

_____

_____

_____ 5. Dogs talk with their tails.

_____

_____

_____ 6. Goats will eat almost anything.

_____

_____

_____ 7. Snakes bite with their tongues.

_____

_____

_____ 8. Raccoons wash their food.

_____

_____

Lauber, Patricia. ***Dinosaurs Walked Here and Other Stories Fossils Tell.*** **New York: Bradbury, 1987.** An introduction to the study of fossils and how these relics disclose the characteristics of the dinosaur world. Updated information with full-color photographs.

Materials Needed for Optional Activities

(See 2.C and E.2 below.)

1. Plaster of Paris "fossil": enough plaster of Paris for each student to implant one small artifact, creating a fossil facsimile; one artifact brought by each student.
2. "Fossil layers" for a fossil dig: enough plaster of Paris for each student to have four layers of the substance in a half-pint or pint milk carton; blue, green, red, and yellow food coloring; a kitchen knife for each pair of students (CAUTION: to be used only under adult supervision); student-brought artifacts: small, flat, thin objects, such as a leaf or stone (four for each student).

Optional Materials to Show Students Plant or animal fossils, layered rock.
 Also, before reading the book, request student-brought fossil contributions.

Directions

1. Introduce the topic of fossil data about dinosaurs—and the book—by examining available fossils (or use photographs) and asking students to ponder the questions:
   - What is a fossil?
   - How could layers of rock and fossils give us information about the characteristics of dinosaurs and how they lived?
2. Read the book and complete the activity sheet:
   A. Read the book to students, through chapter 4, one chapter at a time.
   B. Coordinate completion of each activity sheet section with the appropriate chapter. Students write the information as a whole group, in pairs, or individually.
   C. Completing Chapter 1 reading and the activity sheet section:
      (1) Additional discussion points and questions:
      - page 1: Define a fossil
        Name several kinds of fossils (shells, bones, feathers).
      - page 2: What happens to most living things when they die?
      - page 6–7: Describe how an animal becomes a fossil. Why have most fossils come from the remains of plants and animals that died where there was water?
      (2) *Optional activity*: Make a plaster of Paris "fossil"
        Each student implants a flat, thin artifact, such as a shell or twig, onto one layer of the plaster to simulate the starting of a fossil imprint. *Plaster/water proportions*: ½ cup water, ¼ cup plaster
   D. Completing chapter 2: as directed. Suggested answer for "Fossils tell us about" *(changes in plants, animals, and climate)*
   E. Completing chapter 3:
      (1) Additional discussion points and questions:
      - page 22: Fossils and sedimentary rock form in _____.

- page 24: Studying layers of rock tells us that plant and animal fossils in the same layer must have lived _____ .

(2) *Optional activity*: Making "fossil layers" and conducting a fossil dig

- Measure each student's milk carton and divide plaster allotment into four parts. *Note:* Mix only enough plaster for one layer and for a few students at a time to prevent hardening. *Plaster/water proportions:* ½ cup water, ¼ cup plaster.

- Provide each layer separately to students (each colored differently with the food coloring), and while still wet, students press one object into each layer. *Note:* Set each layer before adding the next.

- Before plaster is set too hard, pair students to *carefully* carve apart each other's "fossil layers" (with kitchen knife) to examine the effects of the layering and the imprints. *Note:* Carving outdoors eliminates dust problems.

  Variation: use four colors of clay instead of plaster.

F. Completing chapter 4:

- page 31: Studies of dinosaur tracks show that many earlier ideas about dinosaurs are now _____ .

G. Additional discussion point: What are the most important clues fossils have given us about how dinosaurs lived? Why?

Additional Books *The News About Dinosaurs*, by Patricia Lauber, Bradbury 1989; *Dinosaur Mountain: Graveyard of the Past*, by Caroline Arnold, Clarion, 1989; *If You Are a Hunter of Fossils*, by Byrd Baylor, Atheneum, 1980.

Extended Activity   "Footprints of Note"
Students give uses for and identification of tempera paint footprints:

1. Students put one shoe each into a box.
2. Teacher secretly selects from three to six shoes and imprints each one on paper, with tempera paint.
3. Later, students in small groups are given an imprint to describe at least two things the owner could do with that type of shoe and to identify its owner.

Name _____

Directions: A diary is a record of what happens to people and things. Tell what happened to dinosaurs and other fossils by finishing the sentences.

I. ENTRIES ABOUT FOSSILS (Chapter 1)

Studying fossils can give information about

dinosaurs because _____

_____

_____

Bones or wood have become purified by _____

_____

Optional: Make a plaster of Paris "fossil."

II. MORE ENTRIES ABOUT PRESERVING (Chapter 2)

Three more ways animals have been preserved

are _____

_____

Fossils tell us about _____

_____

III. AN ENTRY ABOUT LAYERS OF FOSSILS (Chapter 3)

Studying fossils from the same layers of rock

tells us what kind of _____ and

_____ lived when dinosaurs did.

Optional: Make "fossil layers" and conduct a fossil dig.

IV. ENTRIES ABOUT DINOSAUR TRACKS (Chapter 4)

List two *wrong* ideas we've had about dinosaurs. Write on back.
List three *new* ideas we've learned about studying their tracks.

Lauber, Patricia. *VOLCANO*. New York: Bradbury, 1986. Powerful full-color photographs and engaging text tell the story of the eruption and healing of Mount St. Helens from an environmental viewpoint.

Materials

1. For the volcanic eruption simulation: soda bottle (narrow top), baking pan, sand or dirt, baking soda, red food coloring, one cup vinegar.
2. For paper chains: pastel green and blue construction paper strips, cut to 1″ × 9″, at least five per student. See 3. D and G below.

Optional Transparencies of pages to be read to students; enlargement of volcano diagram on page 2.

Background Information for Students Secure basic information, and illustrations if possible, about volcanoes, to present to students before reading the book.

Note: Adapt the amount of information presented in this lesson to the age and tolerance of the group.

Directions

1. Introduce the book to students by showing and discussing the photographs on pages 1 (opposite), 8, 18, and 19. Refer to a map.
2. Next, include the following in basic information about the formation and eruption of a volcano:
    A. What is a volcano?
       • Hot gases, lava, and rock fragments burst through an opening in the earth's surface.
       • The mountain itself is a volcano, the cone being built by lava and other materials.
       • The word *volcano* comes from the Latin word, *Vulcan*, the name given to the god of fire.
    B. What causes an eruption to begin? Most scientists believe that some rock inside the earth becomes so hot that it melts. It is called *magma*; it is light, and it rises.
    C. How does a volcano erupt? The solid surrounding rock puts pressure on the lighter magma and pushes it up and out of the opening in the mountain.
    D. What kinds of materials erupt? Mostly lava, rock fragments, and gas. What erupts depends on how sticky or runny the magma is.
3. Read the book to students, conduct completion of the activity sheet, and direct the volcanic eruption simulation as follows:
    A. Pass out the activity sheet.
    B. Present the information structure for chapters 1 and 2, as given on the activity sheet.
    C. Assist students in filling in the information at appropriate intervals during the chapter reading. Additional helps:
       (1) Point out chapter headings and subheadings on sheet.
       (2) Ask students to use short, succinct phrases or sentences, and to write small.

D. Next, conduct the volcanic eruption simulation with extreme caution:

(1) Put bottle in pan and build a mountain around it using the dirt.

(2) Put one tablespoon of the baking soda and the food coloring into the bottle.

(3) Rapidly pour in the vinegar.

(4) Reaction: Foam spews over the top and runs down the sides.

(5) Why: Pressure created by formation of carbon dioxide gas (reaction from baking soda and vinegar together) forces the liquid out the top.

E. Read chapter 3 to students, asking the following questions:

- After page 27: Would more or fewer plants and animals have survived if the blast had occurred in January? Why? What conditions could allow plants and animals to survive?

- After page 30: What *kinds* of animals survived? (hibernating, those in logs and lakes)

- After page 34: Name some ways that plants and animals depend on and help each other to survive.

Then complete the activity sheet.

F. Read chapter 4 to students, discussing additional information about how plants and animals depended on and helped each other survive.

G. Students make paper survival chains as follows:

(1) Give examples of links between the surviving plants and animals, such as in paragraph 2, page 39: A plant provided food for aphids, aphids gave honeydew to ants, and so on.

(2) Students write five steps in an animal/plant survival chain, one step on each chain link. Number. Glue links together.

H. Chapter 5 is optional.

Extended Activity Look up volcano records in the *Guinness Book*.

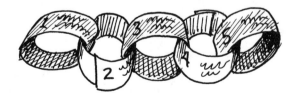

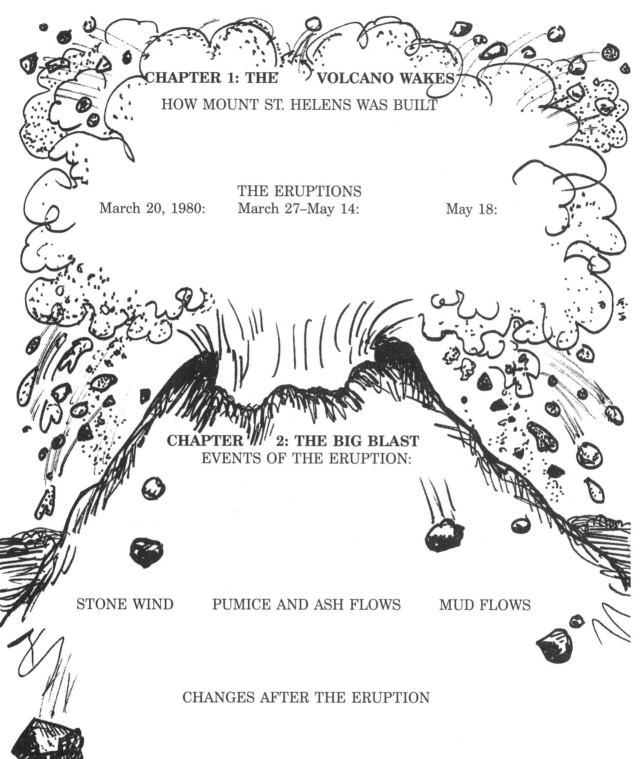

CHAPTER 1: THE   VOLCANO WAKES

HOW MOUNT ST. HELENS WAS BUILT

THE ERUPTIONS

March 20, 1980:   March 27–May 14:   May 18:

CHAPTER   2: THE BIG BLAST
EVENTS OF THE ERUPTION:

STONE WIND   PUMICE AND ASH FLOWS   MUD FLOWS

CHANGES AFTER THE ERUPTION

CHAPTER 3: SURVIVORS AND COLONIZERS

PLANTS   ANIMALS

Simon, Seymour. _Icebergs and Glaciers._ **New York: William Morrow, 1987.**
Basic, interesting facts about the formation, types, and journeys of glaciers and icebergs, and their impact on our planet.

Recommended Material

Physical map of the world.

1. Introduce the book to students.
   A. Show the front and back cover photographs, and ask students to share their knowledge about icebergs and glaciers.
   B. Next, ask these questions:
      - How does a single snowflake finally become a glacier?
      - How many miles long was the largest iceberg ever measured?
      - The world's biggest ice sheet is as tall as how many Empire State Buildings?
   C. Assure students that the above questions will be answered and other very interesting pieces of information will be given about the size, strength, and function of these giant frozen structures.
2. Read the book to students and discuss. Make size comparisons of the various kinds of icebergs and glaciers to objects students are familiar with.
   A. Point out information contained on the activity sheet.
   B. Point out continents, mountains, etc., on the map.
   C. Possible questions, discussion points, and comparisons:
      - When does an ice field become a glacier?
      - What could be some reasons that glaciers in Antarctica move mostly by creeping?
      - Why do you think different parts of a glacier move at different speeds?
      - Compare how slowly the slowest glacier moves with how fast the fastest one moves.
      - Compare the size of the U.S., Mexico, and Central America with the size of the Antarctic ice sheet.
      - Brainstorm ways that icebergs could be moved to dry land.
3. Complete the activity sheet:
   A. Reinforce concepts as needed.
   B. Students complete the statements. Check.
   C. Students follow directions at the bottom for making the snowflake. Additional _hints_:
      (1) Check student work for folding and cutting accuracy to ensure uniform placement of points and cut patterns.
      (2) Give a demonstration run-through if needed.
      (3) _Optional_:
         - at step 5, scallops or other "fancy" cuts can be made on the cut line.
         - at step 6, fold in half again and make notch-cuts.
   D. After the cutting is completed, students read the questions and answers again, with

some of the information missing—similar to the Cloze technique for reading comprehension evaluation. Students exchange and read information.

E. Point out the similarities and differences in each of the snowflakes.

Extended Activity   Enjoy poetry about snowflakes, such as "Snowflakes," by David McCord, in *Sing a Song of Popcorn*, Scholastic, 1988, page 24.

Answer Key to Activity Sheet

1. ice, 6
2. ice, glaciers
3. crevasse
4. faster
5. grind and crush
6. 10
7. 200
8. fresh water

Directions : 1. Fill in the blanks. Check. 2. Cut out the square. SAVE THE PICTURES AT THE BOTTOM. 3. Make a SIX-SIDED snowflake, using the square. Follow the picture directions carefully.

1. Each snowflake is a feathery crystal of _____ .

Every snowflake has ____ ⬡ sides.

2. Single snowflakes pack together to become _____ fields. When these fields move, they become _____ .

3. When the ice from the glacier cracks, a crack is called a _____ .

4. Thicker glaciers move _____ than thinner ones.

Fold 1 _____

5. When glaciers move they _____ and _____ all things in their way.

6. The biggest ice sheet in the world is about the height of _____ Empire State Buildings.

8. Icebergs may be used in the future as _____ for dry lands.

7. The largest iceberg measured was about _____ miles in length.

Fold 3

Fold 2

©1991 by The Center for Applied Research in Education

Ride, Sally, with Susan Okie. *To Space and Back*. New York: Lothrop, Lee & Shepard, 1986. High-interest details, with NASA photographs, of life aboard a space shuttle—as children want to hear it.

Materials

1. Styrofoam meat trays or plates, one for each student to cut a five- to six-inch "person."
2. Popped popcorn, a few pieces for each student.

Optional Materials Photographs of the moon landings to compare with concepts from the present lesson.

Directions

1. Before introducing the book, review:
   A. the major points of the space shuttle program
   B. concepts of gravity and weightlessness, including:

   gravity—the force between objects and the earth pulling on each other. Gravity causes objects to have weight.

   weightlessness—without weight, zero gravity, or a force that neutralizes gravity.

   Interesting fact: A nine-pound baby would weigh about 90 million pounds on the surface of a neutron star because of the strong gravitational pull (*Usborne Book of Facts and Lists*, EDC, 1987).

2. Read the book to students and discuss:
   A. Introduce the book by asking what would be some of the most interesting things you would do as an astronaut? The most fun things?
   B. Read to students or summarize the information from pages 7 through 27.
   C. Carefully read and discuss pages 29 to the end of the book. *Optional, but recommended*: After page 35, ask students to write three questions they have about life in space, leaving lines to write answers if they are given in the course of reading the book. Possible questions to discuss:
   - page 39—Why would food get to the stomach without a problem when eating upside down in space?
   - page 41—What are some foods you couldn't eat in space?
   - page 42—What's another game besides catch you could play with peanuts or cookies? (Keep-away? "Peanut Hockey"?) Could you play Monopoly® in space? Why or why not? Two games that couldn't be played in space are _____ _____ . Why?
   - page 46—What do you think would be the most fun about sleeping weightless? Why can't you choose to sleep on your back, or side, or stomach?
   - page 53—Would your clothes ever get "static electricity" in space?
   - page 54—The four reasons astronauts go to space are: _____
   - page 58—How many more miles above the earth are spaceships than commercial airplanes?
   - page 59—What are some important questions that need to be asked and answered about the effects of weightlessness on the body for a two-year trip to Mars? (body hygiene, muscle maintenance, eating, storage of waste material)

- page 66—If an astronaut floated away without being tethered, could the person get back to the spaceship on his or her own?
- page 81—Weightlessness compared to the pull of gravity may be somewhat like wearing regular shoes and then roller skates or _____
- page 85—Additional activity illustrating gravitational pull and the earth's orbit:

  Materials: ball (earth), string (gravity), person (sun)

  Procedure: Attach the ball to the string. Student swings the ball on the string over his or her head. Why does the ball travel in a circle? What would happen if the string were cut?

3. The activity sheet may be completed independently, except for numbers 2, 5, and 6 or, students complete the entire sheet with partners or in small groups.

   Prompts for question 2:

   - Think about a time on earth when a person seems lighter . . . (in water)
   - It's like holding . . . (a big "nothing," a texture instead of weight)
   - Use descriptive words . . . (powerful, strong)

Related Books   *Space Station*, by Charlene W. Billings, Dodd, 1986; *Junk in Space*, by Richard Maurer, Simon & Schuster, 1989; *The Day We Walked on the Moon*, by George Sullivan, Scholastic, 1990.

Related Science Experiences   *Earth Science Activities for Grades 2–8*, by Marvin N. Tolman and James O. Morton, Parker, 1986.

7–8 WEIGHTLESS WONDERS

Name _____

Directions: Sally Ride says that being weightless is the best part of being in space. The activities and questions below are for exploring some interesting and fun concepts about weightlessness. Answer in complete sentences.

1. Describe three things Sally says feel wonderful to do in space because of being

   weightless. _____

   _____

   _____

   _____

2. Make a "weightless person" from styrofoam. Describe how you would feel holding a

   weightless person in space.   _____

   _____

3. What bodily functions do not change when you are weightless (four functions) _____

   _____

   _____

4. If you are _____ inches (or cm) tall on earth, how tall would you be in space?

   _____ . Why? _____

   _____

5. Toss a piece of popcorn up and try to catch it in your *mouth*! What do you have to

   do to get popcorn, peanuts, and other foods into your mouth in space? _____

   _____

   Why? _____

6. Pretend you are in space holding a satellite that weighs 2,000 pounds on earth. What

   can you do with it in space that you can't do on earth? _____

   _____ .

   Write answers to the following items on the back of this page:

   7. Five things I could do in space that I wish I could do on earth are:

   8. Two games I could play inside the spaceplane are; Here are the materials and rules for playing them:

   9. Here are the steps for getting a cardboard puzzle ready to put together in space:

Caney, Steven. *Invention Book.* **New York: Workman, 1985.** All of the know-how for bringing an invention to reality, plus the stories behind thirty-six popular inventions, including the Frisbee™, Life Savers™, Levis®, and sneakers.

Materials

Scrap or inexpensive materials such as styrofoam cups, string, pipe cleaners, straws, buttons, cardboard tubes, enough for every one or two students. (See 3 below.)

Before reading the book to students   Select two or three inventions from those starting on page 89. Tell about them to students, as an interest-builder.

Directions

1. Introduce the book by recounting the important and interesting information about the selected inventions and selecting two or three students to find an additional invention to read about later and share with the class. *Optional*: Lend the book to a student overnight.

2. Present the book background information for prospective student-created inventions:

   A. Pages 15 to 17:

      • What is an invention?

         Dictionary definition: a new, useful process, machine, improvement, etc.

         Book definition: Someone's idea about ways things can be improved.

            Some ideas have never been done,
            Others make old inventions better, or make jobs easier or more fun

      • What is an inventor? Anyone can be one. Every invention started as a person's idea, and everyone has ideas!

      • What "does it take" to be an inventor? A person must let his/her mind explore *many* possible solutions to each invention problem. He or she must think like an inventor:

            —build on other people's ideas and keep trying, even when there are "accidents"

            —use the fewest materials, with the lowest cost possible

         Note: different results than expected are not necessarily failures

   B. Show students the simple inventions on pages 17, 18, 28, and 41. (Transparency optional.)

      Discuss extensions and modifications of these or other ideas that students become interested in.

3. Students complete a simple invention by modifying materials to create new uses. After assembling the materials, invite students to experiment (individuals or pairs) with the materials and create a new object using one or more of the items. Sample inventions: "Basket Button Game" (flip a button into a cup mounted on a straw), "Walkie-Talkie" (straws, two cups).

4. Facilitate student completion of the activity sheet invention as follows:

   A. Decide whether students will do the invention at home or at school. If completed at school, assemble more "odds and ends" in addition to those used above: styrofoam meat trays, tongue depressors, paper clips, etc.

B. Present the basics for getting started:

    (1) Decide on something you'd like to build or test.

    (2) Assemble the materials, tools, and space.

    (3) Write all of the information you collect on your Inventor's Notebook sheet.

C. Review the steps on the activity sheet with students.

    Sample objects to invent: mouse trap with wood, plastic tube, and peanut butter; doorbell with a box, wood, bell, etc.—"knocking is a boring way to enter a room"; bubble machine; solar radiometer.

D. Intersperse the invention completion with stories about more inventions from the book, including the Frisbee™ and the Dixie® Cup.

E. Key points about the invention to clarify with students:

    (1) A clear, focused goal to begin with will help narrow the steps and eliminate unnecessary experimenting.

    (2) Results different than expected can still be successful!

    (3) Question 6 is to be filled out if the goal and result are changed.

    (4) Steps, details, and how materials are used are needed for completing question 3.

Related Books   *The Problem Solvers*, by Nathan Aaseng, Lerner, 1989; *Inventions No One Mentions*, by Chip Lovitt, Scholastic, 1987; *Homer Price*, by Robert McCloskey, Penguin, 1976.

7–9   INVENTORS NOTEBOOK

Name _____

1. I am planning to invent a (an) _____ _____. This seems like a good thing to have because _____ _____

2. The materials and tools I plan to use are:

Materials: _____

Tools: _____

3. I am now experimenting with designing my invention. Here are the steps I'm going through to make it work: (Give step details and include how materials are used).

A. _____

B. _____

C. _____

D. _____
   Use back of paper for any more steps.

4. Problems and possible solutions I see are:

Problem: _____

Possible solution: _____

5. I think I've done it! Here's why: _____ _____

OR:
↓

6. I've changed how I'll get my invention to work: _____

Symes, Dr. R. F. *Eyewitness Books: Rocks & Minerals.* **New York: Alfred Knopf, 1988.** Clear, interesting photographs and well-written, appealing text give the basics for understanding the creation, importance, and uses of rocks and minerals.

Directions

1. Ask anyone who has or who knows of someone who has a rock collection to share information and the collection.

2. Show students the cover and flip through several interesting pages.

3. Peruse background information contained in the parts called "The Earth," "What Are Rocks and Minerals?", and "How Rocks Are Formed."

   Point out the following key concepts:

   A. The study of the history of the earth is called *geology*. Rocks give us important information about what happened on Earth long ago.

   B. *Rocks* are natural mixtures of one or more minerals. *Minerals* are nonliving substances that have pressed together. The minerals are made of *elements* such as oxygen, iron, and carbon. All minerals appear within rocks, and many times make up part of the rocks.

   C. The rocks, minerals, and chemical elements within the earth are continuously being moved by natural changes within the earth and through surface processes.

4. Read the book information as follows:

   A. Read and discuss the important points of these four kinds of rocks:

   • Volcanic rocks, beginning on page 18

   • Fossils, page 38

   • Crystals, page 44 (include the first paragraph on page 46)

   • Gemstones, page 50

   B. Define each of the four kinds.

   C. Emphasize information contained on the activity sheet.

5. Complete the activity sheet as follows:

   A. Reinforce information! (Most groups will need the information presented more than once.)

   Particularly emphasize concepts for statements B, E, K, and N.

   B. Discuss the concept of "nature" and of rocks as part of nature. Point out that rocks are composed of natural materials (as opposed to man-made) and continue to change because of nature. See page 12, "Weathering and Erosion."

   C. Point out that rocks are a good source of "natural toys."

   D. Students complete the worksheet as a group, in pairs, or independently, depending on the lesson objectives and the group's expertise.

Additional Information About Rocks and Minerals   Filmstrip with cassette "Rocks and Minerals," available from National Geographic Society Educational Services, Dept. 5350, Washington, D.C. 20036-3652.

Additional Activities

1. "A Friend Rock"
   A. Read the book *Everybody Needs a Rock*, by Byrd Baylor (Macmillan, 1985) to students.
   B. Students find their own special rock.
   C. Students each devise a game "that takes just me and one rock to play." Examples: flip the (coin) rock; hide and seek the rock (close eyes, throw rock in air, try to find it); create a house for a rock (including pictures of father and mother—the little rock looks like his mother—and books to read: *Rocks and Minerals, The Rock and the Three Bears* . . .)
2. "It's A . . ."
   Students each write a description of a rock (with optional illustration) for others to identify.

Answer Key to Activity Sheet

A. TRUE
B. TRUE
C. FALSE
D. FALSE
E. TRUE
F. FALSE
G. TRUE
H. TRUE
 I. FALSE
J. TRUE
K. FALSE
L. TRUE
M. TRUE
N. FALSE
O. TRUE
P. FALSE

Message: ROCKS ARE NATURAL FUN

7–10 ROCKS: GEMS UNDER FOOT

Name _____

Directions: Write letters above the correct numbers after deciding whether a statement is TRUE or FALSE. Correct letters will reveal a message about rocks.

— — — — — | — — — | — — — — — — — | — — —
1 2 3 4 5 | 6 7 8 | 9 10 11 12 13 14 15 | 16 17 18

VOLCANIC ROCK

A. Rocks and lava do blow apart to become "fire-broken" volcanic rocks.
   If the statement is TRUE, write the letter K above 4. If FALSE, write P above 10.

B. The wind can carry volcanic ash for thousands of miles.
   TRUE: A above 10, FALSE: L above 13.

C. Pumice is not the only rock that floats in water.
   If TRUE: O above 6. FALSE: A above 6.

D. Obsidian, or natural glass, is chemically different than pumice.
   If TRUE: write B above 3. FALSE: R above 7.

FOSSILS

E. Rocks that feature parts of once-alive plants and animals are called *fossils*.
   TRUE: T above 11. FALSE: R above 11.

F. The bones or shells of animals tend to rot away and therefore are not usually part of fossils.
   If TRUE: S above 8. FALSE: A above 14.

G. Many of the plants and animals in fossils are now extinct.
   If TRUE: E above 8. FALSE: E above 14.

H. Because of details contained in fossils, scientists can usually date those rocks.
   If TRUE: U above 17. FALSE: R above 5.

CRYSTALS

I. Crystals are "frozen ice." If TRUE: M above 12. FALSE: U above 12.

J. Crystals have "faces." If TRUE: N above 18. FALSE: D above 16.

K. Two crystals can be exactly the same. If TRUE: A above 4. FALSE: L above 15.

L. Natural crystals look like someone has cut and polished them.
   If TRUE: O above 2. FALSE: N above 7.

GEMSTONES

M. Gemstones are valued because they are beautiful, rare, and strong.
   If TRUE: R above 13 and N above 9. FALSE: G above 13 and A above 17.

N. Gemstones usually show color and shine without cutting and polishing.
   TRUE: S above 14. FALSE: F above 16.

O. The diamond is the hardest mineral.
   TRUE: C above 3 and S above 5. FALSE: E above 4 and O above 14.

P. A diamond's color is not important to its quality.
   TRUE: C above 11. False: R above 1.

Health With Children's Books

Decision making, Self-belief

Waber, Bernard. *Ira Sleeps Over*. Boston: Houghton Mifflin, 1972. Ira is afraid to take his teddy bear to Reggie's until he discovers something about Reggie he didn't know.

Note about the appropriateness of the book   Although students may have heard the story before, the timeliness of the themes and characters for this age group will most likely generate enthusiasm for a re-reading.

Materials

Duplicate enough copies of the activity sheet for whole group contributions to parts A and B of #2 below, at least one copy for each part.

Directions

1. Read the book to students, empathizing with Ira over the universal problem of fear of being laughed at because of a decision.
   Discuss:
   A. Why did Reggie keep avoiding Ira's questions about what he thought about teddy bears?
   B. Why did Ira believe his sister rather than his parents?
   C. What important lessons did both Ira and Reggie learn from the sleep-over? (Listen to parents, don't let brothers and sisters talk you out of something you believe in, don't be afraid to acknowledge fears—others probably have them, too)
   D. Apply the concepts to classroom and individual student decision making.
2. Completion of the activity sheet(s):
   A. Brainstorm fears that two or more students have in common. Point out that it often helps to know that others are afraid of the same things you are. Record these fears on the activity sheet(s), and title the page: "Beary Unforgettable Fears." Then, brainstorm ways of coping with these common fears.
   B. Next, ask students to tell about situations where they have decided to do something they believed in, even at the risk of being laughed at. Point out the value of sticking by ideas you believe in. Record these beliefs on the activity sheet(s). *Optional*: students write their individual accounts on separate activity sheets. Title the page "Beary Good Beliefs."
3. Display the activity pages for students to peruse.

Additional Activities

1. "Beary Beary Stuffed Animal Party"

   Students bring their favorite bear or other stuffed animal to class.
   "Character sketch cards" are filled out for each animal, describing its looks, special "talents," etc. *Optional*: Have a "slumber party" with pillows, nightclothes, flashlights, etc. Students tell ghost stories, hot chocolate is served, and so forth.

2. "Beary Scary Stories to Write in the Dark"

   Students write individual or group ghost or scary stories in the dark, with flashlights or other lighting creating the atmosphere. Record stories on the activity sheet. *Optional*: Have a slumber party (in the classroom), as above, and share stories.

Name _____

Coping With Loss; Describing a Personality

Viorst, Judith. *The Tenth Good Thing About Barney*. New York: Atheneum, 1971. Remembering nine, and finally ten good things about his cat, Barney, helps a boy deal with its death.

Materials

Copy the activity sheet on gold or yellow paper to simulate a plaque.

Directions

1. Read the book to students, pointing out ways that the boy accepted and dealt with his cat's death:
   - He admitted his sadness and cried to "get his feelings out."
   - He recounted the happy times and the good times about his cat.

   Possibility for handling question of heaven vs. no heaven (page 14): Present this as one person's view. Point out that some people stand assured that there is a heaven, and others negate the concept of heaven entirely.

2. Ask students to share their personal methods of coming to terms with losing a person or animal through either separation or death.

3. Preparation for completing the activity sheet:
   - Brainstorm kinds of special people or animals to write about (living or dead). Examples: grandparents, parents, a friend, coach, pet
   - Brainstorm descriptions: what the person/animal looks like (clothes, color of fur)
   - Brainstorm character traits: actions and behavior (brave, clever, truthful)
   - Brainstorm things done well (play the guitar, catch a ball)
   - Brainstorm how the person/animal helped others (taught swimming, kept company when sick)
   - Brainstorm how the person/animal made others feel good (believed could win a game, stood by as a friend)

4. Students complete the writing either independently or with help from a partner. *Note:* If it becomes difficult for a student to write about a person or animal that has died, help with another selection.

5. Students cut out their "plaque." *Optional*: Students read their tribute to the group.

Directions: Write ten good things about a person or animal that is very special to you. They don't have to be alive now. You can write the items in sentences or make a list.

_____
(Name of person or animal)

_____ is (or was) _____

_____

_____

_____

_____

_____

_____

_____

And that's a pretty good job for a

_____
Kind of person or animal (grandma, cat, etc.)

Cole, Joanna. *The Magic School Bus Inside the Human Body.* **New York: Scholastic, 1989.** A classroom trip on a magic school bus through the body, with its major parts and functions depicted with hype and humor.

Optional Materials

Charts and pictures of the major body systems

Directions

1. Read the book to students and enjoy the humor that makes the learning interesting.
2. Point out the major body parts and functions both during and after reading. Include concepts contained in the riddles. Note particularly riddles 3, 8, and 9. Riddle 10 is a *bonus* riddle.
3. Complete the activity sheet with one of the options, depending on the age and skill level of the students:
   A. Older, higher-performers: Complete independently or in pairs. *Note:* these students could have fun composing additional answers.
   B. Third and fourth grade middle to high performers: Find correct answers for as many riddles as possible individually or in pairs.
   C. Younger and/or lower-performers: Complete partially or wholly as a group, with optional use of a transparency.

Extended Activity For older students: Writing—"More Body Riddles"
Students make up their own riddles working with partners or individually.

Additional Activity For older students: "To Tell the Truth—the Human Body"
Students, in groups of three, assume the role of a body part or system, for example, the brain or muscles, and give a talk about that body part. Only one of the three students tells "the whole truth," with two students giving one or two minor false details, thereby being "imposters." The rest of the group tries to determine who the "real" body part/system is. Students in the class must have access to the information presented, either through the book, or as a class study. See Activity 2–10, To Tell the Truth: Zeus and His Family for the structure of a similar activity. *Additional Magic School Bus Titles: The Magic School Bus at the Waterworks* (Scholastic, 1989) and *The Magic School Bus Inside the Earth* (Scholastic, 1987).

Answer Key to the Activity Sheet

1. C
2. F
3. A
4. D
5. J
6. I
7. B
8. E
9. G
10. H

8–3 BODY RIDDLES

Name _____

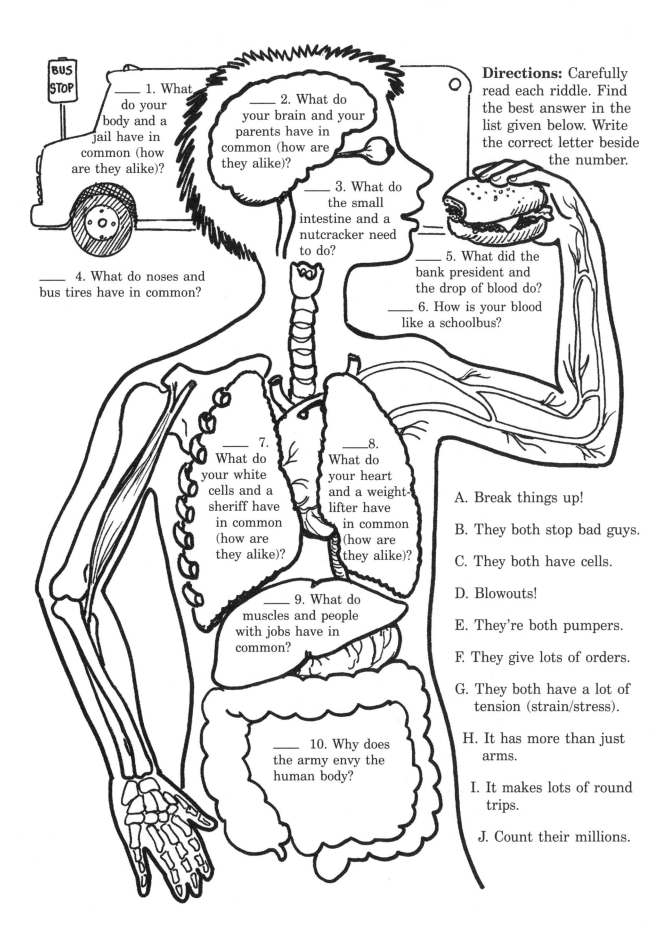

____ 1. What do your body and a jail have in common (how are they alike)?

____ 2. What do your brain and your parents have in common (how are they alike)?

____ 3. What do the small intestine and a nutcracker need to do?

____ 4. What do noses and bus tires have in common?

Directions: Carefully read each riddle. Find the best answer in the list given below. Write the correct letter beside the number.

____ 5. What did the bank president and the drop of blood do?

____ 6. How is your blood like a schoolbus?

____ 7. What do your white cells and a sheriff have in common (how are they alike)?

____ 8. What do your heart and a weight-lifter have in common (how are they alike)?

____ 9. What do muscles and people with jobs have in common?

____ 10. Why does the army envy the human body?

A. Break things up!

B. They both stop bad guys.

C. They both have cells.

D. Blowouts!

E. They're both pumpers.

F. They give lots of orders.

G. They both have a lot of tension (strain/stress).

H. It has more than just arms.

I. It makes lots of round trips.

J. Count their millions.

Marshall, James. *Yummers!* **Boston: Houghton Mifflin, 1973.** Emily Pig's life takes on large dimensions as she satisfies her increasing hunger during her "exercise walk."

Directions

1. Ask students whether they have ever been upset because they didn't get to eat all of the ice cream, soft drinks, and cookies they wanted. Tell them to listen to what happened to Emily Pig when she "pigged out." Read and discuss tne book.

2. Reinforce or review nutritional information as follows:

   A. Foods Emily ate and which of the four food groups they belong to.

   B. The three basic functions of nutrients (the chemical makeup of foods):
      - build, repair, or maintain bones and tissues (give growth)
      - make sure body processes, such as the heart and blood path, run smoothly
      - give energy (measured in calories)

      Optional: Reinforce or review the specific components of the six nutrients: carbohydrates, fats, proteins, minerals, vitamins, water.

   C. Point out the harmful effects of eating too much of the "extra foods," such as cola, banana splits, cookies, jam, and butter. These are usually high in fat or sugar or are used for flavorings. They add unnecessary calories, tear down or get in the way of good foods that are building bones and tissues, give only temporary energy, and can cause high cholesterol levels, increasing the risk of heart disease and stroke.

   D. Review the components of being healthy:
      - proper diet: foods low in fat and sugar and high in complex carbohydrates (for energy), proteins (for growth and maintenance of body structures), minerals, vitamins
      - exercise
      - rest
      - low stress

   E. Discuss why many young people are either overweight or underweight today. Review ways to control weight: calorie counting, controlling cholesterol and fat intake, exercise, etc.

   F. Review ways to describe a character—how he/she acts and behaves.

      Also ask: What kind of a friend was Eugene? Possibilities for his "motives" include: (a) trying to gently lead Emily to walking and cutting down on calories and junk food; (b) afraid to lose Emily's friendship if he pointed out her eating faults; (c) thought how Emily ate was her own business.

3. Complete the activity sheet:

   A. Students work individually, in pairs, in small groups, or as a whole group to finish statements 1 through 5, depending on age and ability of students. *Option for older students:* Complete statements 1 through 5 rapidly in small groups orally or in written form, spending more time on the bonus and extended activities.

   B. Bonus (*) questions: Discuss criteria needed or desired, including the following:

   (1) The healthy snacks fill-ins can provide a lively post-answer discussion as to what constitutes a healthy snack.

(2) Calories for the four foods (approximations):

peach ice cream—300; one (average) slice of cheese pizza—720; tuna sandwich on white bread—280; peanut butter and jam sandwich—380. Total—1,680 calories.

Note: Giving students examples of calorie amounts of similar foods can be helpful. Examples: hot dog—270; four slices of bacon—700; grilled cheese sandwich—340.

Extended Activity   Older Students: "Fascinating Food Records and Facts"

Students, in small groups or individually, find interesting information on the following topics and give reports:

• From *The Second Kids' World Almanac of Records and Facts,* by Margo McLoone-Basta and Alice Siegel, Pharos, 1987:
"Fun Foods for Fitness," page 25 (foods for fresh breath, quick energy)
"Fun Facts About Food," page 113 (facts about popcorn, pizza, etc.)
"The Inside Story on Foods," page 120 (food additives, flavorings, etc.) plus page 124–129

• From *Guinness Book of World Records,* 1989 edition
"Food and Drink Records," page 407ff.
"Eating Records," page 495ff. (see note, top of page 496)
See also Activity 8–8, 4-4-3-2 and Yummers, Too!

Name _____

Directions: To be happy and healthy and still say "yum yum" to good food, Petunia Pig should think about the suggestions YOU give her!

* List three *healthy* snacks Petunia could eat. Use your favorites!

1. _____
2. _____
3. _____

1. Petunia Pig should eat lots of

_____ _____ _____
    (three kinds of foods)

2. She needs good food for _____
    (how nutrients from good food help body)

3. She should NOT eat a lot of _____

because _____

_____

4. Petunia should do the following three things each day to be healthy: A. _____

B. _____   C. _____

4. She can keep her weight down by: A. _____

B. _____   C. _____

5. My favorite pig character is _____ because

_____

*Write the names of book characters and a favorite food for each on the back. Example: Winnie the Pooh, honey.

*How many **calories** do each of these four foods have? ESTIMATE!
peach ice cream _____
one slice pizza _____
tuna sandwich _____
peanut butter sandwich _____
TOTAL

Sharmat, Marjorie Weinman. *The 329th Friend.* **New York: Four Winds, 1979.**
Emery Raccoon discovers that he is his own best friend.

Viorst, Judith. *If I Were in Charge of the World . . . and Other Worries.* **New York: Atheneum, 1982.** Title poem, page 2. Oatmeal, Monday mornings, sisters, and bedtime would all be cancelled "If I Were in Charge . . ."

Directions

1. Overview of the activity:

    A. A student is selected to be "Person of the Day," with the activity sheet as a basis for pointing out the unique and special contributions of each student. (This is an excellent activity for the beginning of the school year.)

    B. The activity sheet can be completed by each student individually, either as a class project, or by the individual student on the selected day. Or, the teacher can record the information while the class listens.

    C. A "Person of the Day" construction-paper badge, completed and worn by the selected student, adds interest, as does a special bulletin board for displaying the activity sheet, etc. The selection for Person of the Day can be made from the badges or the activity sheets.

2. Introduce the books and the activity through the following:

    A. Ask the question: "Why do you like to be thought of as 'neat and special'?"

    B. Outline the parts of the activity.

    Optional for older students: Summarize the content of *The 329th Friend.*

3. After reading *The 329th Friend,* point out *how* and *why* Emery learned to like himself and his friends. Ask students to think about *why* each person should be a friend to himself.

    After reading the Viorst poem, ask students to decide on something each would do to improve the world. Eliminate the opportunity for ideas such as "cancel school or homework."

4. Before completion of the activity sheet, give students examples of *quality responses*, so as to establish the activity as a "fun but responsible" one. If students have several favorite foods, animals, etc., suggest that they select one of those.

    • Note regarding the "We like ___ because ___ . . ." section: This can be completed by the group after the Person of the Day is selected. Several students contribute reasons why the student is liked (special abilities, personality traits) and one or two are chosen to be recorded on the sheet. Examples include: We like ___ because she is a good sport when the team loses/he treats everyone fairly.

    • *Optional*: Free time (one-half hour, suggested) for recreational reading, art or a game, for the Person of the Day.

    • *Optional*: Compile sheets into a class book. (Can provide insightful reading for the principal or guidance counselor.)

Additional Activities

1. "What's In A Name?" *Note:*   can be used with person chosen for Person of the Day.

    A. Read *Tikki Tikki Tembo,* retold by Arlene Mosel (Holt, 1989), to students.

B. Choose a student for the class to describe with positive attributes, using adjectives that begin with the letters in name. Example:

C onsiderate
H onest
U sually smiling
C ourteous
K ind

C. Write description in attractive format and display.

D. *Optional*: Explore meanings of names. One source: *Steven Caney's Kids' America,* (Workman, 1978), page 30ff.

2. "Creative Writing With Sentence Starters"

A. Students use sentence starters such as, "The important thing about the 329th friend is _____," or "The best way to have a friend is to _____," to write a sentence or paragraph.

B. Illustrate and compile individual pages into a class book. Example: "The Twenty-Six Ways to Have Friends." Students read book to younger groups.

8–5 PERSON OF THE DAY! Name _____

_____ _____

My favorite food is _____

My favorite animal is _____

My favorite sport is _____

My favorite book is _____

My favorite author is _____

My favorite subject is _____

Three things I like about school are _____

_____

Something I can do very well is _____

I am a friend to myself because _____

We like _____ because _____
         (student's name)   (written by other students)

_____

I like my parent(s) because _____

_____

A very special time with my family was when _____

_____

It was special because _____

_____

If I were in charge of the world, I would _____

_____

_____

_____

> **Miles, Miska. *Annie and the Old One.* Boston: Little, Brown and Company, 1971.** A Navajo girl learns to accept the death of her grandmother and weaves a rug of understanding about life and the marching on of time.

Optional Materials

1. A simple loom or paper weaving materials for demonstrating the basics of weaving on a hand loom or providing a simple weaving experience for students.
2. Egg timer for bonus activity.

Directions

1. Introduce the book by asking students to think about a problem they can't do anything about but are having a hard time accepting. Tell them to listen for how Annie deals with a situation she can't change.
2. Read and discuss the story with students, pointing out:

   A. the meaning of weaving-related words: *warp, shed, weft*

   B. Annie's reluctance, but final understanding and acceptance of her grandmother's impending death:

      (1) At first, Annie didn't want to understand what was happening with her grandmother

      (2) Annie appeared to be doing "babyish" or trivial things to slow down the death. When someone wants something badly enough, they sometimes lose the ability for logical thinking.

      (3) Annie finally accepted the death, because she learned that the passing of time is a natural event over which she has no control

3. Direct the completion of the activity sheet as follows:

   A. Review concepts as needed by students.

   B. Next, instruct them to finish the first five statements.
      Possible prompts: the first letter of a word.

   C. Before students finish statements 6, 7, and 8, point out the difference between problems that really *are* unsolvable and those that *appear* to be. For example: Having to wear braces or glasses, not staying up late on schoolnights, parents getting divorced, are all problems or situations that must be accepted, but not having friends or being too fat are problems that usually have a workable solution.

   D. Bonus activity:

      (1) Practice making words with the group using another phrase, such as, "Annie and the Old One." Use these strategies:
         • Make words from letters in the normal order
         • Add endings (*s, ed, ing*) to the words already made
         • Add prefixes and suffixes
         • Change the first letter
         • Combine words

      (2) Students use above strategies for "A Rug of Understanding." Suggested time for completion: 6 minutes. Use egg timer.

4. *Relevance for the beginning of the school year:*
Use the theme of solvable problems to set realistic goals, both for the class and individual students.

Film available   Annie and the Old One

Additional Activity   Social Studies, "Weaving Patterns"
Students research weaving patterns used by different Indian tribes and create a rug pattern on graph paper using appropriate colors.

Name _____

Directions: There are some situations that we must accept the way they are. Annie couldn't change the fact that her grandmother was going to die. But some problems are just waiting for us to put a solution into action!

Start from the bottom and fill in the blanks—one blank for each word. The ideas are in the order they happened in the story. BONUS activity at the bottom!

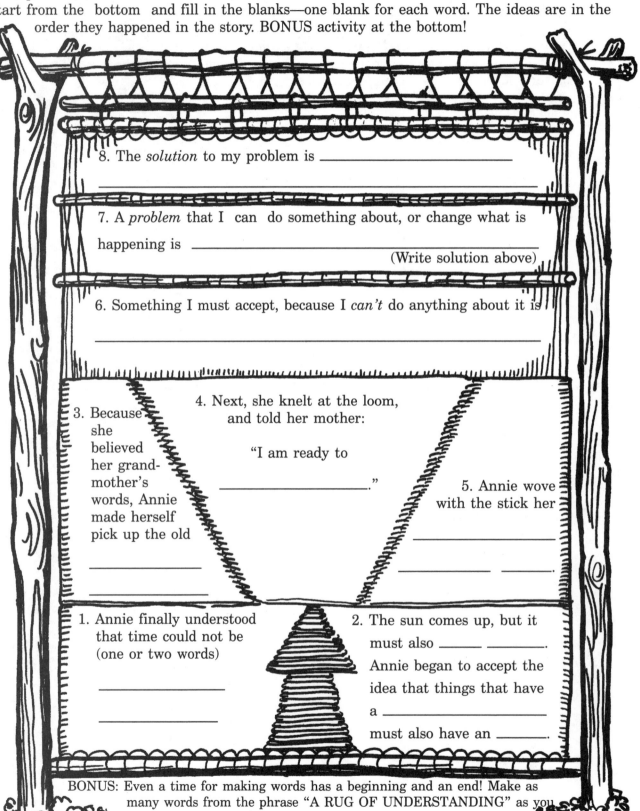

8. The *solution* to my problem is _____

_____

7. A *problem* that I can do something about, or change what is

happening is _____
(Write solution above)

6. Something I must accept, because I *can't* do anything about it is

_____

3. Because she believed her grand- mother's words, Annie made herself pick up the old

_____

_____

4. Next, she knelt at the loom, and told her mother:

"I am ready to

_____."

5. Annie wove with the stick her

_____

_____.

1. Annie finally understood that time could not be (one or two words)

_____

_____

2. The sun comes up, but it must also ____ _____.

Annie began to accept the idea that things that have

a _____

must also have an _____.

BONUS: Even a time for making words has a beginning and an end! Make as many words from the phrase "A RUG OF UNDERSTANDING" as you can in _____ minutes.

Sharmat, Marjorie. *The 329th Friend* (Macmillan, 1979); Lobel, Arnold.
Frog and Toad Are Friends, "A Swim" (Harper, 1985); Spier, Peter. *People*
(Doubleday, 1989); Miles, Miska. *Annie and the Old One* (Little, 1985); Viorst,
Judith. *Alexander and the Terrible, Horrible, No Good, Very Bad Day*
(Macmillan, 1972); Stevens, Janet. *The Tortoise and the Hare* (Holiday, 1984);
Waber, Bernard. *Ira Sleeps Over* (Houghton Mifflin, 1975); Marshall, James.
Yummers! (Houghton Mifflin, 1986).

Directions

1. Read or summarize the unfamiliar books from the list. Point out to older students that these familiar books are being used in this activity to develop ways of dealing with stress. *Alternative to reading books to students:* Rotate students through a center where students read individually or in pairs over several days.

2. Reinforce the main ideas contained on the activity sheet for each of the books.
   * For older students, give the general concept.
   * For younger and/or low-performers, *orally* use the *actual phrases* and words.

3. Students complete the activity sheet by following the directions on the sheet. Students may work individually, in pairs, or with the large group—depending on their level.
   Notes:
   * If students have difficulty, supply the first letter of the word.
   * For younger students: Words and phrases can be displayed in random order on a transparency or the board.
   * The *number under the letter* contained inside a sketched book is the number for the letter after it is unscrambled. For example, in the first book, the *N* is in *fourth* place in the message when it is written *correctly*.
   * Tell students to enjoy finding ways of making their lives more stressless. Point out and relate the KEY symbol to ways of relieving stress.

4. After completion, check the activity sheet with students and elaborate on the concepts that directly relate the ideas to reducing stress. Examples:
   * Emery Raccoon: Being a friend to yourself means that if you like yourself, you will always have a friend. Not having to look for a friend can reduce stress.
   * Toad: Being able to "ask others to laugh *with* you," takes away the temptation for them to laugh *at* you, keeping stress lower.

   Ask students to contrast the impact of "Thinking About Happy Things" with that of Eeyore (*Winnie the Pooh* series by A. A. Milne) who sends himself negative messages.

Answer Key to Activity Sheet FRIEND; YOURSELF, WITH YOU; DIFFERENT; "GOOD-BYE," "HI"; EVERYONE, NEW; HEALTHY, WISE; FEAR, GEAR; INPUT, OUTPUT. Message: THINK ABOUT HAPPY THINGS

8–7 STRESSLESS BOOKS

Name _____

Directions: 1. Unscramble the words and fill in the blanks. 2. Next, find the letters with numbers below them. For a STRESSLESS message, write those letters above the correct number here:

__ __ __ __ K__ __ __ __ __ __ __ __ __ __ __ __ __ __ __ __ __
1 2 3 4 5 6 7 8 9 10 11 12 13 14 15 16 17 18 19 20 21

Emery Raccoon from *The 329th Friend* says:

Be a friend to yourself and you have a good

R N F E I D
④

for life!

The book, *People*, says:

It's OK to be

T F E D I N E F R
①

Alexander, from *Alexander and the Terrible, Horrible, No Good Day* says:

Bad days happen to

V E O Y R E N E ,
but tomorrow is a

___ ___ ___ day!
E W N
⑲

The book, *Ira Sleeps Over*, says:

Telling a

E A F R
⑥

helps you get back

in ___ ___ ___ ___
E A G R
⑫ ⑳

Toad, from *Frog and Toad are Friends*, says:

Laugh at

S R L F E O Y U
㉑   ⑧   ⑨

and the world laughs

T I H W   O Y U
⑯   ⑮ .

The book, *Annie and the Old One*, says:

Be able to say

O D G O – Y E B
⑦

so you can think of

saying ___ ___ to new
things. ③ ②   I H

Tortoise, from *The Tortoise and the Hare*, says:

Eat right and exercise to be

E T H L Y H A ,
⑪   ⑰

wealthy, and

S I W E
⑱

Emily Pig from *Yummers!* should have said:

Good body

I U P N T
⑬ ⑩

gives good body

O T U U T P
⑭

©1991 by The Center for Applied Research in Education

Marshall, James. *Yummers!* **Boston: Houghton Mifflin, 1973.** Emily Pig's life takes on large dimensions as she satisfies her increasing hunger during her "exercise walk."

Materials

1. Black copies of the activity sheet for every two or three students
2. Game markers. *Optional*: small food objects, such as Starburst® wrapped candies (from M&M / Mars Co., available at many grocery stores)
3. Die for each group of two or three students
4. Jump rope
5. Plain paper cut into "note cards" for "Congratulations" note (space 22). *Optional*: "Congratulations" sticker for front of note
6. Play-Doh® for space 8 (optional)

Directions

1. Proceed through steps 1 and 2A through E from Activity 8—4, *Pigging Out on Health.*
2. Point out a few of the game components (not the rules) which have important nutritional and fitness information. Example: At space 3, Petunia eats many less scones and has a balanced breakfast, with attention to calories. In the book version, the pig has (probably) a snack, with "all the scones, butter and jam that she wants." Point out that a tomato is a *fruit,* and that *protein* builds strong bones.
3. Teach the game rules. Supplement the rules with the following:

    A. Divide group into teams of two or three (game is faster with two).

    B. Reinforce: "Do not begin your turn until the other player is finished."

    C. Fill in answers on the sheet only *once,* but all other activities must be done again *each time* you land on that space.

    D. Point out the spaces which have blanks to be filled in: 7, 20, 25, 26, 28. (*Optional*: Circle those numbers in red.)

    E. Point out where the additional game materials will be located (jump rope and note paper). *Optional*: Write format for "Congratulations" note (space 22) on board:

    "Congratulations, Petunia, for passing up the banana split!"
    Your friend, _____

    F. Tell students to raise their hand when they reach space 29, to be checked out on correctness of written answers. *Note:*   Some students may need hints for space 25, such as: "What would it cost if you bought *two* half-dozens?"

Optional   Students classify foods from the game according to 4-4-3-2, either during or after the game.

Here is Petunia Pig's new game for being healthy and fit. See if you can win the health game, too!

Game Rules: 1. Roll to see who starts.
2. Roll a ONE to start. 3. THREE players: use one through four; TWO players, use one through three 4.To win, land on space 29, with all BLANKS filled in, answers checked. 5. Start over when a person wins. Only fill in blanks once. WAIT for a player to complete a turn before you begin yours!

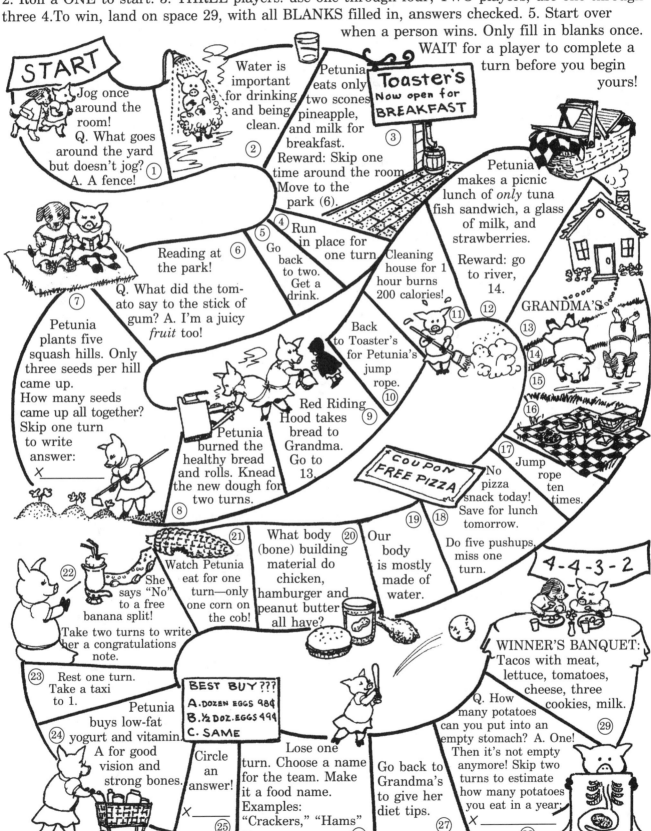

START

Jog once around the room!
Q. What goes around the yard but doesn't jog? A. A fence! ①

② Water is important for drinking and being clean.

③ Petunia eats only two scones pineapple, and milk for breakfast. Reward: Skip one time around the room Move to the park (6).

Toaster's Now open for BREAKFAST

Petunia makes a picnic lunch of *only* tuna fish sandwich, a glass of milk, and strawberries. Reward: go to river, 14.

④ Run in place for one turn

⑤ Go back to two. Get a drink.

⑥ Reading at the park!

⑦ Q. What did the tomato say to the stick of gum? A. I'm a juicy *fruit* too!

Cleaning house for 1 hour burns 200 calories! ⑪

⑫ GRANDMA'S ⑬ ⑭ ⑮ ⑯

Petunia plants five squash hills. Only three seeds per hill came up. How many seeds came up all together? Skip one turn to write answer:
X_____

⑧ Petunia burned the healthy bread and rolls. Knead the new dough for two turns.

⑨ Red Riding Hood takes bread to Grandma. Go to 13.

⑩ Back to Toaster's for Petunia's jump rope.

COUPON FREE PIZZA

No pizza snack today! Save for lunch tomorrow.

⑰ Jump rope ten times.

⑱ Do five pushups, miss one turn.

⑲

⑳ Our body is mostly made of water.

㉑ What body (bone) building material do chicken, hamburger and peanut butter all have?

Watch Petunia eat for one turn—only one corn on the cob!

4-4-3-2

⑳ She says "No" to a free banana split! Take two turns to write her a congratulations note.

㉒

㉓ Rest one turn. Take a taxi to 1.

㉔ Petunia buys low-fat yogurt and vitamin. A for good vision and strong bones.

BEST BUY ???
A. DOZEN EGGS 98¢
B. ½ DOZ. EGGS 49¢
C. SAME

Circle an answer!
X____ ㉕

Lose one turn. Choose a name for the team. Make it a food name. Examples: "Crackers," "Hams"
X_____ ㉖

Go back to Grandma's to give her diet tips. ㉗

WINNER'S BANQUET: Tacos with meat, lettuce, tomatoes, cheese, three cookies, milk.
Q. How many potatoes can you put into an empty stomach? A. One! Then it's not empty anymore! Skip two turns to estimate how many potatoes you eat in a year:
X_____ ㉘

㉙

Parker, Steve. *Eyewitness Books: Skeleton*. New York: Alfred Knopf, 1988.
Lifelike pictures and interesting facts about human and animal skeletal systems and their structure and function.

Note: This activity sheet is designed as a review of some of the basics of the human skeletal system and can be used as a springboard for further exploration of these concepts.

Directions

1. Introduce the book by displaying the cover and several appealing pages. Further engage students with the following questions:

   A. What does the term "big headed" have to do with the human skull and brain? (p. 6)

   B. How many times a year do the bones that enable you to breathe have to move? (p. 8)

   C. What is the largest bone in the human body? the smallest? Why are some people midgets—what caused their bones not to grow as large? (p. 10, 58–59)

   D. How many different bones do you have in your body? (p. 62)

2. Present book information for the activity sheet:

   A. Read and discuss the following pages as the basic information, underlining the importance of the skeletal system's functions of support, movement, and protection of muscles, tissues, nerves, and organs: pages 6, 14, 26–27, 38, 42, 48, 54–55

   B. Point out the following key bones and their functions:

      • Skull—shields the brain and the delicate organs of sight, hearing, smell, and taste (p. 6, 14, 26)

      • Teeth, jaws—chop through ½ ton of food per year (p. 6)

      • Knee—the largest joint in the body, carries almost half of the body's weight (p. 10, 54)

      • Spine—the backbone, supports the head, arms, and legs and protects the spinal chord (p. 38–39)

      • Ribs—guard the heart and lungs, a flexible cage with moveable bars (p. 42)

      • Arm and hand—engage in precise movements which show great strength and accuracy (p. 48)

      • Leg—thick and strong enough to carry the body's weight (p. 54)

   C. Additional points for discussion:

      • How is a bat's skeleton the same as a human's? How is it different? (p. 16)

      • Compare a cat's skeleton to that of a human (p. 16)

      • Compare a bird's skeleton to a human's (p. 18)

3. Completing the activity sheet:

   A. Review important information as needed, with students identifying each of the bones that are reviewed.

   B. Ask students to supply answers to the riddles individually, in pairs, or in small groups. Point out that these riddles were written by fifth graders. *Optional*: Give students the first word or letter of the answer.

Extended Activities

1. "No spineless spinal chords here!"

   Students examine the spine and spinal chord from available animal skeletons, such as a chicken, fish, or rabbit. See pages 20–21 and 38–39. Note the large holes in each vertebra that line up to protect the delicate spinal chord.

2. "Boning up on bones"

   Students bring bones from available animal skeletons to compare with those from the book. Drawing bones and comparing the drawings with those of Leonardo Da Vinci is another possibility.

Answer Key to Activity Sheet

1. protecting precious things
2. brain
3. weight lifting
4. cap
5. hold up the head
6. spineless
7. hitting the bull's eye
8. phony bone
9. pressure is put on them
10. chop things
11. chopper
12. rib cage has flexible bars

8–9 BONY CRACK-UPS!

Name _____

Directions: Identify the bones. Next, write answers to the riddles by unscrambling *either* the words or the letters in the words.

What is a skeleton when it's fast asleep? <u>Dead to the world</u>

1. What do your skull and a safe have in common?

_____

_____

things protecting precious

2. What did the skeleton forget to take when it crossed the road against the red light?

a _____

abnri

3. Since the knee joint carries half of the body's weight, what sport could it turn out for?

_____

giwhte tlgnifi

4. What did the knee wear to keep its top warm? a _____

apc

5. What do a spine and a lettuce stem both do?

_____

the up head hold

6. Why didn't the jellyfish stand up for its rights when it got knocked down?

it's _____

npisleses

7. What was the bull scared of when the arm and hand bones threw the dart? _____

eye the hitting bull's

8. What is a funny bone?

a _____

npohy nobe

9. What do a fat person's leg (which carries a lot of weight) and a winning athlete have in common?

_____

_____

put them pressure on is

10. How do teeth and the jaw bones act like an ax?

they _____

ohcp nghtis

11. What is the name used for both your teeth and a helicopter?

a _____

pohcrep

12. Why would an animal rather live in a rib cage than a cage at the zoo? a _____

_____

has rib flexible cage bars

*BONUS: Write your own "bony riddle"!

_____

_____

Creative Arts with Children's Books

Art: Line and Shape; Writing: Descriptive Phrases

Oakley, Graham. *Magical Changes.* **New York: Macmillan, 1979.** A picture book with pages cut horizontally so the reader can mix and match top and bottom halves.

Materials

For Second and Third Grades

1. Draw two sets of vertical lines on 8½-by-11 inch white paper, as shown here.

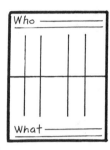

2. Next, draw a horizontal line across the middle.
3. Write *WHO* and draw two writing lines near the top. Write *WHAT* and draw similar lines at the bottom.
4. Reproduce one copy (black preferable) of the paper for each student on 9-by-12-inch white drawing or manila paper.
5. Secure crayons and other coloring materials.

For Fourth and Fifth Grades

1. Draw four sets of vertical lines, each ½ inch wide, as shown. (This is a facsimile of lines in the book on the right-side pages.)

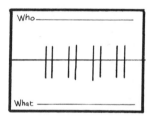

2. Follow steps 3, 4, and 5 from above.

Directions

1. Introduce the book by showing the first four pages with their "basic" top and bottom halves. Then start mixing and matching. Once the magic is understood, the visual and vocal involvement will become high.
2. Complete the activity with the following:
   A. After distributing the copies, tell *younger* students to make the two sets of lines part of the picture. Tell *intermediate* students to make the vertical lines into the main objects for the picture.
      • The sets of lines should feature (or be the basis for) the *same* object, duplicated one (or three) times.
      • The top half should feature what the objects look like, and the bottom half should show what has happened to them.

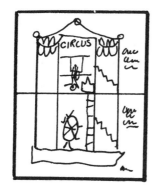 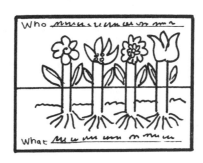

B. Show examples from the book
  - *Jack and the Beanstalk:* TOP—beanstalk climbing to the sky; BOTTOM—was cut down by Jack
  - *The Trojan Horse*: TOP—the wooden horse with people inside; BOTTOM—was pushed and pulled by the soldiers
  - *The globs of wax*: TOP—soft, squishy wax; BOTTOM—was melted by the fire

C. Generate student examples, such as the following:
  - WHO—The half-opened flowers
  - WHAT—Were carefully planted

D. Instruct students to draw the basic shapes of their picture lightly with pencil.

E. Next, students write about the objects they have drawn: "who" (or what object) is doing something on the first set of lines, and "what" the person, animal, or object is doing (or what happened to the person) on the second set. Use the past tense of verbs: Pencils *scribbled,* cans of soda *fizzed,* flowers *were planted.*

F. Special writing directions for older higher performing students: Expand the writing part to teach subject and predicate, modifiers, and direct objects, as appropriate to student level:

  (1) Subject: Describe the "who" and use at least 3 adjectives and/or adverbs—*"Four frantic, wiggly, speeding pencils . . .*

  (2) Predicate: Include modifiers and direct object— *. . . wildly scribbled crafty words."*

G. Students trace objects and writing with black felt-tip pens and add color.

H. Pages are cut in half diagonally and put into a class book. Then watch the "magical changes" occur as students "perform" their book.

  Note: although students initially will want to keep their work, the excitement with the group interchange will override the sense of individual ownership.

Extended Activity   Students create a skit with roles for the top and bottom halves of the object(s).

Martin, Bill Jr. and John Archambault. *Listen to the Rain.* **New York: Holt, 1988.** Lyrical words that vibrantly express the sounds and feelings of rain, highly complimented by watercolors that capture their moods.

Materials

1. Rhythm instruments such as sand blocks, triangles, and drums, that will enhance the spoken imitations of the rain sounds.
2. *Optional*: copies of the poem for students or a transparency.

Directions

1. Read the poem twice to students, the first time without showing the illustrations. Point out the potential for making the words "sing" and for voice imitation of the various rain sounds.
2. Direct students in executing the poem as choral speaking:
   A. Experiment with large group, small group, and individual speaking of the various lines.
   B. Help students practice portraying the sounds of rain with their voices. Work on inflection and volume.
   C. Add instruments where appropriate.
   Optional: Present to an audience with enlargements of the illustrations or slides.

Suggested Rhythm Instruments

"whisper"—sand blocks

"tinkle"—finger cymbals, triangle

"wet whisper of the rain"—wind chimes

"singing"—strum autoharp, no buttons down

"tiptoe pitter-patter"—two woodblocks

"splish, splash, splatter"—anything that shakes, maracas

"steady sound"—hand drum

"roaring"—bass drum roll

"lashing, gnashing, teeth of rain"—cymbals

"lightning-flashing"—cymbals crash

"thunder-crashing"—drum roll

"mishy mushy"—sucking sounds with mouth

"quietude, silence"—total silence, pause

"dripping, dripping, dropping"—finger cymbals

"the fresh . . . after-time of rain"—windchimes

Additional Activity   Try creative writing with "Listen to the _____"

Neumeier, Marty and Byron Glaser. *Action Alphabet.* **New York: Greenwillow, 1984, 1985.** "Active" alphabet letters act out the sample words they depict.

Materials

1. White 9-by-12-inch construction paper (one piece per student); scissors.
2. One of the following: black 9-by-12-inch construction paper (one per student), white chalk; OR black, narrow and wide felt-tip pens.

Directions

1. Present and enjoy the book with students. Point out that the letters are acting out the words they represent. For example, the *A* is an acrobat doing acrobatic tricks; the *B* is a big letter, acting or being very large.

2. Students draw, or draw and cut, their own action letter depicting a newly created action, through one of the following procedures:

   A. For younger or lower performing students:
      (1) Group brainstorms action words, enough for one per student.
      (2) Students draw the action letter-object on the black paper, using chalk.
      (3) Students cut out the letter-object and glue it onto the white paper.
      (4) Students write the letter and word.

   B. For older students:
      (1) Follow the above steps, OR
      (2) Students or teacher select(s) an action letter-object to be drawn with felt-tip pens:
         (a) Students lightly draw the shape and other picture objects in *pencil*, then trace with felt pens.
         (b) Students write the letter and word.

      Optional: Students write a descriptive or other paragraph, or combine black paper cutting with the drawing techniques

3. *Optional*: Make copies of individual work for a class book.

Additional Activity Students make name tags, book titles, or books about themselves using action letters/words. Example:

Drawing: Line; Writing: Poetry

Livingston, Myra Cohn. *Celebrations.* **New York: Holiday House, 1985.** The popular holidays in poetry combined with Leonard Everett Fisher's stunning paintings.

Materials

1. One piece of white 9-by-12-inch paper per student
2. Crayons or felt-tip markers, wide and narrow, or oil crayons
3. *Optional*: larger pink or red construction paper to be cut into heart shape for mounting drawing. Also, small paper to be cut into heart shape for completing the writing; scissors.

Directions

1. Read the poem "My Valentine" to students for pleasure.
2. Student drawing of "My Valentine":
    A. Distribute the white paper and coloring materials.
    B. Instruct students to outline the shapes lightly in pencil first
    C. *Drawing instructions for younger students:*
        (1) Draw a square head almost *as large as your paper.*
        (2) Draw two eyes, with twenty eyebrows.
        (3) Draw "something else besides a brain" in his/her head.
        (4) Draw four ears "twitching," and noses that "shine."
    Reread the poem to students, asking them to note color details

D. *Drawing instructions for older students:*

(1) Reread the poem, slowly, to students asking them to think about the features of the "Valentine":

- how many eyes, eyebrows, ears, noses
- shapes of the features
- colors and textures

(2) Students draw either a head or the full character, *as large as the paper.*

E. Students add color. *Optional, but attractive*: Outline features in black.

F. Students give their "Valentine" a name ("Nosey," "Dreamy").

G. Acknowledge the *unique* and *creative* results from each student—although each started with the same data!

H. *Optional*: Students mount Valentine on larger heart shape.

3. Writing completion by older students:

A. Select one or two student drawings to write a group sample poem about.

B. Students describe the character and tell what the character does, using couplets or other rhyme forms. Example:

> *Nosey*
> Nosey's always slick and clean;
> He scrubs the spots and in between.
> He's got two mouths instead of hair;
> A white tuxedo he'll proudly wear.

C. Students complete individual writing at bottom of page or on small heart.

Art: Defining Objects, Space; Writing: Action Words

Jonas, Ann. *Round Trip.* **New York: Greenwillow, 1983.** Striking black-and-white, positive and negative images depicting a trip to the city and back again.

Materials

1. One piece of either 9-by-12-inch or 5-by-7-inch black construction paper for each student (see 2A below)
2. One piece of 9-by-12-inch white construction paper per student
3. Glue and scissors
4. *Optional*: white chalk

Directions

1. Read the book to students, enjoying the excitement of the positive and negative images—the black being defined because of the white, and vice versa.
2. Completion of the drawings:

   A. Give *younger* students the whole piece of black paper; *older,* the half sheet.

   B. Students cut an unknown or unnamed shape/object:

   • Shape should not be a predetermined image, such as a house or a tree.

   • Object should be as large as the paper.

   • *Optional for younger students*: Students draw an outline of the object with chalk before cutting.

   Note: Students tend to be more creative if they do not predetermine an object to cut.

   C. Display student work to the group when one or two have a recognizable shape. Identify it, then turn it upside down, and generate group ideas for naming.

   D. Next, present the examples given in this activity. *Note:* If the group has difficulty getting started, present the objects earlier.

This cool and comfortable shirt keeps the heat away on hot summer days.

The heavy hammer strikes the sturdy nail three times.

A black bear can feel snug in his cozy winter grotto.

The slim, slick rocket blasts off for a quick trip to the moon.

This shrill bike horn warns
people when I whiz through the
streets.

The lonely tree stands
straight through the
brisk wind.

E. Continue to feature creative work to motivate others. If needed, elicit group help with naming individual student's objects.

F. Students should make minor cutting adjustments to give appropriate detail.

G. Objects are glued to the white paper, leaving space at the top and bottom for writing.

3. Completion of the writing:

A. Complete a group writing example, using a student's work.

B. The following format is suggested:

(1) Describe what the object looks like and what it is doing (or can do, or is used for).

(2) Give other information about the object.

C. Students complete individual writing.

Optional: Students draw light pencil lines on the paper for straight writing.

Optional: Compile a copy of work into a class book for the library, where it will attract a lot of attention!

Extended Activity Make "up and down" bookmarks from black paper scraps.

Additional Activity Write words with "up and down" letters. Example: *top, dot*.

Base, Graeme. *Animalia.* **New York: Abrams, 1987.** Extraordinary use of color and composition feature animals and objects that are set with both reality and imagination in this unusual alphabet book.

Materials

1. If possible, make a *black* copy of the activity sheet for each student, as this page is intended as a souvenir of the book and the artistic process it represents.

2. Coloring materials: colored pencils (recommended) or crayons. *Optional*: fine-point black pen for completing drawings.

   Note: Either seat students close to the book or circulate among students as pages are presented.

Pre-Book Skills

Gear reinforcement or review of the following elements and principles of design to student age and ability to facilitate book discussion and activity sheet completion:

1. Elements of Design: line, shape, color, texture
2. Principles of Design: unity and variety

Directions

1. Introduce the book by asking students to imagine what "horrible hairy hogs hurrying homeward on heavily harnessed horses" would look like. Display that page and discuss.

2. Present the pages of the book to students, discussing or pointing out:

   A. Objects beginning with the letter—"the more you find, the more you discover"

   B. the following design components from selected pages (letters *D* and *G* offer good examples):
   - basic shapes (circle, rectangle, cube)
   - basic colors and textures
   - repeated shapes, colors, and textures
   - unity of each scene—all the animals and other objects *belong* together; the shapes, colors and textures work together to create an effect
   - variety of each scene—the elements (line, shape, color) are modified to create visual interest. Note the interest and variety of typefaces announcing each letter's theme.
   - composition—all of the above comprises this. Base's artistry in putting the animals and other objects together on the page and integrating color, line, shape, size, space, and so forth are evident.

3. Present completion of the activity sheet as follows:

   A. Promote the page as a work of art that will be a souvenir or remembrance of the book art. (It was designed by artist Susan Jerde.)

   B. Invite students to point out objects, including the less obvious ones (Clydsdale, cantering, chariot, curb bit, chaps, cinch, cantle)

   C. Discuss and relate applicable book design elements:
   - lines, shapes, textures, size

- repeated shapes and textures (circle, trapezoid, triangle; spots—leopard, girl; dots—China, chimney stones, chimney smoke; stripes—chrysanthemum petals, chimney bricks)
- unity and variety as related to the elements of size, space, line, shape

D. Drawing completion: (*Note:* Instructions are given here as opposed to on the activity sheet so as to preserve the picture quality of the activity sheet. Write instructions for students to refer to.)

(1) Students finish drawing the chain and the diamonds on the horse's neck, fill in the unshaded blanket section, and texture the Cheetah's leg and chimney sections

(2) Students add three objects of their own beginning with *C.* Brainstorm objects if needed

(3) Students add color, building on the principles of unity and variety

Extended Activity   Students create their own picture using design elements.

Name _____

Cheerful Chimp in Chaps on Champing Chestnut Charger

—Susan Jerde

Student- or teacher-selected fiction or nonfiction, one book for each student that features steps in a process, a developmental cycle, or a simple subject whose actions easily lend to animation. Examples: *The Sunken Treasure,* by Gail Gibbons (Harper, 1988); *Volcano,* by Patricia Lauber (Bradbury Press, 1986); "Humpty Dumpty" by Mother Goose; *Rain Rain Rivers,* by Uri Schulevitz (Farrar, Straus & Giroux, 1988).

Materials

1. 3-by-5-inch index cards, approximately six to eight per student, stapled as shown; alternative: 3-by-5-inch scratch pads, 15 to 25 pages per student
2. Black felt-tip pens, crayons
3. Student or teacher created example flip book.
4. *Optional*: Samples of commercially made flip books.

   Note: Maurice Sendak uses the concept of the flip book in his drawings. See *One Was Johnny* (Harper, 1969) and *Alligators All Around* (Harper, 1962)

Directions

1. Subjects for the drawings are selected by the teacher or students, depending on the purpose of the lesson/activity. Examples: plants growing from seeds, the water cycle from cloud to rain or from river to ocean, treasure being retrieved from a sunken ship, Pinocchio growing his nose, Leslie swinging across the water and falling (*Bridge to Terabithia* by Katherine Paterson, Harper, 1987).

   Assist students in selecting a *simple* subject, concept, object, to draw—one which the student feels capable of executing successfully.

2. Prepare students for completing the drawings:

   A. Contrast the difference between a storyboard (or separate parts of a story) or several processes and one action of a story or one process or part of a process. Explain that students will be illustrating through animation—a sequence of drawings where each one is slightly different from the preceding one so that when the pages are "flipped through," the figures seem to move. Demonstrate, and show examples.

   B. Tell students to make the drawings *simple* so what is happening can be quickly and easily seen.

   C. Drawings should be a little less than half the page size.

   D. Students should plan ahead, so that:
   • drawings are in the "right place,"
   • drawings are kept the same size, where appropriate,
   • there will be room for the conclusion, or punchline

   E. Students draw in pencil, starting with the *second* card (page), or *last* page depending on choice. *Note:* tracing object from previous page is usually a good option.

   F. Students write the name of the book used, and the author on the front cover. They also indicate where to begin the flipping, front or back.

   G. If students are focusing on a problem, usually a solution should be included.

   H. Fine-point black felt-tip pen should be used, and color may be added.

3. Optional, students write poetry featuring concepts from the drawings (usually done only when the six to eight *cards* are used):

A. Organize the steps for writing:

1. Choose free or structured style, such as rhyming or cinquin.

2. Use one to three words for each card.

3. Write the poetry for a particular illustration on the *back* of the previous card, that is, the words for the first illustration are written on the back of the cover.

4. Sample poem (created from *Rain Rain Rivers* and *Cloudy With a Chance of Meatballs*).

> When a cloud
> bursts,
> it doesn't
> shatter a mirror
> It creates
> one!

B. Complete the poetry for one or two sample books as a group.

Option: Complete all writing for books with small groups or the large group.

Books to be selected by students.

Directions

1. Talk about the kinds of chants and cheers done at football and basketball games. Share examples.

2. Conduct student writing of a chant or cheer from a favorite book in the following manner:

    A. Select a book known to all students and write a group chant or cheer. Examples include: *Cloudy With a Chance of Meatballs* by Judith Barrett, Atheneum, 1978:

    > Stringy Spaghetti, tasty pies;
    > Hamburgers, meatballs, fall from the skies;
    > Ra, Chewandswallow!

    "The Camel Dances," from *Fables* by Arnold Lobel, Harper, 1980:

    > Dance Camel, step camel;
    > Rah, rah, rah!
    > Leap camel, twirl camel;
    > Go-o, camel!

    The Tortoise and the Hare by Janet Stevens, Holiday, 1984:

    > We're gonna F-I-G-H-T,
    > We're gonna S-C-O-R-E,
    > We're gonna fight, we're gonna score;
    > We're gonna win once more,
    > So go-o-o TORTOISE!

    B. Discuss possible books, characters, and plots that students could choose.

    C. Students select a book familiar to most students and decide what character or plot detail to focus on.

    D. Students write a rough draft of a chant or cheer. Write actions that could be used. Share good initial student examples with the group to motivate those needing a start. Explain to students that when the chants are completed, groups of students can practice and perform the chants for the class.

    Note: Most students will be able to "naturally" evolve a rhythmic pattern for the writing, without a teacher-given structure. For those having difficulty, model one of the basic patterns above.

3. When each final copy is completed, conduct group practice of the chants for class performance with the following steps:

    A. Assign students to groups of three to four, with copies of each chant for each student in the group either made by the students or the teacher.

    B. Students in the group learn and practice each other's chant, complete with actions.

    C. Each group performs their chants for the class. *Optional*: Videotape the groups and analyze the replay.

Art: Drawing Focal Object; Writing: Rhyming Poetry

> **Siebert Diane.** *Heartland.* **Paintings by Wendell Minor. New York: Crowell, 1989.** A tribute to the spirit and everyday life of the Midwest farmer in poetic text and stunning paintings.
>
> *Note:* the book and activity coordinate well with a study of U.S. regions.

Materials Needed to Complete Wall Hanging

1. Iron-on interfacing (Pellon Craft Bond,™ Craft Fuse,™ etc.) enough for one eight-inch square for each student

2. Backing material (cotton-poly combination is fine) for squares to be adhered to

3. *Optional but attractive*: three-quarter inch ribbon for border between squares and on sides, and Stitch Witchery™ to adhere ribbon to backing. Materials available at fabric stores. No sewing necessary!

4. Oil crayons and/or fabric pens, pens (some fine-point) to complete drawing and writing.

5. *Optional*: Transparency of map of the United States.

Directions

1. Introduce the book with the following:

   A. Present the cover and tell students that *Heartland* is a celebration of an important part of the United States.

   B. Tell them that after the book is shared, each person will celebrate by helping to create a wall hanging featuring the interesting details of the particular area.

   C. Present the transparency map, wall map, or globe.

   D. Ask students to name states that would make up the "heart," or middle of the land. Then outline the twelve Midwestern states, Illinois, Indiana, Iowa, etc.

   E. Ask students to share highlights about the states (products, cities, etc.). Add a note about the world record for corn growing: 31-foot high cornstalk grown in Washington, Iowa in 1946, according to *Guinness Book,* 1989. Compare height with classroom height.

2. Present the book with the following:

   A. Point out that the land, products, and objects are *personified,* or given the qualities of a person. The poetic text is in the first person.

   B. Ask students to listen for interesting phrases that describe this land, and to enjoy the beautiful paintings that add interest and understanding.

   C. Read poem to students.

3. After the reading, discuss the important concepts, including:

   * the specific and special qualities of the personification
   * the meaning of *Heartland* (central area that can usually survive on its own)
   * nature's power over people
   * the spirit of the American farmer to survive, be successful, and to supply America with the basic foods for life.

4. Complete the wall hanging as follows:
   A. Reread, assigning each student a phrase or concept to illustrate and write a two-sentence poem for. Give other examples of couplets prior to writing.
   B. Give format for poem:
      (1) "I am a (the) _____ that (where)
          (object)

          _____.
              (what happens)
          I _____."
      (2) Both sentences rhyme.
   C. Students complete a rough draft of the illustration and poem on paper. Important instructions:
      • Feature one large object, land shape, and so forth rather than several small objects.
      • Leave *half-inch margins* on all four sides.
   D. Final copy is then drawn (with pencil first) on interfacing, with color added. *Cautions:* Make sure students draw on proper side and make sure students do not put felt pens over oil crayons.
   E. Pieces are ironed onto backing material with ribbon, etc.

Additional Book   by Siebert and Minor: *Mojave,* Crowell, 1988.

Lilly, Kenneth. *Kenneth Lilly's Animals.* Text by Joyce Pope. New York: Lothrop, Lee & Shepard, 1988. Magnificent, realistic illustrations and lively, readable text depicting wild animals from six habitats around the world. Also:

- Base, Graeme. *Animalia.* New York: Abrams, 1987. With extraordinary use of color and composition, this sophisticated alphabet book features animals set in a surrealistic style. *Note: Surrealistic* is used here in general rather than historic context.
- Bayer, Jane. *A, My Name Is Alice.* New York: Dial, 1984.
- Animal characters in the cartoon-like style in books by Steven Kellogg that sell "humor and fun from *A to Z.*"

Materials

1. Reproduce the activity sheet on white tag or other heavy paper. Have available crayons and colored pencils.
2. *Optional*: oil crayons and three pieces of yarn for each student.

Directions

1. Reinforce or review the following elements of art with students:
   - Line—shows direction or path of motion. Can be thin, wide, light, heavy, jagged, straight, or curved. Can change in length, width, color, or direction.
   - Color—creates or expresses mood and emotion.
   - Shape—lines join and intersect to form outlines of shapes.
   - Texture—line, color, shape, and contrast create it, gives the illusion of how something would feel.
2. Reinforce or review the concept of *design:* organizing the elements of line, color, shape, texture and value into a unified picture.
3. Reinforce or review the concept of common media, or materials, used:
   - color—watercolors, acrylics, pastels
   - line and wash
   - collage
   - woodcuts
4. Present the three *exciting* books, the analysis of the art of each, and the activity sheet in the following manner:

   A. Instruct students to carefully cut out each of the three gorillas.

B. Present Kenneth Lilly's book and the paintings of the gorillas on page 12.

(1) Discuss the paintings in terms of line, color, shape, and texture.

(2) Define the style as *realistic*—the subjects look as they do in nature. Lines are very important, as they show motion and texture.

(3) Compare Lilly's gorilla with that of Steven Kellogg's. Discuss the idea that Kellogg's art is *cartoon-like,* in that it exaggerates the shapes and details to make people laugh. Also compare Graeme Base's gorillas. This is an example of surrealistic art where realism is combined with imagination. Color and lines are used to create humorous details.

(4) Next, students discuss and write the following information on the *back* of the "walking" gorilla, the one that will represent Lilly's art:

KENNETH LILLY'S REALISTIC ART:

  I. The most important thing about realistic art is that the animal looks as it is seen in nature.

  II. This artist's purpose is to show how the animals really look in their habitats.

  III. Lilly emphasizes line and color (light and dark tones—value) to create texture, and to make objects appear three-dimensional.

C. Next, present Graeme Base's tigers. Compare with Lilly's and Kellogg's. Students discuss and write the following information on the back of the "standing" gorilla, representing Base's art:

GRAEME BASE'S SURREALISTIC ART:

  I. The most important thing about surrealistic art is that realism is used with imagination. Base uses color and lines to create humorous details.

  II. This artist's purpose is to create realism with humor.

  III. Base emphasizes color to bring objects together that he's placed in unusual and exaggerated settings.

D. Next, present Kellogg's rhino. Compare with Lilly's and Base's. Students discuss and write the following information on the back of the "sitting" gorilla:

STEVEN KELLOGG'S CARTOONISH ART:

  I. The most important thing about cartoon-like art is that the shapes and details are exaggerated to make people laugh.

  II. This artist's purpose is to entertain with humor.

  III. Kellogg emphasizes lines, and accents with color.

E. Students now create their own examples of the three styles of art, on the front of the gorillas. Do the following:

(1) Review the components of each style of art.

(2) Provide the art materials listed above.

(3) Display books for students to look at.

(4) When one or two students begin to create good examples, display to group.

(5) Punch holes as noted, tie strings, and hang as mobiles around the room! *Hint*: bend paper clips and hang the mobiles from light fixtures. Be sure to make the top string long.

Additional Activity Students practice realistic and surrealistic drawing from steps given above.

Name _____

Directions: 1. *Carefully* cut out the gorillas. 2. Write the information about the art of the three illustrators on the back of each. 3. Complete the drawing and coloring of each gorilla according to the illustrator's style. 4. Punch one hole in each, tie string, and hang as a mobile.

A, My Name Is Alice Across the Curriculum

10–1 APPRECIATING THE ANTICS OF ALICE AND COMPANY

Reading: Appreciating Character Humor

1. Read and enjoy with students the liveliness and humor of both the text and illustrations.
2. Point out the playfulness or whimsicality between who the characters are and what they do: Alex, an anteater, sells and eats ants; Fifi, a fox, sells feathers instead of fetching the feathers from fowl.

10–2 POINTING OUT PLACES

Social Studies: Identifying Cities and Countries on a Map

1. Point out to students the various cities, states, countries, and so forth on a map or globe.
2. *Optional*: Students write one interesting fact about each of the twenty-six places on a miniature "flag" and place on a map. Possible source: *The Usborne Book of Facts and Lists,* EDC Publishing, 1987. Contains over half of the places. Example: Brazil has the widest road in the world: 820 feet wide, enough for 160 cars side by side.

10–3 CURIOSITY ABOUT THE CREATURES

Science: Facts About Unusual Animals

1. Point out to students, "Some facts about less familiar creatures . . ." inside the back cover.
2. *Optional*: Find an interesting fact about each of the animals and play a match-up game with the name and the facts. Possible sources: *The Big Book of Animal Records,* by Tison and Taylor, Grossett, 1985; and *Guinness Book of World Records.*

10–4 ALPHABETIZING ALICE AND FRIENDS

Spelling: Alphabetizing Words

Students alphabetize a group of names and other words to the second letter.
Examples: *F*—feathers, Fifi, fox, Fred; *P*—Paul, pebbles, pig, Polly, puffin.

10–5 NOTHING BUT NOUNS
Language (Grammar): Identifying Nouns

Students identify and list all of the nouns, possibly in a competition. Also, categorize as common or proper nouns.

10–6 MY NAME IS
Writing, Art: Creating a Character

1. Give students the book format for creating their own characters in writing and illustration. Simplified: Leave out "my husband . . . "
2. *Optional*: Students each choose different letters so that a class alphabet book can be made.
3. *Optional*: Make a class quilt, with iron-on or other material. Use 7-inch squares.

10–7 AMUSING MASKS
Art: Creating a Character Mask

1. Students create paper masks using the characters developed in the writing.
2. Students speak the lines for their character, wearing their masks, for other groups of students.

10–8 ALICE'S STORE-Y PROBLEMS
Math: Solving Story Problems

1. Supply numbers for the following problems, according to student level, and present:
   A. Doris and Dave delivered $_____ worth of dust to their friends. If the friends gave back $_____ worth, how much did Doris and Dave really earn? _____
   B. Gertrude and George sell giggles for $_____ each. Rabbit wouldn't quit giggling, so they charged him for _____ giggles. How much did the giggles cost him altogether? _____
   C. Make up other problems as desired.
2. Additional problem activities:
   A. Information to students: *"A Giggleless Minute?"*

      In a group of three, take turns keeping one person from giggling or laughing for 2 minutes. One person is "it" and tries to get the second person to giggle. The third person is the timekeeper. *Important rule*: You may not touch the "giggler."

Information to teacher:

When someone giggles, it's the next person's turn; and after the group session, all the non-gigglers can be in a final contest where the rest of the class tries to get them to giggle.

B. Information to students: *"A Secret Number of Kisses"*

Keith gave Karen a secret number of kisses.

Follow the steps below to see if your teacher can figure out the secret number of kisses:

(1) Choose any number above 10 and below 30.

Write it at the side of the page. (This is the secret number!)

(2) Add 4.

(3) Multiply that answer by 2.

(4) Subtract 8.

(5) Multiply that answer by 4.

The new answer is _____

(6) Give the new answer to your teacher, who will tell you *without looking* what your original number—the secret number of kisses—is!

Information to teacher:

Divide 8 into the student's final answer to get the secret number. Example: $1944/8 = 243$.

3. Set up a store to sell everyday and interesting items.

10–9   ALPHABET BALL BOUNCING _____
P.E., Health: Physical Exercise, Coordination

Refer to the author's note at the back for rules for the playground game using a ball. Students can use verses from the writing activity.

Activities for Any Book Across the Curriculum

11–1 READING TOGETHER

Recreational Reading Fluency

Materials

1. Duplicate four copies of the "Reading Together" activity sheet (one sheet for each of four weeks) for each student.
2. Write a letter to parents explaining the activity. See step 2 below.
3. *Optional*: Books for younger students, such as David McPhail's *Fix-It* (Dutton, 1984); pictures from the *Babar* books by Jean and Laurent de Brunhoff showing the family reading together.

Directions

1. Motivate students for this reading-with-parents project by asking them "How many of you like it when your parents spend time doing things with you and pay attention to you?" For younger children, read the above mentioned books (if available).
2. Explain the program:
   A. Read with your parents for ten to fifteen minutes each night for two or four nights per week for four weeks.
   B. Alternate the reading either by pages in a book or by nights. *Note:* Older siblings grandparents, etc., can substitute for parents.
   C. The books you read can be any that you and your parents choose.
   D. Complete the "Reading Together" record page each day and turn it in on _____.
3. Share positive experiences among the students each week for reinforcement.

11–2 HAPPY BIRTHDAY WITH A BOOK

Book Selection

Materials

Duplicate the "Happy Birthday! Happy Reading!" activity sheet for the class.

Directions

On a student's birthday, ask the other students to suggest a good book for the birthday person to read. Write it on the activity sheet, along with a message to the student. *Alternative:* Ask the birthday student to suggest a favorite book to be read to the class.

READING TOGETHER

Date _____ Author _____

Title _____

Comments: _____

Student _____ Parent _____

Date _____ Author _____

Title _____

Comments: _____

Student _____ Parent _____

Date _____ Author _____

Title _____

Comments: _____

Student _____ Parent _____

Date _____ Author _____

Title _____

Comments: _____

Student _____ Parent _____

RECOMMENDED BOOK:

BIRTHDAY:

MONTH

NAME:

Materials

1. Duplicate the book chart for each student onto various colored papers. Select a space in the classroom where a set can be displayed with an appropriate statement or sign.

2. *Optional:* Poem beginning "Books to the ceiling, books to the sky . . ." from Arnold Lobel's *Whiskers & Rhymes* (Greenwillow, 1985); James Marshall's *Red Riding Hood* (Dial, 1987); and Reading Is Fundamental's *Once Upon a Time* (currently out of print).

Directions

1. Motivate student interest in recreational reading by displaying and talking about books the students and you consider "favorite good books." Read the above mentioned books, if available.

2. Present a copy of the book chart to each student.

3. Describe the program to students as follows:

   A. Color one book picture for each group of _____ pages read. (See the list below.)

   B. Groups of pages can be added together when reading a longer book. When twenty book pictures have been colored in, you will receive a _____ (sample rewards include extra free time, new package of colored markers or pencils). You decide on the exact number of pages, depending on the group.

4. Students complete some, most, or all of reading outside of school. Verification of pages read at home can be done through requiring the signature of a parent below the listed titles and pages read.

5. Display the book charts so that students can note each other's progress as well as their own.

Suggested Pages of Reading per Grade Level

grade 2 — one picture book or I Can Read Book® (published by Troll)

grade 3 — 25 to 50 pages

grade 4 — 75 to 100 pages

grade 5 — 100 to 125 pages

grade 6 — 150 pages

BOOKS– ____

I love them!

BOOKS– ____

I love them!

11–4 GOOD BOOK HANGMAN

Identifying Words/Titles/Sentences

Directions

1. Draw a gallows on the chalkboard. *Variation:* Omit gallows and draw the person standing on the ground.
2. Select a word from a book familiar to students.
3. Draw a line for each letter of the word.
4. Ask students to name letters; fill in the correct ones. List the incorrect letters.
5. Draw one part of the person each time a letter is incorrect, up to six parts.
6. The object is to complete the letters in the word before completing the six parts of the person.

Variation   Use the title of a book, a character, or a sentence from a book. Add four more parts (two hands and two feet) to the person.

11–5 GOOD BOOKS SEVEN-UP

Identifying a Main Character or a Title

Materials

Choose one of two options: seven familiar titles *or* main character names. Write one each on 9-by-12-inch paper. (Use titles for younger students.) *Note:*   When using titles, make sure the main character can be easily identified. Make up extra titles or characters for subsequent games to replace correctly identified ones.

Directions

1. Play the game in the usual manner, with the following modification: Students must identify a book character or title in addition to identifying the person who tapped them.
2. Method of playing:
   A. Seven students who are "it" hold up but conceal the writing on the paper until a tapped student correctly identifies the correct "it."
   B. A tapped student must identify the main character for a given title, or the title for a given main character, in addition to identifying the student who tapped him or her. If only the person is identified correctly, the two do not exchange places.

Variations   Younger students can read the title or character name correctly, or spell the words. Older students can identify the author, give a character trait, or give the theme.

11–6 GOOD BOOKS MATCH-UP
Matching Words

Directions

1. Select characters, titles, or authors for matching either as two different words (or groups of words) or as two words that are the same. (If the same, select ten to twelve; if different, twenty to twenty four.) *Variation:* Select key vocabulary from a book (eight to twelve words). Write the pairs of words (either different or same) each on a 3-by-5-inch card. *Note:* Make sure the writing does not show through the back of the card.

2. Mix up the sets and lay the cards face down on the table or floor.

3. A student is selected to turn two cards face up for a match. If a match is made, the student continues playing. If the words or groups don't match, the next student takes a turn.

4. The game continues until all matches have been made.

5. The winner is the student with the most sets.

11–7 BOOK ACTIVITIES CLUB
Book Appreciation

Directions

1. Organize a time period where students can come together to share extended interests with books. Suggested structure:

   A. Meet twice a month after school.

   B. Sample activities:
      - Games adapted to books, such as charades, book tag, treasure hunt (interesting questions written for students to find and answer)
      - Put on or go to a play
      - Book trades where students bring used paperbacks to exchange
      - Art projects that explore styles of illustrators

   C. Time: 1 to 1½ hours per session

   D. Participation: voluntary

   E. Transportation: usually arranged by parents and carpools

   F. Refreshments: optional but fun! Try treats with book themes, such as gelatin cubes from *Cloudy With A Chance of Meatballs* by Judith Barrett (Atheneum, 1978), doughnuts from *Homer Price* by Robert McCloskey (Penguin, 1976), everything from *Yummers!* by James Marshall (Houghton Mifflin, 1973).

2. Send an information letter to parents, outlining the objectives and structure, and giving time choices.

   Note: A shortened version could be done during school hours.

11–8 WHO AM I?
Asking and Answering Questions

Directions

1. Select enough books familiar to students so that each student can be given a major character.

2. Write each character's name on a separate 3-by-5-inch card.

3. Reinforce or review the meaning of *character descriptions* (what the character looks like) and *character traits* (how a character acts or behaves). Give examples.

4. Pin a character card to the back of each student (without that student knowing the identity).

5. The pinned student asks other students questions about his or her character's description and traits so as to identify the character.

6. *Only Yes/No questions may be asked.*

7. Pinned students must ask a minimum of five questions before attempting an identification. A different student must be asked each question.

11–9 BOOK REVIEW: A GOOD BOOK?
Evaluating a Book

Materials

Duplicate copies of "Book Review: A Good Book?" according to your intended use (as a whole group project, for selected students or individuals, or as a choice).

Directions

1. Define *book review* for students:
   - Describes and evaluates a book
   - Includes comments about the characters and a summary of the plot (also usually comments about the setting, author's style, and themes)
   - Tells what the reviewer likes about the book and what the reviewer doesn't like

2. Define each of the *kinds of books*:
   - Fantasy: about things that cannot really happen or people and creatures that do not exist
   - Humor: sparkling ideas told in an amusing way to make people laugh
   - Mystery: plot and characters centered on an element of the unknown, frightening adventures, and suspense
   - Science Fiction: a form of fantasy in which imaginative science possibilities are used in plot, often with future society as the setting
   - Realistic Fiction: real people and events tell a modern imaginary story

- Historical Fiction: tells a story about the past with major facts about characters, ideas, and customs being true; but details, such as conversations, are made up
- Biography: the authentic facts of the lives of individual people done as a work of literature

3. See activity 2–9, "A Good Story—What Are the Parts?" for practice with concepts of character and plot.

4. Uses for the book review sheet:
   - Practice with completing an analysis of a book (the class, group, or individuals read the books)
   - Books to recommend for other students to read
   - New books that have not been critiqued by the librarian or teacher

11–10   BOOK TALK
Speaking With Fluency

Directions

1. A student is selected to talk for one minute about a book without saying "um."
2. The student chooses his or her own title, is given time to think about what he or she is going to say, and begins when the selected timekeeper says "Go." *Note:* Note cards may be used as prompts.
3. The timekeeper keeps the time and records the number of "successful" seconds.
4. If the student says "um" before five seconds into time, the student is given a second start. Students may pause no more than five seconds between words.

11–11   CALENDAR BOOKNOTES
Writing Annotations

Materials

Duplicate at least thirty of the "Calendar Booknotes" activity sheet onto heavy, light-colored paper (in several colors). Cut them out.

Directions

1. Students each select a favorite but different fiction title to write an annotation for.
2. Teach the definition of *annotation:* An annotation is a short idea or remark about a book that explains enough about the book so that others will want to read it, but not so much that they know the story beforehand. An annotation gives the problem but not the solution, or the question but not the answer. Give examples.
3. The group of students complete enough annotations for each day of the month. The "booknotes" are numbered according to the calendar display.
4. Each day, the booknote for that day is read to the group, thereby presenting the opportunity for another book for student reading.

Directions

1. For at least the first few games, divide the class into groups of twelve to fifteen students.

2. Group members each give the name of a book and a one-sentence fact about the plot or a character. Students listen to each other's statements carefully.

3. Next, go around the group a second time, with each student giving the book and statement of another selected student.

4. Each student's statement may be chosen for repetition only once, so that all the statements will be used.

1. Title: _____

2. Author: _____

3. Kind of Book: (Underline one) fantasy, humor, mystery, science fiction, realistic fiction, historical fiction, biography

4. A main character: (name) _____

   description: (how looks in two or three words or phrases) _____

   _____   _____

   traits: (how acts or behaves in two or three words or phrases) _____

   _____   _____

5. Summary of plot:

   Problem (one or two sentences) _____

   _____

   _____

   Solution (two or three sentences) _____

   _____

   _____

   _____

6. Tell how a character or event made the story interesting (two or three sentences)

   _____

   _____

   _____

   _____

7. Tell something that was unique, different, or surprising in the solution (two or three sentences, use the back of the paper)

8. On a scale of 1 to 10 (1 is terrible, 10 is excellent) rate the book:

   1 2 3 4 5 6 7 8 9 10 (circle number)

© 1991 by The Center for Applied Research in Education

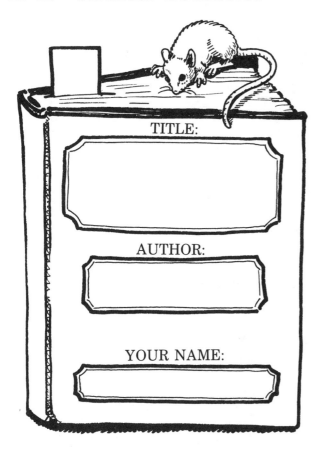

TITLE:

AUTHOR:

YOUR NAME:

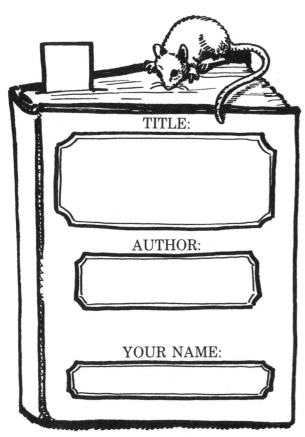

TITLE:

AUTHOR:

YOUR NAME:

Annotated List of Titles Used in This Book

A, My Name Is Alice, Jane Bayer (New York: Dial, 1984). Ball-bouncing rhymes and Steven Kellogg illustrations that "sell humor from A to Z."

Action Alphabet, Marty Neumeier and Byron Glaser (New York: Greenwillow, 1984, 1985). "Active" alphabet letters act out the sample words they depict.

Alexander and the Terrible, Horrible, No Good, Very Bad Day, Judith Viorst (New York: Atheneum, 1972). Some days are bad—even in Australia.

Animal Fact/Animal Fable, Seymour Simon (New York: Crown, 1979). Common beliefs about popular animals are given, and then the facts are distinguished from the fables, with the reasons being noted.

Animalia, Graeme Base (New York: Abrams, 1987). With extraordinary use of color and composition, this unusual alphabet book features animals and objects that are set with both reality and imagination.

Annie and the Old One, Miska Miles (Boston: Little, Brown and Company, 1971). A Navajo girl learns to accept the death of her grandmother and weaves a rug of understanding about life and the marching on of time.

Banner in the Sky, James Ramsey Ullman (New York: Harper & Row, 1954). Young Rudi Matt carries on the dream of his father to reach the summit of the Citadel, the highest mountain in Switzerland. A compelling drama of determination, skill, pride, and jealousy that prompts discussions of the value of life.

Be a Perfect Person in Just Three Days!, Stephen Manes (New York: Bantam-Skylark, 1983). Is being perfect the answer to Milo's—and everyone's—problems?

Bet You Can't!, Vicki Cobb and Kathy Darling (New York: Avon, 1983). A collection of more than sixty mostly impossible-to-do but highly motivating-to-try tricks.

The Boy of the Three-Year Nap, Dianne Snyder (Boston: Houghton Mifflin, 1988). Taro, the lazy son of a Japanese seamstress, who spends his life taking naps and eating, finds out that laziness doesn't pay—or does it?

The Boy Who Was Followed Home, Margaret Mahy (New York: Dial, 1975). A growing number of hippos follow Robert. The "solution" has a surprise permanency to the problem!

Buffalo Woman, Paul Goble (New York: Bradbury, 1984). A young hunter's love for a buffalo in the form of a beautiful maiden requires that he become a buffalo to remain with her.

The Bug Book, Dr. Hugh Danks (New York: Workman, 1987). An excellent child-oriented field guide for catching, identifying, and caring for twenty-six bugs, including grasshoppers and sowbugs.

Celebrations, Myra Cohn Livingston (New York: Holiday House, 1985). The popular holidays are celebrated in poetry, with stunning paintings by Leonard Everett Fisher.

Children of the Wild West, Russell Freedman (New York: Clarion, 1983). Historical photographs and informative text chronicling the American West from 1840 to the early 1900's.

Cinderella, Charles Perrault, retold by Amy Ehrlich, illustrated by Susan Jeffers (New York: Dial, 1985). Exquisite illustrations highly compliment the retelling.

Cloudy With a Chance of Meatballs, Judi Barrett (New York: Atheneum, 1978). The weather in the town of Chewandswallow, where it rains soup and snows mashed potatoes, is delicious—until it takes a turn for the worse.

D'Aulaires' Book of Greek Myths, Ingri D'Aulaire and Edgar Parin D'Aulaire (New York: Doubleday, 1962). The gods, goddesses, and heroes of ancient Greece come to life with all their heroic, powerful, mischievous, tricky, and winsome characteristics.

Destination: Antarctica, Robert Swan (New York: Scholastic, 1988). British explorer Robert Swan and two others trek 900 miles over treacherous, icy terrain to the South Pole, tracing the footsteps of early explorer Robert Scott.

Dinosaurs Walked Here and Other Stories Fossils Tell, Patricia Lauber (New York: Bradbury, 1987). An introduction to the study of fossils and how these relics reveal the characteristics of the dinosaur world. Complete with full-color photographs.

Eyewitness Books: Rocks and Minerals, Dr. R. F. Symes (New York: Alfred A. Knopf, 1988). Clear, interesting photographs and well-written, appealing text give the basics for understanding the creation, importance, and uses of rocks and minerals.

Eyewitness Books: Skeleton, Steve Parker (New York: Alfred A. Knopf, 1988). Lifelike pictures and interesting facts about human and animal skeletal systems and their structures and functions.

Fables, Arnold Lobel (New York: Harper & Row, 1980). Short, original fables with inviting animal characters.

Flowers, Fruits, Seeds, Jerome Wexler (Englewood Cliffs, NJ: Prentice-Hall, 1987). Highly appealing full-color photographs with short, informative text depicting the cycle of a plant from flower to fruit to seed to flower.

Handtalk, Remy Charlip and Mary Beth and George Ancona (New York: Macmillan, 1974). The basics of two kinds of sign language: finger spelling and signing.

Heartland, Diane Siebert, paintings by Wendell Minor (New York: Thomas Y. Crowell, 1989). A tribute to the spirit and everyday life of the midwest farmer in poetic text and stunning paintings.

A House for Hermit Crab, Eric Carle (Saxonville, MA: Picture Book Studio, 1987). The true habits of the hermit crab are shown in this modern-day fable as one crab copes with growth, change, and friendship.

How Much Is a Million?, David M. Schwartz (New York: Lothrop, Lee & Shepard, 1985). Concepts, examples, and the numbers for a million, billion, and trillion—with humor and accuracy.

The Hundred Dresses, Eleanor Estes (San Diego: Harcourt Brace Jovanovich, 1944, 1973). A poor Polish girl is teased because she wears the same blue dress every day, although she says she has one hundred dresses all lined up in her closet. Good material for discussion of stereotyping, prejudice, teasing, and friendship.

Icebergs and Glaciers, Seymour Simon (New York: William Morrow, 1987). Basic, interesting facts about the formation, types, and movement of glaciers and icebergs, and their impact on our planet.

The Inside-Outside Book of Washington, D.C., Roxie Munro (New York: E. P. Dutton, 1987). An artist for *The New Yorker* artistically and architecturally creates the unique atmosphere of both the inside and outside views of Washington, D.C.'s most famous buildings.

Invention Book, Steven Caney (New York: Workman, 1985). All of the know-how for bringing an invention to reality *plus* the stories behind thirty-six popular inventions, including the Frisbee®, Life Savers™, Levis®, and sneakers.

Ira Sleeps Over, Bernard Waber (Boston: Houghton Mifflin, 1972). Ira is afraid to take his teddy bear to Reggie's, until he discovers something about Reggie he didn't know.

The Jolly Postman, Janet and Allen Ahlberg (Boston: Little Brown and Company, 1986). A book of real letters written by well-known fairy tale characters to each other. Demonstrates and stimulates imagination.

Kenneth Lilly's Animals, Kenneth Lilly, text by Joyce Pope (New York: Lothrop, Lee & Shepard, 1988). Magnificent realistic illustrations and lively, readable text depicting wild animals from six habitats around the world.

Large as Life Animals, Joanna Cole (New York: Alfred A. Knopf, 1990). Life-sized paintings with brief, high-interest text, giving the characteristics of various small nocturnal and daytime animals. Included are the greater Indian fruit bat and the fennec.

Listen to the Rain, Bill Martin, Jr. and John Archambault (New York: Holt, 1988). Lyrical words vibrantly express the sounds and feelings of rain, complemented by watercolors that capture the moods.

The Magic School Bus Inside the Human Body, Joanna Cole (New York: Scholastic, 1989). A classroom trip on a magic school bus through the body, with its major parts and functions depicted with hype and humor.

Magical Changes, Graham Oakley (New York: Macmillan, 1979). A picture book with pages cut horizontally so the reader can mix and match the top and bottom halves.

A Medieval Feast, Aliki (New York: Thomas Y. Crowell, 1983). The preparation and celebration of a feast at an English manor house—fit for the king who *is* coming to visit!

Mufaro's Beautiful Daughters, John Steptoe (New York: Lothrop, Lee & Shepherd, 1987). An African tale in which kindness wins over pride and greed. Stunning illustrations enrich a meaningful story.

The Owl and the Pussy-Cat, Edward Lear, illustrated by Paul Galdone (New York: Clarion, 1987). Lear's classic nonsense poem with Galdone's fanciful design and features. (Other illustrators include Lorinda Bryan Cauley.)

People, Peter Spier (New York: Doubleday, 1980). We are alike, but we are also unique and different individuals—Isn't it wonderful!

Red Riding Hood, retold and illustrated by James Marshall (New York: Dial, 1987). Granny is most disturbed about having her reading interrupted, and her granddaughter promises "never to talk to strangers again."

Round Trip, Ann Jonas (New York: Greenwillow, 1983). Striking black/white and positive/negative images depicting a trip to the city and back again.

Sarah, Plain and Tall, Patricia MacLachlan (New York: Harper & Row, 1985). The tender bonding between Sarah, plain and tall, from Maine and a motherless prairie family.

Scaly Babies: Reptiles That Grow Up, Ginny Johnston and Judy Cutchins (New York: Morrow, 1988). Photographs and text describing interesting physical and behavioral characteristics of young reptiles.

The Secret Soldier, Ann McGovern (New York: Four Winds Press, reissued 1987). A brief biography of Deborah Sampson, a young woman who disguised herself as a man to fight with the Continental Army during the Revolutionary War.

Sing a Song of Popcorn, selected by Beatrice Schenk de Regniers (New York: Scholastic, 1988). Four appealing limericks on pages 110–111 from a collection of 128 poems that are illustrated by nine Caldecott artists.

Sir Cedric, Roy Gerrard (New York: Farrar, Straus & Giroux, 1984). Sir Cedric, the brave knight, receives more than honor when he battles Black Ned. Satirical comedy poking good-natured fun at chivalry.

Sir Francis Drake: His Daring Deeds, Roy Gerrard (New York: Farrar, Straus & Giroux, 1986). Drake's battles with the Spaniards, told from an Englishman's point of view.

Squeeze a Sneeze, Bill Morrison (Boston: Houghton Mifflin, 1977). Witty and wacky rhyming word play that starts the reader creating rhymes.

Stone Fox, John Reynolds Gardiner (New York: Harper & Row, 1980). Ten-year-old Willy is determined to save his grandfather's farm—and his grandfather—by entering a dog sled race against the legendary Indian, Stone Fox.

Sunken Treasure, Gail Gibbons (New York: Thomas Y. Crowell, 1988). Treasures from the Atocha, a Spanish galleon sunk in 1622 and found in 1985. Readable, interesting nonfiction.

A Taste of Blackberries, Doris Buchanan Smith (New York: Harper & Row, 1973). Since Jamie liked to tease and act, it was difficult to tell whether he was acting when he fell to the ground after one bee sting. Tasteful treatment of coping with the sudden death of a best friend.

The Tenth Good Thing About Barney, Judith Viorst (New York: Atheneum, 1971). Remembering nine and, finally, ten good things about his cat, Barney, helps a boy deal with its death.

That Snake in the Grass, Lilo Hess (New York: Scribners, 1987). Engaging facts are elaborated and superstitions are dispelled in this accounting of snakes in the wild and as pets.

The 329th Friend, Marjorie Weinman Sharmat (New York: Four Winds, 1979). Emery Raccoon discovers that he is his own best friend.

To Space and Back, Sally Ride with Susan Okie (New York: Lothrop, Lee & Shepard, 1986). High-interest details, with NASA photographs, of life aboard a space shuttle—as children want to hear it.

The Tortoise and the Hare, adapted and illustrated by Janet Stevens (New York: Holiday House, 1984). Tortoise eats right, works out, and jogs over the finish line while watching Hare in his pink jogging shorts try to catch up.

A Tournament of Knights, Joe Lasker (New York: Thomas Y. Crowell, 1986). Justin, a brave young knight about to fight his first tournament, learns that courage is only one of the virtues of the encounter.

Volcano, Patricia Lauber (New York: Bradbury, 1986). Powerful full-color photographs and engaging text tell the story of the eruption and healing of Mount St. Helens from an environmental viewpoint.

The War with Grandpa, Robert Kimmel Smith (New York: Dell, 1984). First-person account of a ten-year-old boy who struggles to maintain two separate emotions—his love for his grandfather and his desire for independence in decision making.

We the People, Peter Spier (New York: Doubleday, 1987). American diversity and unity are presented in detailed illustrations, celebrating the concepts of the Preamble, as well as the Constitution itself.

What the Moon Is Like, Franklyn M. Branley (New York: Thomas Y. Crowell Junior Books, 1986). Details about the moon's surface as described by astronauts.

Where the Sidewalk Ends, Shel Silverstein (New York: Harper & Row, 1974). Everyone wants to know what's in the traveler's sack in "What's in the Sack!"—but that's not the real question, says the traveler.

The Whipping Boy, Sid Fleischman (New York: Greenwillow, 1986). Newbery-winning novel about a spoiled prince and his whipping boy. They run away and are caught by two ruffians who are fooled as to their identities.

Yummers!, James Marshall (Boston: Houghton Mifflin, 1973). Emily Pig's life takes on large dimensions as she satisfies her increasing hunger during her "exercise walk."